MIGRA

How To Books on Living & Working Abroad

Applying for a United States Visa	Living & Working in Britain
Become an Au Pair	Living & Working in Canada
Do Voluntary Work Abroad	Living & Working in China
Doing Business Overseas	Living & Working in Hong Kong
Emigrate	Living & Working in Israel
Finding a Job in Canada	Living & Working in Saudi Arabia
Finding a Job in New Zealand	Living & Working in the Netherlands
Finding Work Overseas	Master Languages
Finding Temporary Work Abroad	Migrating to Canada
Get a Job Abroad	Obtaining Visas & Work Permits
Get a Job in America	Rent & Buy Property in France
Get a Job in Australia	Rent & Buy Property in Italy
Get a Job in Europe	Retire Abroad
Get a Job in France	Selling into Japan
Get a Job in Germany	Setting Up Home in Florida
Get a Job in Hotels & Catering	Spending a Year Abroad
Get a Job in Travel & Tourism	Study Abroad
Live & Work in America	Teach Abroad
Live & Work in Australia	Travel Round the World
Live & Work in France	Working Abroad
Live & Work in Germany	Working as a Holiday Rep
Live & Work in the Gulf	Working in Japan
Live & Work in Italy	Working in the Gulf
Live & Work in Japan	Working on Contract Worldwide
Live & Work in New Zealand	Working on Cruise Ships
Live & Work in Portugal	Your Own Business in Europe

Other titles in preparation

The How To Series now contains more than 170 titles in the following categories:

Business Basics
Family Reference
Jobs & Careers
Living & Working Abroad
Student Handbooks
Successful Writing

Please send for a free copy of the latest catalogue for full details (see back cover for address).

LIVING & WORKING ABROAD

MIGRATING TO CANADA

How to apply successfully for permanent residence

M. J. Bjarnason

Cartoons by Mike Flanagan

British Library Cataloguing-in-Publication data
A catalogue record for this book is available from the British Library.

© Copyright 1996 by M. J. Bjarnason

Published by How To Books Ltd, Plymbridge House,
Estover Road, Plymouth PL6 7PZ, United Kingdom.
Tel: (01752) 202301. Fax: (01752) 202331.

All rights reserved. No part of this work may be reproduced, or stored in an information retrieval system (other than for purposes of review), without the express permission of the Publisher given in writing.

Note: The material contained in this book is set out in good faith for general guidance and no liability can be accepted for loss or expense incurred as a result of relying in particular circumstances on statements made in the book. The laws and regulations are complex and liable to change, and readers should check the current position with the relevant authorities before making personal arrangements.

Produced for How To Books by Deer Park Productions.
Typeset by Kestrel Data, Exeter.
Printed and bound in Great Britain by
Cromwell Press, Broughton Gifford, Melksham, Wilts.

Contents

List of illustrations — 8

Preface — 9

1 The immigration categories — 11

Sponsored Dependants — 11
Independent Applicants — 12
Withdrawn categories — 13
Accompanying family members — 13
How to choose the right categories — 15
A cautionary note — 16

2 Sponsored Dependants (Family Class Relatives) — 18

Overview of the process — 18
The forms required — 19
Documentation required — 37
Your interview at the Canadian Immigration Office — 38

3 Independent Applicants — 40

Documentation — 40
Overview of the process — 41
Processing and Right of Landing fees — 42
The Point System: an overview — 43
The Point System in detail — 43
A self-assessment — 50
Self-assessment charts for employment in Canada — 50
Summary — 54
Applicants destined to the Province of Quebec — 54

4	**Specific Vocational Preparation and Occupational Demand**	66
	Specific Vocational Preparation (SVP)	66
	Occupational Demand	67
5	**Entrepreneurs, Self-Employed Persons and Investors**	69
	Entrepreneurs	69
	Self-employed	71
	Investors	72
	Recommendation	74
	Business Immigrant Coordination Centres	76
	Additional documentation—business applicants	78
6	**The application forms and documents**	87
	Gathering information	87
	Contacting the immigration office	89
	Reply from Immigration	90
	The Application for Permanent Residence	91
	Submitting your completed application	109
	Cautions	111
7	**The priority system and interview**	113
	The priority system	113
	Preparing for the interview	114
	Outcome of the interview	116
8	**The clearance checks**	117
	Your security check	117
	Your medical check	117
	When to depart	118
9	**What is an immigrant visa?**	119
	The Record of Landing	119
	The port of entry check	122
	What is a Landed Immigrant or Permanent Resident?	122
	Applying for Canadian citizenship	123
	How not to lose your immigrant status	123

Contents	7

10 Conclusion	125
Appeals	125
Family businesses	126
Obtaining professional help	126

Appendices

A Designated Occupations List	128
B General Occupations List	130
C Alphabetical Listing of Occupations	163
D Immigration application Processing Fee and Right of Landing Fee	197
E Sample CCDO Job Descriptions	200
F Canadian Immigration Offices abroad	205

Other useful addresses	218
Further reading	226
Index	227

List of Illustrations

1. Sponsorship Kit — 21
2. Assessment under the Point System — 44
3. Self-assessment chart for employment in Canada — 51
4. Self-assessment chart for entrepreneur or investor — 52
5. Self-assessment for self-employed persons — 53
6. The Quebec point system — 56
7. Self-assessment chart for Quebec — 62
8. Business Applicant Summary — 79
9. Personal Worth Statement — 83
10. Sample letter to the immigration authorities — 90
11. Application for Permanent Residence in Canada (Form IMM 8) — 92
12. Record of Landing (Form IMM 1000) — 120

Preface

The Canadian immigration process has long been a mystery to most applicants who, as a result, are disadvantaged in submitting their applications because they do not understand the process and how to handle it. As well, applicants often are unable to obtain straightforward information from Canadian Immigration authorities.

This book is intended to resolve this mystery by providing prospective immigrants with the information necessary to assess their qualifications beforehand. They can submit their applications with a complete knowledge of the procedures and enhance their prospects of success.

Based on more than 35 years' experience, *Migrating To Canada* has been written to aid prospective immigrants to Canada, primarily persons residing outside of Canada who wish to follow the legal process to become permanent residents of Canada. It tells how to complete, document and submit an application with confidence.

It applies to all provinces and territories of Canada including the Province of Quebec which has its own immigrant selection system. Included are appendices essential to the self-assessment process as they contain necessary specific technical data. *Migrating to Canada* also includes all the necessary sample forms, addresses, charts, information and recommendations needed to assess your own qualifications and properly submit your application. My objective is to help you to maximize your chances of success.

This book is designed to offer you a clear understanding of Canadian immigration procedures, so that you may determine whether or not you can comply with the requirements. It explains how to go about applying for permanent residence, and what to expect as you go through each stage of the procedure.

Migrating to Canada is presented in simple language, without any direct reference to sections of the Immigration Act and Regulations. I want you to be able to use it as a practical and step-by-step guide to the Canadian immigration process. The book outlines the different categories in which you can apply and helps you determine which is best suited to your circumstances.

You are then guided through the process that you will have to follow, from the gathering of information and documentation for the application to actually coming to Canada as an immigrant. In short, this book should answer all the essential questions you have if you are contemplating emigrating to Canada.

M. J. Bjarnason

1
The Immigration Categories

In order to begin the process of assessing your prospects of successfully immigrating, it is necessary that you have a knowledge of the basic immigration categories and some specific definitions. I will explain these as simply as possible.

Basically, there are only two categories under which you can apply to become a permanent resident of Canada: **Sponsored Dependants** and **Independent Applicants**.

The following definitions will make it easier for you to understand the two main categories and the various subsections under the independent category.

SPONSORED DEPENDANTS

These are close relatives of a Canadian citizen or of a permanent resident who is at least 19 years of age. Relatives eligible for admission in this category include:

- husband or wife
- fiancé or fiancée with accompanying dependent children
- father or mother
- dependent children
- grandparents
- unmarried orphaned brothers, sisters, nephews, nieces or grandchildren under 19 years of age.

There are certain very limited exceptions under which you can apply as a Sponsored Dependant even if you are not very closely related to a Canadian citizen or permanent resident.

For example, if you have a relative of any degree who is a Canadian citizen or permanent resident who has no very close relatives in Canada or anywhere else in the world, you might be able to be sponsored by that person as a Sponsored Dependant. Your relative in Canada would have to be unmarried (or divorced) and without children, parents or grandparents. It should be noted that this exception rarely applies, as most people have a close relative somewhere.

If you think you might fall into this category, or there are other very special circumstances about your situation, it would be best for you or your relative in Canada to seek the advice of a professional immigration consultant.

INDEPENDENT APPLICANTS

There are four categories of Independent Applicants:

- Skilled Immigrants
- Entrepreneurs
- Investors
- Self-Employed

Skilled Immigrants

Skilled Immigrants are individuals intending to seek employment in Canada in an occupation which is in demand. (An arranged job in Canada is not necessary, although it helps.)

Entrepreneurs

Entrepreneurs are persons who have the intention and ability to establish, purchase, or make a substantial investment in a business venture in Canada in which *the applicant will actively be involved in the management of the business.*

The business must make a significant contribution to the economy and result in the creation or maintenance of employment opportunities for at least one or more Canadian citizens or permanent residents, other than the entrepreneur and his dependants. This category is attractive to experienced business persons whose background is oriented towards the ownership and management of small to medium size enterprises.

Investors

Investors are persons who have a proven managerial track record in business, and have a personal net worth of Cdn$500,000 or more. Investors are required to make an investment of a minimum of

Cdn$250,000 for at least five (5) years in a specific project or investment syndicate. From 1 July 1996, applicants are only allowed to invest in government-administered venture capital funds. The only exception is in the Province of Quebec where investments can be made in privately administered investment syndicates.

Self-Employed

A Self-Employed immigrant is a person who has the intention and ability to establish a business in Canada that will employ only the applicant. The business must make a significant contribution to the economy, or to the cultural or artistic life of Canada. This category accommodates individuals who, although they may not create or preserve jobs for Canadians, nevertheless make a significant contribution in economic and artistic terms, such as farmers, sports personalities, artists, authors, members of the performing arts, and operators of small outlets which certain communities may need.

WITHDRAWN CATEGORIES

Retirement Category

It was previously possible to apply as a Retired Person. This provision of the Immigration Regulations has been withdrawn. It is no longer possible for an applicant without relatives in the Sponsored Dependant category in Canada to apply on the basis of retirement.

Assisted Relatives

Prior to February 1993, it was possible for a Canadian Citizen or Permanent Resident to sponsor a brother, sister, uncle, aunt, nephew or niece for admission into Canada. This provision of the Immigration Regulations has been rescinded. Such relatives must now comply as Independent Applicants, although they will receive some limited benefit for having a relative in Canada. This is explained in detail in Chapter 3 in the self-assessment process.

ACCOMPANYING FAMILY MEMBERS

New Immigration Regulations have been implemented which determine who may be included in the Canadian immigration application of the principal applicant and his/her spouse for the purpose of accompanying them to live in Canada. Formerly, all never married children of any age could be included as dependants on their parents' application, regardless of whether they were in fact truly dependent on their parents.

New definition

The new regulations allow you to include on your application as your accompanying dependants only the following:

(1) Your and/or your spouse's unmarried children under age 19 at the time your application is submitted. They must be unmarried when they apply for a visa, and still unmarried when the visa is issued.

(2) A son or daughter who is 19 or over at the time the application is submitted, but who is continuously enrolled and in attendance as a full-time student in an academic, professional or vocational program at a university, college or other educational institution, and has been during that time wholly or substantially financially supported by his/her parents. Such a child could be married.

(3) A son or daughter of any age who is suffering from a physical or mental disability, is wholly or substantially supported by his/her parents and is incapable of supporting him/herself by reason of that disability.

(4) The unmarried children under age 19 of the persons referred to in (1) to (3) above.

Key points concerning children

There are some important points to remember when deciding which children can be included as accompanying dependants on your application form:

- Your dependants, to be eligible to accompany you to Canada, must be able to show that they meet the foregoing requirements regarding marital status and dependency both at the time the application for permanent residence is received by the immigration office and when the immigrant visa is ready to be issued. For example, if a child over 19 is a full-time student when an application is submitted, but has left school by the time the case is finalized, he/she will no longer be eligible to be included on your application.

- A child under 19 when the application is submitted but over 19 when it is ready to be finalized is *not* disqualified as a result of passing the age limit while the application is in process.

- A student referred to in (2) above who has interrupted studies for an aggregate period of less than one year is still considered to be in 'continuous' enrolment.

- If you have a child over 19 whom you believe meets the requirements set out in paragraphs (2) or (3) above and is thereby eligible to be included in your application, you must:

    (a) clearly indicate this fact on your application and provide information and documentation in respect of that child with your application, such as letters of acceptance from your dependants' educational institutions, cancelled cheques showing tuition, room or board you have paid or other papers telling how you support your dependants,

    (b) attach a written explanation to your application form indicating why this child is dependent upon you, and

    (c) submit any required processing fees in respect of that child, pursuant to the instructions regarding fee payment which are included in the application package.

Finally, it should be noted that your ineligible children are not by their exclusion from your application disqualified from later immigrating to Canada. However, they must at the time when they wish to proceed meet the selection criteria in the appropriate immigration category.

HOW TO CHOOSE THE RIGHT CATEGORIES

Let us consider how best to opt for the right category. First, go back to the definition of the Sponsored Dependant category.

Do you have any of those relatives in Canada who are at least 19 years of age and willing and able to help you?

If you do, you are in the best possible position to have an application approved.

If you do not have a relative in the Sponsored Dependant category, do you or your spouse have a relative (closer than a cousin) who is a Canadian citizen or permanent resident, 19 years of age or over, and willing to help you?

If you do, that's good. It's not as good as having a relative under the Sponsored Dependant category in Canada, but it does put you in a better position to be successful in your application to emigrate.

Do you have substantial assets and business experience?

If so, you may be able to submit an application as an Entrepreneur, Self-Employed person or Investor.

If you do not have a relative in Canada and your assets are limited, you should not abandon hope of immigrating to Canada.

Remember, you may also apply to come to Canada to take up employment as a skilled immigrant. There might be very few people in Canada with your qualifications, and your occupation might be strongly in demand. If so, your application may be accepted in a Designated Occupation or under the General Occupations List. A complete listing of all occupations currently in demand are listed in Appendices A, B and C.

Don't be concerned if you have not fully understood these various options. As we proceed, each will be dealt with in turn as we go through the application process.

A CAUTIONARY NOTE

Before we begin to describe the application process, there is one piece of advice applicable to every case.

The Immigration Categories

> **Do not write or say anything throughout the appl**
> **process is not truthful. Be completely truth**
> **your application!**

If you have had trouble with the law in the past, provide complete details. Often applicants are refused not because of the offence, but because they fail to be completely truthful in their application. If you or a dependent family member has serious health problems, be sure to provide particulars. It is to your long term advantage to provide complete details of your situation.

2
Sponsored Dependants (Family Class Relatives)

OVERVIEW OF THE PROCESS

This chapter deals only with Sponsored Dependants. If you determined in the previous chapter that you cannot apply in this category, please go on to Chapter 3. The process you will follow in your application as a Sponsored Dependant is very different from the one you would follow as an Independent Applicant. The Sponsored Dependant is the simplest category under which to emigrate.

The initial forms and interview

You should begin by asking your relative in Canada to contact the nearest Canada Immigration Centre. Your relative will then be given or sent certain forms to fill out. The forms will include an **Undertaking Of Assistance** and another form called a **Financial Evaluation**. A sponsoring guide will also be provided. Samples of both these forms and the instructions for their completion follow.

Your relative will complete these forms and mail them to the local Canadian Immigration Centre. Once approved, a copy of the Undertaking will be sent to the Canadian High Commission, Embassy or Consulate in your area of the world. You will be sent a letter by that office stating that an Undertaking of Assistance has been filed and approved in Canada and that you must now complete an **Application for Permanent Residence**. Once your completed application has been received by that office, a date and time will normally be set for you to meet an immigration officer.

Security and medical checks

After your interview, providing the immigration officer is satisfied with the results, a security check will be done on you and you will be asked to undergo a medical examination. This does not mean the immigration officer thinks you are sick or a subversive. These are routine checks done on every applicant, regardless of the immigration category in which you apply.

Once you have had your medical examination, the completed medical examination forms will be sent to Canadian immigration doctors by you or by the physician that examined you. You must be examined by a doctor in your country who is approved by the Canadian government to conduct such examinations.

Your immigration document

After the Canadian doctors have reviewed the results of the examination, they will transmit their decision back to the Immigration Office you are dealing with. Assuming you pass the medical examination and the security checks, you will then receive a document called an **Immigrant Visa and Record of Landing**. This is your 'immigrant visa' for Canada. You may then leave your country and travel to Canada as an immigrant. (See Figure 12.)

Keep in mind that:

- You must enter Canada before the expiration date on the visa, which is usually some months from the date of issue.

- Visas will not be extended under any circumstances.

- There is no Canadian visa impressed in your passport.

- You must present your Immigrant Visa and Record of Landing to a Canadian immigration officer at the port of entry to Canada.

At the port of entry you will be asked to sign the Immigrant Visa and Record of Landing to verify the information it contains. The officer will record your entry and stamp your passport with a small stamp. You are then a permanent resident (**landed immigrant**) of Canada.

THE FORMS REQUIRED

The above description is only an overall picture of the process you will have to go through to become a landed immigrant through sponsorship by a close relative in Canada. I mentioned two forms your relative will have to fill out. Samples are included on the following pages, which reproduce a typical Sponsorship Kit provided by Immigration Offices in Canada.

IMMIGRATION Canada

Sponsoring a Family Class Relative
Forms and Instructions

IMM-5196E (02-96)

Fig. 1. Sponsorship Kit.

Migrating To Canada

BEFORE YOU START...

Helping families be together is a very important part of Canada's immigration policy. Remember, when you sponsor family class relatives, you must look after their shelter and care for up to ten years. This application will help you decide if you can make this promise or not.

- ☐ Read through all the instructions detailed on the following pages before completing the forms.
- ☐ Please photocopy the blank forms and use one copy of the form as a working copy. Keep it for your records.
- ☐ Gather all the documents that you and your relatives need. These are listed under **Document Checklist – Undertaking**.
- ☐ You should now carefully complete the forms by following the step-by-step instructions. Sign and date your forms.
- ☐ Attach all the required documents to your application forms. Be sure to complete the **Document Checklist – Undertaking** and include it with your completed application.
- ☐ Calculate the fee you need to send using the **Immigration Fees Calculation Table**.
- ☐ Put one original and two photocopies (three photocopies if you reside in Quebec) of your **Undertaking** and **Financial Evaluation** forms, one copy of the **Document Checklist** form, supporting documents and appropriate fees in the return envelope.
- ☐ When filling in the return address on the envelope, ensure
    - a) you have entered **5196E** in the spaces provided for the type;
    - b) you have entered **Case Processing Centre** on the first line of the address box;
    - c) you have entered **P.O. Box 6100** on the second line of the address box;
    - d) entered **Adoption** on the last address line provided if this is an adoption case; and
    - e) you have entered **Mississauga** in the spaces provided for the City, **ON** in the spaces provided for the Province, and **L5A 4H4** in the spaces provided for the Postal Code.

    The following is an example of how that area should be completed:

    ```
                                            5196E
    ┌─────────────────────────────────┐
    │ Case Processing Centre          │
    │ P.O. Box 6100                   │
    │ (Adoption, if applicable)       │
    └─────────────────────────────────┘
            CITY/VILLE        PROV     POSTAL CODE POSTAL
           MISSISSAUGA         ON         L5A 4H4
    ```

- ☐ Clearly print your name and address in the space provided at the top left-hand side on the face of the return envelope.
- ☐ Have the post office weigh your envelope to ensure sufficient postage. The post office will return your application to you if there is not enough postage.
- ☐ If properly completed, your application will be processed within approximately 6–8 weeks and the decision will be sent to you by mail.
- ☐ If you wish to enquire about the status of your application, please telephone the nearest Immigration Telemessage Service as per the enclosed list.
- ☐ If you move, please contact your nearest Immigration Telemessage Service to advise them of your new address.

Things that slow down processing:
- Incomplete, unsigned or undated application forms
- Missing documents
- Incorrect or missing fees
- Not enough postage
- Incorrect or incomplete addresses

Sponsored Dependants

INSTRUCTIONS FOR COMPLETING FORM IMM 1344 UNDERTAKING

USE A BLACK PEN OR A TYPEWRITER. PRINT IN BLOCK LETTERS.
Add Chinese characters for any names and addresses in Chinese. Add Farsi script for names and addresses of persons residing in Iran.

PART A. SPONSOR

This section applies to the sponsor.

1. **Surname (family name) and given name(s):** Print all names in full. Do not use initials. This name will appear on all official documents issued in Canada.
2. Print an "x" in the appropriate box to indicate your **sex**.
3. **Date and place of birth:** Please provide your date of birth by the day, month, year. Print the name of the country where you were born.
4. Print the name of the country of your **citizenship**.
5. If you were born **IN CANADA**, do not complete this box. If you were born **OUTSIDE** of Canada, you **MUST** complete this box.

   Date of landing in Canada: This is the date you arrived in Canada and were granted permanent resident status.

   Record of Landing document number: This number can be found on your Record of Landing document in large, bold type.

   Name of country where my application for permanent residence was processed: At what office did you submit your application for permanent residence? Write the name of the country in this box.
6. Are you a **Canadian citizen?** Print an "x" in the box to indicate "YES" or "NO." Print your citizenship certificate number, if applicable.
7. Print an "x" in the box that indicates your **marital status**. Check one or more, for example, divorced but now remarried. Remember to send a copy of the Court judgement for your divorce or the death certificate of your deceased spouse.
8. **Current address in Canada:** Print the home address where you live now: include the street address, your apartment and/or your unit number, the city, province and your postal code.
9. **Mailing address:** Print your mailing address *if it is different* from your current home address.
10. Print your home telephone number, including the area code.
11. **Telephone number for messages:** If you have access to a telephone where a message can be left for you to call Canada Immigration, print this number here.
12. **What is the most convenient time for you to receive telephone messages?:** Print the time here.

PART B. FAMILY MEMBERS BEING SPONSORED AND THEIR DEPENDANTS

This is where the sponsor should enter the information about the relatives being sponsored.

NOTE: If you are sponsoring a spouse who is ethnic Chinese, you must complete the section on the back of the UNDERTAKING form in addition to the questions in Section B. If you are sponsoring a spouse from Iran, you must complete the section on the back of the UNDERTAKING form in addition to the questions in Section B.

13. **a) Family member you are sponsoring:** Print your spouse's name on the first line, the surname (family name) first, then the given name(s). Continue across the line and print the information requested in boxes 14–20. (See instructions for completing these boxes below.)

    b) His or her accompanying dependants: Enter the name of your spouse's dependent children who are in Canada. Continue across the line and print the information as requested.

    c) His or her dependants not accompanying: List your spouse's dependent children residing abroad. You **must** list these children in this space even though they are not coming to Canada at this time.

14. Print your relative's **relationship** to you (for example: *spouse, son, daughter*).
15. Please provide the **date of birth** (by the day, month, year) of your spouse and his/her dependent children.
16. Print the **name of the country** where your spouse and dependent children were **born**.
17. Print the **name of the country** where your spouse and dependent children are **citizens**.
18. Print the **marital status** of your spouse and dependent children. Refer to box 7. for types of marital status.
19. Put an "x" in the box indicating the **sex** of the person concerned.
20. **Type of dependent child:** Put an "x" in the box 1, 2 or 3 to indicate if your spouse's dependent children are:
    - **1:** unmarried and under 19 years of age
    - **2:** full-time students and financially dependent on your spouse
    - **3:** disabled and financially dependent on your spouse.

    These boxes are only to be filled in for dependent children.
21. **Current mailing address of persons named above:** Print your spouse's address. Please be sure the address is correct and complete. If not, visa offices will not be able to contact your relatives to send them application forms.
22. **a)** If you have previously sponsored other relatives, mark an "x" in the "YES" box. If you have not previously sponsored other relatives, mark an "x" in the "NO" box.

    b) If you have previously sponsored other relatives, and these relatives have **not** asked for money from the federal government or provincial government, mark an "x" in the "YES" box. This will confirm that you have supported these relatives. If your sponsored relatives **have** received money from the federal or provincial government in Canada, mark an "x" in the "NO" box.

PART C. DECLARATIONS

23. **and 24.** Answer all question in this section which relate to you. Failure to do so will result in your **Undertaking** being returned to you.
25. **Signature:** You must sign and date this undertaking. Failure to do so will result in your application being returned to you.

REMEMBER: **If the spouse you are sponsoring is ethnic Chinese or from Iran, you must complete Part D on the back of the Undertaking.**

Sponsored Dependants 25

INSTRUCTIONS FOR COMPLETING FORM IMM 1283 FINANCIAL EVALUATION

This form will help to determine if you have enough money to sponsor your relatives.
USE A BLACK PEN OR A TYPEWRITER. PRINT IN BLOCK LETTERS.
Add Chinese characters for any names and addresses in Chinese. Add Farsi script for names and addresses of persons residing in Iran.

1. **Surname (family name):** Print your family name.
2. **Given name(s):** Print all names in full. Do not use initials.
3. **Date of birth:** Print your date of birth, using the day, month, year.
4. **Size of family unit:** Count all of your family members (including yourself) who depend on you for support. Print the total number in box 4.
5. **Your employment:** Print the information as requested. Print the name, address and telephone number of your employer, as well as your occupation. Enter your gross annual income on the corresponding line in Section 7.
6. **Your spouse's employment:** Print the information as requested. Print the name, address and telephone number of your spouse's employer, as well as your spouse's occupation. Enter your spouse's gross annual income on the corresponding line in Section 7.
7. **Income from all sources:** Print the information as requested. If you are self-employed you must include with your application a copy of your most recent **Notice of Assessment** from Revenue Canada.

   Total income: Add the income from all sources and insert the total in box 7 (right-hand side of form). This will give you your total income.
8. **Debts:** Print the information as requested and insert the total in box 8 (right-hand side of form).
9. **Total income available:** From your total income (box 7), subtract your total debts (box 8). This will give you the amount of money you have available.

   Now look at the chart on the following page. What is the size of the community/city where you live? If it is 500,000 or over, see column **A**. If your community is smaller, go to the appropriate column: **B, C, D** or **E**. Go down the column until you come to the line where the number of persons you are responsible for crosses with the size of the community where you live. This will give you an estimate of how much money you will need to have each year to sponsor your relative(s).

   The amount of money available to you (TOTAL INCOME AVAILABLE) should be close to or higher than the number you found on the chart.
10. **Assets:** Please detail all of your assets and indicate the worth/value of each item listed. Worth/value should be based on current "Fair Market Value." If there is a debt to the item listed, please indicate the total debt amount as shown in the following example: House ($79,000 mortgage) − − $125,000
11. Both you and your spouse must sign the **Financial Evaluation**. Failure to do so will result in your application being returned to you.

LOW INCOME CUT-OFF OF FAMILY UNITS (effective April 1, 1994)

Size of Family Unit	SIZE OF AREA OF RESIDENCE				
	A	B	C	D	E
	500,000 and over	100,000 – 499,999	30,000 – 99,999	** Less than 30,000	Rural Areas
1 person	$15,452	$13,572	$13,259	$12,087	$10,520
2 persons	$20,945	$18,398	$17,973	$16,383	$14,261
3 persons	$26,624	$23,385	$22,844	$20,824	$18,126
4 persons	$30,655	$26,922	$26,302	$23,977	$20,869
5 persons	$33,492	$29,416	$28,737	$26,196	$22,801
6 persons	$36,356	$31,928	$31,192	$28,434	$24,749
7 persons	$39,101	$34,343	$33,551	$30,585	$26,620
For Each Additional Person	$2,800	$2,460	$2,410	$2,190	$1,915

**Includes cities with a population between 15,000 and 30,000 and small urban areas (under 15,000).

ATTENTION RESIDENTS OF QUÉBEC

The ministère des Affaires internationales, de l'Immigration et des Communautés culturelles of the Québec government (MAIICC) has income standards that differ from those of Immigration Canada.

If you wish to sponsor a family member other than your spouse or minor child, you must prove to the MAIICC that you have sufficient income to see to the basic needs of your immediate family and of the persons you wish to sponsor. The ministère will also take into consideration the basic need of the persons you have already sponsored. Below are the standards in force from January 1 to December 31, 1996. These amounts are indexed every year.

Basic needs of sponsor and dependant persons	
Number of dependant persons	Gross annual income of sponsor
0	$15,610
1	$21,074
2	$26,017
3	$29,920
4	$33,302
Required gross annual income is increased by $3,382 for each additional dependant.	

Basic needs of sponsored persons		
Persons 18 and over	Persons under 18	Annual gross amount required by sponsor
0	1	$5,403
0	2	$8,565
The annual gross amount required is increased by $2,855 for each additional person under 18		
1	0	$11,420
1	1	$15,343
1	2	$17,322
The annual gross amount required is increased by $1,980 for each additional person under 18		
2	0	$16,744
2	1	$18,759
2	2	$20,247
The annual gross amount required is increased by $1,488 for each additional person under 18 and by $5,325 for each additional person 18 or over.		

Sponsored Dependants 27

INSTRUCTIONS FOR COMPLETING FORM IMM 5287
DOCUMENT CHECKLIST – UNDERTAKING

The documents you need to send are listed below. Please gather up these documents, then complete the **Document Checklist – Undertaking**. Return the **Document Checklist** with your other forms and documents.

The Document Checklist – Undertaking will help you remember what to send and it will help us check that you have sent the correct documents and forms.

If any of the required documents is missing, your application form may be returned to you. All documents in a language other than English or French must be translated by a professional translator. Provide a photocopy of the original document and the translation in English or French.

FORMS
- Undertaking (IMM 1344)
- Financial Evaluation (IMM 1283)
- Document Checklist – Undertaking (IMM 5287)

IDENTIFICATION DOCUMENTS – PHOTOCOPIES ONLY
- Record of Landing (IMM 1000) or Permanent Resident Card (for persons who have immigrated to Canada) **and**
  both sides of a Canadian citizenship card (if you are now a Canadian citizen), **or**
  a Canadian birth certificate, **or**
  the identity pages from a Canadian passport.
- T-4 slip for income tax purposes, or letter from your employer, or most recent income tax return (or other evidence of residence in Canada)
- Divorce, annulment or death certificate from prior marriage(s)

FEES (as determined on form IMM 5214, Immigration Fees Calculation Table)
- **Processing Fee**: Fee for your application.
  The processing fee is for service only. It does not guarantee approval of your application for landing. It is not refundable. If your request is refused, you will have to submit a new processing fee to apply again.
- **Right of Landing Fee** (effective February 28, 1995)

28 Migrating To Canada

Example	
Basic needs of sponsor: (sponsor, spouse and 2 minor children)	$29,920
Basic needs of sponsored person: (main sponsored person, spouse, 1 child of major age and 2 minor children)	$25,572
Income necessary to acceptance of undertaking application	**$55,492**

The above amounts will enable you to determine whether you have the financial capacity for such an undertaking. However, your calculations will be only an estimate for a Québec immigration officer will make the definitive calculation.

If you have already sponsored a member of your family and you failed in your obligations, your application will probably be refused, even if you meet the financial requirements.

For further information, please do not hesitate to contact the office of the ministère des Affaires internationales, de l'Immigration et des Communautés culturelles in your region.

Montréal Direction régionale de Montréal 415, rue Saint-Roch Montréal (Québec) H3N 1K2 Tel.: (514)864−9191	**Montérégie** Direction régionale de la Montérégie 2533, rue Cartier Longueuil (Québec) J4K 4G5 Tel.: (514)928−7715
Québec, Chaudière-Appalaches, Bas-Saint-Laurent, Gaspésie, Saguenay-Lac-Saint-Jean, Côte-Nord and Îles-de-la-Madeleine regions Direction régionale de Québec 500, avenue de Lévis Québec (Québec) G1S 3E1 Tel.: (418)643−1435	Bureau de Trois-Rivières 100, rue Laviolette Édifice Capitanal, 1er étage Trois-Rivières (Québec) G9A 5S9 Tel.: (819)371−6011
Estrie and Mauricie-Bois-Francs regions Direction régionale de l'Estrie 740, rue Galt Ouest, bureau 400 Sherbrooke (Québec) J1H 1Z3 Tel.: (819)820−3606	**Outaouais, Abitibi-Témiscamingue and Nord-du-Québec** Direction régionale de l'Outaouais 259, boul. St-Joseph, Bureau 101 Hull (Québec) J8Y 6T1 Tel.: (819)772−3021
Laval, Laurentides and Lanaudière regions Direction régionale Laval, Laurentides et Lanaudière 1005, boulevard Pie X Chomedey, Laval (Québec) H7V 8A9 Tel.: (514)681−2775	

Sponsored Dependants 29

IMMIGRATION TELEMESSAGE SERVICE

Use the following telephone numbers to get access to the Immigration Telemessage Service in your area. An automated voice response will help you get answers to a wide range of Immigration questions any time of day or night. By using the touch-tone features of your telephone, you can even order an application kit or get an update on the status of your case.

ATLANTIC REGION	
Saint John's, *serving all of Newfoundland*	(709)722–5388
Halifax, *serving all of Nova Scotia*	(920)426–2970
Saint John, *serving all of New Brunswick*	(506)636–4587
Clients in Prince Edward Island may obtain service from any of the above numbers	
QUÉBEC REGION	
Hull, *serving Hull, Maniwaki and northern Québec*	(819)997–2911
Montréal, *serving surrounding area*	(514)496–1010
Québec City, *serving surrounding area*	(418)648–3625
Sherbrooke, *serving surrounding area*	(819)564–5722
Trois-Rivières, *serving surrounding area*	(819)371–5282
ONTARIO REGION	
Toronto, *serving the Greater Toronto and Mississauga areas*	(416)973–4444
St. Catharines, *serving the Niagara Peninsula from Lake Erie to Stoney Creek*	(905)988–2840
Sudbury, *serving north-eastern Ontario, from Georgian Bay. to the Québec border and north to James Bay*	(705)671–0725
Kitchener, *serving Cambridge, Guelph, Kitchener. Wellington, Waterloo, Huron & Perth*	(519)571–6674
Oshawa, *serving Durham Region, Oshawa. Peterborough, Ajax, Whitby & Pickering*	(905)721–7516
Ottawa, *serving Ottawa, Kingston and surrounding area*	(613)995–8131
Hamilton, *serving surrounding area*	(905)572–2787
London, *serving surrounding area*	(519)645–4113
Windsor, *serving surrounding area*	(519)966–8173
PRAIRIE REGION	
Winnipeg	(204)983–2043
Winnipeg, *serving all of Manitoba*	(800)663–9640
Regina	(306)780–6190
Regina, *serving Regina and southern Saskatchewan*	(800)667–9229
Saskatoon	(306)975–4117
Saskatoon, *serving Saskatoon and northern Saskatchewan*	(800)361–5148
Calgary	(403)292–5724
Calgary, *serving Calgary and southern Alberta*	(800)806–3706
Edmonton	(403)495–2100
Edmonton, *serving Edmonton and northern Alberta*	(800)313–4303
BRITISH COLUMBIA/YUKON REGION	
Vancouver	
– *serving the Vancouver calling area*	(604)666–2171
– *serving the rest of British Columbia and the Yukon*	(800)665–9100

Migrating To Canada

Citizenship and Immigration Canada / Citoyenneté et Immigration Canada

UNDERTAKING

PROTECTED WHEN COMPLETED - A

Please Print or Type

A - SPONSOR

1. SURNAME (FAMILY NAME) (and maiden name, if applicable) | GIVEN NAME(S) | CLIENT ID NUMBER
2. SEX: ☐ MALE ☐ FEMALE
3. DATE OF BIRTH (D M Y) | COUNTRY OF BIRTH
4. COUNTRY OF CITIZENSHIP
5. DATE OF LANDING IN CANADA (D M Y) | RECORD OF LANDING DOCUMENT NO. | NAME OF COUNTRY WHERE MY APPLICATION FOR PERMANENT RESIDENCE WAS PROCESSED
6. CANADIAN CITIZEN: ☐ YES ☐ NO | CITIZENSHIP CERTIFICATE NO.
7. MY PRESENT MARITAL STATUS (if more than one applies, please indicate e.g. divorced but now engaged):
   ☐ NEVER MARRIED ☐ MARRIED ☐ LEGALLY SEPARATED ☐ DIVORCED
   ☐ WIDOWED ☐ ANNULLED MARRIAGE
   SPOUSE'S NAME (WHERE APPLICABLE)
8. MY HOME ADDRESS IS, INCLUDE APT. / UNIT # | POSTAL CODE
9. MY MAILING ADDRESS IS ☐ SAME AS IN BOX 8 OR | POSTAL CODE
10. HOME TELEPHONE NO. — AREA CODE / NO.
11. TELEPHONE NO. FOR MESSAGES — AREA CODE / NO.
12. INDICATE MOST CONVENIENT TIME TO REACH YOU BY TELEPHONE | TIME ☐ AM ☐ PM

B - FAMILY MEMBERS BEING SPONSORED AND THEIR DEPENDANTS - please refer to instructions for part "B"
(for Chinese characters/Farsi script - see part "D")

13 SURNAME (FAMILY NAME) (include birth name/maiden name if applicable)	GIVEN NAME(S)	14 RELATIONSHIP TO SPONSOR	15 DATE OF BIRTH (D M Y)	16 COUNTRY OF BIRTH	17 COUNTRY OF CITIZENSHIP	18 MARITAL STATUS	19 SEX M F	20 TYPE OF DEPENDENT CHILD 1 2 3
a) Family member you are sponsoring							☐☐	☐☐☐
b) His or her accompanying dependants							☐☐	☐☐☐
							☐☐	☐☐☐
							☐☐	☐☐☐
							☐☐	☐☐☐
							☐☐	☐☐☐
c) His or her dependants not accompanying							☐☐	☐☐☐
							☐☐	☐☐☐
							☐☐	☐☐☐

21. PRESENT MAILING ADDRESS OF PERSON(S) BEING SPONSORED (USE CHINESE/FARSI SCRIPT IF APPLICABLE)
    TELEPHONE NO.

22.
   a) I HAVE PREVIOUSLY SPONSORED RELATIVES ☐ YES ☐ NO
   b) IF YES, HAVE YOU SUPPORTED ALL RELATIVES PREVIOUSLY SPONSORED WITHOUT GOVERNMENT ASSISTANCE ☐ YES ☐ NO

CONTINUED ON REVERSE
(DISPONIBLE EN FRANCAIS - IMM 1344 F)

IMM 1344 (12-95) E

Canada

Sponsored Dependants 31

C - DECLARATIONS

23 Answer each of the following statements by entering "YES" or "NO" in the box.   YES / NO

I HAVE READ AND UNDERSTAND THE WARNING INDICATED BELOW

I WILL PROVIDE OR ASSIST IN PROVIDING (AS REQUIRED) ADEQUATE LODGING, CARE AND MAINTENANCE FOR MY FAMILY MEMBERS NAMED ON THIS UNDERTAKING FOR THE PERIOD DETERMINED BY AN IMMIGRATION OFFICER. I UNDERSTAND THAT THIS PERIOD MAY BE FOR AS LONG AS TEN YEARS

I WILL PROVIDE FINANCIAL ASSISTANCE TO THE FAMILY MEMBER(S) NAMED ON THIS UNDERTAKING SO THAT THEY WILL NOT REQUIRE FINANCIAL ASSISTANCE FROM ANY FEDERAL OR PROVINCIAL ASSISTANCE PROGRAM.

24 Answer "YES" or "NO" to (a) or (b) only if you are a Sponsor who is:

a) **RESIDING IN QUÉBEC:**
I UNDERSTAND THAT THE MINISTÈRE DES AFFAIRES INTERNATIONALES, DE L'IMMIGRATION ET DES COMMUNAUTÉS CULTURELLES (MAIICC) WILL ASSESS MY ABILITY TO FULFILL THE FINANCIAL OBLIGATIONS FOR MY FAMILY MEMBER(S) NAMED ON THIS UNDERTAKING.

b) **SPONSORING A FIANCÉ(E):**
I SOLEMNLY DECLARE THAT I AM FREE TO MARRY AND THAT MY MARRIAGE TO MY FIANCÉ(E) AS NAMED ON THIS UNDERTAKING WILL TAKE PLACE WITHIN NINETY DAYS OF MY FIANCÉ(E) BEING GRANTED LANDING. I WILL SEND PROOF OF MY MARRIAGE WITHIN 180 DAYS OF MARRIAGE TO CANADA IMMIGRATION.

25 SPONSOR'S SIGNATURE

SIGNATURE OF SPONSOR	DATE	SIGNATURE OF SPOUSE	DATE

WARNING FOR SPONSOR

THE INFORMATION TO BE PROVIDED ON THIS UNDERTAKING IS REQUIRED FOR THE PURPOSE OF DETERMINING THE ELIGIBILITY OF YOUR RELATIVE(S) FOR PERMANENT ADMISSION TO CANADA AND TO VERIFY YOUR ELIGIBILITY FOR THE PURPOSE OF THE UNDERTAKING AS AUTHORIZED BY THE IMMIGRATION ACT AND THE REGULATIONS THEREUNDER. INFORMATION YOU PROVIDE ON THIS FORM WILL BE HELD IN PERSONAL INFORMATION BANK "SPONSORS OF IMMIGRANTS", EIC PPU 240. YOU HAVE THE RIGHT OF ACCESS TO IT AND TO ITS PROTECTION UNDER THE PRIVACY ACT.

A CHECK OF IMMIGRATION CENTRAL INDICES WILL BE MADE TO VERIFY YOUR CLAIM TO BEING A CANADIAN CITIZEN OR LEGAL PERMANENT RESIDENT OF CANADA

ACCEPTANCE OF THIS UNDERTAKING IS NOT A GUARANTEE THAT YOUR RELATIVE'S (RELATIVES') APPLICATION FOR PERMANENT RESIDENCE WILL BE APPROVED. YOUR RELATIVE(S) MUST ESTABLISH THAT THEY COMPLY WITH THE REQUIREMENTS OF THE IMMIGRATION ACT AND REGULATIONS.

THERE IS A PENALTY FOR DECLARING FALSE INFORMATION AS LISTED IN SECTION 94 OF THE IMMIGRATION ACT.

THE MINISTER MAY ASSIGN INTEREST IN THIS UNDERTAKING TO HER MAJESTY IN RIGHT OF ANY PROVINCE IN WHICH YOUR RELATIVE(S) RESIDE OR RESIDED DURING THE PERIOD OF YOUR UNDERTAKING.

WHERE PAYMENTS ARE MADE TO YOUR RELATIVE(S) FROM ANY OF THE PRESCRIBED ASSISTANCE PROGRAMS, SUCH PAYMENTS SHALL BE DEEMED TO HAVE RESULTED FROM A BREACH OF THIS UNDERTAKING.

HER MAJESTY IN RIGHT OF CANADA OR IN RIGHT OF ANY PROVINCE TO WHICH AN UNDERTAKING IS ASSIGNED MAY TAKE ACTION IN ANY COURT OF COMPETENT JURISDICTION TO RECOVER SUCH PAYMENTS AS A DEBT DUE TO HER MAJESTY.

D - CHINESE CHARACTERS/FARSI SCRIPT

NOTE: IF YOUR RELATIVE IS ETHNICALLY CHINESE, YOU MUST USE THE SPACE BELOW TO WRITE THE CHINESE CHARACTERS FOR ALL NAMES AND ADDRESSES OF RELATIVES YOU ARE SPONSORING AS INDICATED IN BOX 13 ON THE FACE OF THIS FORM. (ATTACH ANOTHER SHEET IF YOU NEED MORE SPACE.)

IF YOUR RELATIVE IS IRANIAN, YOU MUST USE THE SPACE BELOW TO WRITE THE FARSI SCRIPT FOR ALL NAMES AND ADDRESSES OF RELATIVES YOU ARE SPONSORING AS INDICATED IN BOX 13 ON THE FACE OF THIS FORM. (ATTACH ANOTHER SHEET IF YOU NEED MORE SPACE.)

FAMILY NAME	GIVEN NAME(S)
ADDRESS	
FAMILY NAME	GIVEN NAME(S)
ADDRESS	
FAMILY NAME	GIVEN NAME(S)
ADDRESS	
FAMILY NAME	GIVEN NAME(S)
ADDRESS	
FAMILY NAME	GIVEN NAME(S)
ADDRESS	

OFFICIAL USE ONLY

CIC FILE NO	P/S CODE	SETTLEMENT ARRANGEMENTS	MET FOR	PERSON(S)	SPONSOR RECEIVING GOVERNMENT ASSISTANCE	N/A	LENGTH OF UNDERTAKING	YEARS
COST RECOVERY CODE	AMOUNT	RECEIPT NO		PROCESSING OF APPLICATIONS AT			CURRENTLY TAKES A MINIMUM OF	MONTHS
VISA OFFICE		LOCK-IN DATE AT CANADA IMMIGRATION	D M Y	SIGNATURE OF IMMIGRATION OFFICER		DATE SIGNED	D M Y	

IMM 1344 (12-95) E

32 Migrating To Canada

Citizenship and Immigration Canada
Citoyenneté et Immigration Canada

FINANCIAL EVALUATION

PROTECTED WHEN COMPLETED - B

MUST BE COMPLETED BY SPONSOR

WARNING: IT IS AN OFFENCE UNDER SECTION 94 OF THE IMMIGRATION ACT AND SECTION 397 OF THE CRIMINAL CODE OF CANADA TO KNOWINGLY MAKE A FALSE STATEMENT ON THIS FORM.

CLIENT ID NUMBER

1 Surname (Family Name)	2 - Given Names	3 Date of Birth

4 - SIZE OF FAMILY

You ....
Your spouse .... +
Children that depend on you or your spouse for support (regardless of age or degree of dependancy) .... +
Previously sponsored relatives who are still dependent on you or your spouse for support (previous undertaking still valid) .. +
Any other relatives who are dependent on you or your spouse for support .... +
Relatives you are sponsoring on the Undertaking .... +
Other dependent children of the principal applicant who are not applying for permanent residence at this time .... +

Total Size of Family Unit

Total Number of Persons who will be or are dependent upon you or your spouse for support (total of all boxes) 4

5 - YOUR EMPLOYMENT (If you are employed with more than one employer, please detail on a separate sheet and attach to this form)

Are you employed?
☐ Yes ▸ ☐ In Canada ☐ Abroad
☐ No ▸ Are you receiving government assistance?
　　　　☐ Yes (provide details)
　　　　☐ No ▸ How are you supporting yourself? (provide details)

Name and Address of Employer

Supervisor or Personnel Officer's Name

Area Code & Telephone Number

You must attach a copy of your most recent T4 forms, or a copy of your most recent Income Tax return as proof of earnings.

Postal Code

Occupation ▸

☐ Full Time ☐ Part Time ☐ Seasonal

6 - SPOUSE'S EMPLOYMENT (If your spouse is employed with more than one employer, please detail on a separate sheet and attach to this form)

Name of Spouse, including Birth Name/Maiden Name

Is your spouse employed?
☐ Yes ▸ ☐ In Canada ☐ Abroad
☐ No ▸ Is your spouse receiving government assistance?
　　　　☐ Yes (provide details)
　　　　☐ No ▸ How is your spouse supporting yourself? (provide details)

Name and Address of Spouse's Employer

Supervisor or Personnel Officer's Name

Area Code & Telephone Number

You must attach a copy of spouse's most recent T4 forms, or a copy of spouse's most recent Income Tax return as proof of earnings.

Postal Code

Spouse's Occupation ▸

☐ Full Time ☐ Part Time ☐ Seasonal

IMM 1282 (11-95) E

(DISPONIBLE EN FRANÇAIS - IMM 1283 F)

Canadä

Sponsored Dependants

33

- INCOME FROM ALL SOURCES (You must provide proof of this income)   Amount Per Year

Employment   Self .... $
　　　　　　Spouse .... $
Self-employment earnings .... $
Rental Income .... $
Pension Income .... $
Child Tax Benefit .... $
Other Income (please specify) ─────── $

Total Income From All Sources

7 $ |_|_|_|_|_|_|_|

- DEBTS

Amount of Payment Per Year

Rent/Mortgage .... $
Bank Loans.. $
Car Loans... $
Other .... $

Total Debts

8 $ |_|_|_|_|_|_|_|

- TOTAL INCOME AVAILABLE   (Subtract Box 8 from Box 7)

Total Income Available

9 $ |_|_|_|_|_|_|_|

- ASSETS - please detail (If more space required please detail on a separate sheet and attach to this form)

_____ $ _____
_____ $ _____
_____ $ _____
_____ $ _____
_____ $ _____
_____ $
_____ $

Total Assets

10 $ |_|_|_|_|_|_|_|

- I certify that the above information is true and give consent to Citizenship and Immigration Canada to verify any of the information I have provided on this Financial Evaluation.

_____　_____　_____　_____
Signature of Sponsor　　　　　　　　Date　　　　　　　Signature of Sponsor's Spouse　　　Date

- FOR OFFICE USE ONLY

TOTAL INCOME (7)　　−　　TOTAL DEBTS (8)　　=　　AMOUNT AVAILABLE TO SPONSOR (9)　　AMOUNT REQUIRED (low income cut-off figure)

[　　　　　　　]　　　　[　　　　　　　]　　　　[　　　　　　　]　　　　[　　　　　　　]

Settlement Arrangements　　☐ Met　　☐ Not met

Officer's Comments

_____　_____
Signature of Immigration Officer　　Date

The information to be provided on the Financial Evaluation form is required for the purpose of determining your financial ability to provide for your relative(s) seeking admission to Canada and is collected under the authority of the Immigration Act. Information you provide on this form will be stored in personal information bank EIC PPU 0 and is protected and accessible under the provisions of the Privacy Act.

IM 1283 (11-95) E

Migrating To Canada

Citizenship and Immigration Canada / Citoyenneté et Immigration Canada

PROTECTED WHEN COMPLETED - B

IMMIGRATION FEES CALCULATION TABLE (EFFECTIVE FEBRUARY 28, 1995)

Immigration Fees must be paid when you apply to visit, study, work, live in Canada, or are applying to sponsor a relative. This form will help you determine the fees for the service you want. Please note that these fees are subject to change. Once you are satisfied that you are eligible for the service you are requesting, determine the fee amount you must pay by completing the following tables:

CALCULATION TABLE

A PROCESSING FEES: IMMIGRANTS	FEE AMOUNT		NUMBER		TOTAL
APPLICATION FOR MINISTERIAL EXEMPTION: (This refers to applications from within Canada for landing on humanitarian and compassionate grounds) IN-CANADA APPLICATION FOR LANDING: (This refers to applications for permanent residence made by Convention Refugees, Live-in Caregivers in Canada and Post-determination Refugee Claimants in Canada.)					
Applicant and spouse	$ 500.00 each person	X		=	$
Dependent son or daughter 19 years and older	$ 500.00 each person	X		=	$
Dependent son or daughter under age 19	$ 100.00 each person				
SPONSORSHIP OF A FAMILY CLASS RELATIVE:					
All applicants	$ 500.00 each person	X		=	$
Except dependent son or daughter under age 19	$ 100.00 each person	X		=	$
B RIGHT OF LANDING FEE					
RIGHT OF LANDING FEE: (effective Feb. 28, 1995) (This refers to applicants for permanent residence and sponsorship undertakings)					
All applicants 19 years of age and older	$ 975.00 each person	X		=	$
			FEES (A + B) ▶		$

CONTINUED ON REVERSE
(DISPONIBLE EN FRANÇAIS - IMM 5214 F)

IMM 5214 (11-95) E

Canadä

TO BE COMPLETED IF YOU ARE PAYING BY CREDIT CARD

Citizenship and Immigration Canada / Citoyenneté et Immigration Canada

PROTECTED WHEN COMPLETED - B

I agree to pay the Receiver General for Canada $_____ .00 on my credit card for the Immigration services I have requested.	☐ VISA ☐ MASTERCARD (please place an "X" to indicate the type of credit card)
Card Number	Name of Cardholder (please print)
Expiry Date of the Card	Signature of Cardholder
	FOR OFFICIAL USE ONLY ▶ Authorization Number

IMM 5214 (11-95) E

Canadä

Sponsored Dependants 35

C PROCESSING FEES: NON-IMMIGRANTS	FEE AMOUNT		FEES (A+B) ▶ NUMBER		$ TOTAL
VISITOR EXTENSION (Applicable to persons requesting an extension as a visitor-tourist. Please see guidebook for definition.)	$ 65.00 individual	X		=	$
RE-INSTATEMENT OF VISITOR STATUS (You will be informed when to submit this fee)	$ 125.00 individual	X		=	$
STUDENT AUTHORIZATION	$ 125.00 individual	X		=	$
EMPLOYMENT AUTHORIZATION	$ 125.00 individual	X		=	$
Group (2 - 14) Entertainers	$ 250.00	X		=	$
MINISTER'S PERMIT	$ 175.00 individual	X		=	$
Group (2 - 14) Entertainers	$ 350.00	X		=	$
EXTENSION OF MINISTER'S PERMIT	$ 175.00 individual	X		=	$
MAXIMUM RATE: Combination of Non-Immigrant documents	$ 350.00 see below	X		=	$
			FEES (C) ▶		$
		TOTAL FEES (A+B+C) ▶			$

MAXIMUM RATE: COMBINATION OF DOCUMENTS
Applicable only to a visitor extension, employment authorization, student authorization, a Minister's permit or an extension of a Minister's permit. When members of a family apply together or an individual applies for renewal of a variety of visitor documents, the maximum rate for a combination of documents will apply, unless it is beneficial to the family or the individual to pay the individual cost of all documents.

CONVENTION REFUGEES:
As of June 1, 1994, there is a fee for filing a Convention Refugee application for permanent residence. Convention Refugees must submit their application for permanent residence and the processing fee within 180 days of being informed in writing that they have been recognized as Convention Refugees. There is no fee for employment or student authorizations for a Convention Refugee and his/her dependents.

PAYMENT MAY BE MADE BY:
- Certified cheque, traveller's cheque, postal order (make payable to: The Receiver General for Canada)
- Visa or MasterCard (sign the credit card authorization)
- Loan agreement - Right of Landing Fee only (Please consult the Right of Landing Fee Loan Application kit for more details)

DO NOT SEND CASH IN THE MAIL! DO NOT SEND PERSONAL CHEQUES!

IMM 5214 (11-95) E

Migrating To Canada

Citizenship and Immigration Canada

Citoyenneté et Immigration Canada

DOCUMENT CHECKLIST - UNDERTAKING
LISTE DE CONTRÔLE DES DOCUMENTS - ENGAGEMENT

The following is a checklist of everything you must do to make sure that your UNDERTAKING will be processed quickly. If all questions are not answered, if the forms are not signed, or if you do not include the correct processing fee, your complete kit will be returned to you. As well, you must include ALL documents, and information requested. If you do not, there will be a delay in the processing of your UNDERTAKING.

1. Keep a photocopy of all the forms, documents and attachments that you submit to Canada Immigration.

2. Review the forms UNDERTAKING and FINANCIAL EVALUATION to make sure that you have answered all the questions and signed the forms. If all questions are not answered, or if the forms are not signed, your complete kit will be returned to you. No processing will take place on your UNDERTAKING. This will result in a delay in the processing of your UNDERTAKING.

3. Your Processing Fee:

   Review the information to ensure that you have included the correct processing fee. If you wish to confirm the amount you should pay, you can call your nearest Canada Immigration Centre.

4. The following is a list of what you must send to Canada Immigration in the envelope provided:

Le présent document de contôle porte sur tout ce que vous devez faire pour assurer le traitement rapide de votre ENGAGEMENT. Si vous n'avez pas répondu à toutes les questions, si les formulaires ne sont pas signés ou si vous ne joignez pas les droits de traitement appropriés, la trousse vous sera retournée au complet. Vous devez également joindre à votre demande TOUS les documents nécessaires et TOUS les renseigements demandés, à défaut de quoi le traitement de votre ENGAGEMENT sera retardé.

1. Conservez une photocopie de tous les formulaires et documents que vous faites parvenir à Immigration Canada.

2. Assurez-vous d'avoir répondu à toutes les questions des formulaires ENGAGEMENT et ÉVALUATION DE LA SITUATION FINANCIÈRE et d'avoir signé tous les formulaires. Si vous avez omis de répondre à des questions ou de signer un formulaire, votre trousse vous sera retournée au complet. Votre ENGAGEMENT ne fera l'objet d'aucun traitement; ce dernier sera retardé.

3. Vos droits de traitement :

   Revoyez les renseignements pour vous assurer que vous avez inclus les droits de traitement appropriés. Si vous désirez confirmer le montant des droits à payer, vous pouvez appeler le Centre d'Immigration Canada le plus proche.

4. Voici la liste de ce que vous devez envoyer à Immigration Canada dans l'enveloppe prévue à cet effet:

PUT AN "X" IN THE BOX IF YOU SENT THE DOCUMENT

INSCRIRE UN "X" SI VOUS AVEZ ENVOYÉ LE DOCUMENT

- The Undertaking form and one photocopy (two photocopies in Quebec) ☐
- The Financial Evaluation form ☐
- A photocopy of both sides of your Canadian Citizenship card, or ☐
- A photocopy of both sides of your birth certificate issued by the province in which you were born; or ☐
- A photocopy of your Record of Landing document (IMM 1000) ☐
- A copy of divorce judgement if you have been previously married and are sponsoring a fiancé(e) or spouse ☐
- A photocopy of evidence of your income ☐
- The correct processing fee ☐

- Le formulaire d'engagement plus une photocopie (deux photocopies au Québec) ☐
- Le formulaire d'évaluation de la situation financière ☐
- Une photocopie des deux côtés de votre carte de citoyenneté canadienne ou ☐
- Une photocopie des deux cotés de votre acte de naissance délivré par la province où vous êtes né(e). ou ☐
- Une photocopie de votre fiche relative au droit d'établissement (IMM 1000) ☐
- Une copie du jugement de divorce si vous avez déjà été marié(e) et si vous parrainez un(e) fiancé(e) ou un(e) conjoint(e). ☐
- Une photocopie d'une preuve de votre revenu ☐
- Les droits de traitement appropriés ☐

Canada

Undertaking of Assistance Form

This is the form that must be filled out by your relative. Your relative must complete the form as accurately as possible following the detailed instructions. The form also contains a Declaration and a Warning. Acting as sponsor, your relative has certain obligations to you, and this section of the form sets out those responsibilities. These responsibilities include the following: that your relative undertakes to provide for your room and board and general welfare, for a certain specified period, which is usually five or ten years.

This does not mean that you have to live with your relative or take money from your relative. It simply means that, during this specified period, should you become unable to support yourself financially, your sponsor is required to provide for you.

Your relative must sign this form and if your relative is married, his or her spouse should also sign the Undertaking.

Financial Evaluation Form

This is the other form your relative will have to fill out. Its purpose is to determine if your relative has the financial resources necessary to undertake responsibility for you and your dependants accompanying you to Canada.

Your relative needs to complete this form very carefully following the detailed instructions provided. Your relative has to calculate the size of the Family Unit (question 4 on the form, including you and your family) to determine if he or she has the financial resources to support you in Canada, should this be necessary.

Take a look at the 'Low Income Cut-Off of Family Units' provided in the kit. Let's assume you are married with one child. You will see that if your single relative is sponsoring you, resides in a large city, and has never sponsored anyone before, he has to be responsible for four (4) people; himself, you, your wife and your child, and will need to have a total annual income of at least Cdn$30,655 to have his Undertaking approved.

While the family income level required of your relative is relatively modest, it increases quickly depending on the size of his or her family and the number of relatives for whom an Undertaking has been previously submitted.

DOCUMENTATION REQUIRED

Firstly, your relative has to include a copy of his or her **Immigrant**

Visa and Record of Landing and/or **Canadian Citizenship** card for himself/herself and spouse.

Your sponsor also must provide documents to substantiate the funds he or she has indicated on the Financial Evaluation Form, such as bank records, savings account book, certificates of deposit, and so on. Banks in Canada routinely issue letters certifying the amount their clients have on account in the bank, and your relative should approach his bank for such a letter.

Your relative should also provide a letter from his or her employer, which must show the nature of his or her employment, present salary, the length of time employed there, and whether income and other taxes are deducted. If your relative is married, then a similar letter from his or her spouse's employer is also necessary.

Another essential point is that your relative must be able to provide some form of documentation indicating his relationship to you. For example, in the case of a spouse, a marriage certificate is essential. If your brother is in Canada, he should include a copy of his birth certificate and your birth certificate in order to prove the relationship.

Proving a relationship is often a very difficult matter. In some countries a birth certificate is not obtained by parents and may not be registered during the course of one's life. If your relative cannot prove the relationship and if your case is refused on these grounds, or for any reason whatsoever, your relative has a right to appeal to the Immigration Appeal Board in Canada. Note that even though you are the applicant and your relative in Canada is only assisting you, it is your relative who has a right to appeal and not you.

YOUR INTERVIEW AT THE CANADIAN IMMIGRATION OFFICE

As was pointed out in the overview of the process you will have to follow, you will normally be called for an interview with a Canadian immigration officer. This will take place after the Canadian High Commission, Embassy, or Consulate has received instructions from Canada that your relative's Undertaking of Assistance has been accepted and after you have submitted an Application for Permanent Residence in Canada.

The documentation required at your interview varies from office to office. You will normally receive a letter listing the specific documents required by the Canadian High Commission, Embassy, or Consulate dealing with your application.

You should take along your passport and other travel documents. If you are married, you should take your marriage certificate. You should also take along proof of your assets, such as bank books and statements, certificates of deposit, and so on.

If you have any degrees or other educational certificates, diplomas, trade certificates, or professional membership letters, you should take the originals to the interview with you.

At the interview you will be asked some questions by the immigration officer. The most common of these are the following:

- Do you intend to work in Canada?

- Who are your relatives in Canada?

- How does the relationship come about?

- Why do you want to live in Canada?

- Have you visited Canada before? If so, where did you go? How long did you stay? What was the purpose of your trip? What were your impressions of Canada?

- How much money will you take with you to Canada? How much will you transfer later?

The above questions are only meant as guidelines for you to prepare for the interview. Keep in mind that as a Sponsored Dependant your educational and occupational qualifications are not taken into account. Basically, all you have to do is prove your relationship to your sponsor. But, you need to answer all the questions put to you, which may or may not include any or all of the above questions.

Answer each question as truthfully and completely as possible. There is a special section in Chapter 7, dealing exclusively with interviews for independent applicants. Some of it is relevant to you, too, so you might wish to read through it.

The next few chapters deal with Independent Applicants, and not Sponsored Dependants. If you are applying as a Sponsored Dependant, please skip to Chapter 6 entitled 'The Application Forms and Documents' and read through that chapter and subsequent chapters.

3
Independent Applicants

The process for an Independent Applicant to immigrate to Canada is much more involved than the one for a Sponsored Dependant.

DOCUMENTATION

Your first step is to consider all the documents you may need. The documents you will need might include the following, if applicable:

- your birth certificate

- your passport

- your marriage certificate

- your children's and spouse's birth certificates

- your divorce certificate or death certificate of your spouse

- police certificates of No Criminal Record

- military records

- passport size photographs of yourself and spouse and your dependants accompanying you

- evidence of your relationship to any relative in Canada

- your relative's Canadian passport, citizenship card, or Immigration Record and Visa

- any offers of employment in Canada you might have, or

Independent Applicants

detailed business plans for Self-Employed Persons and Entrepreneurs

- evidence of investment in an Investment Syndicate in Canada

- records of all your assets, including your bank books, certificates of deposit as well as tax returns

- records of your past employment, including letters from your previous employers stating dates of employment, nature of work, etc.

- all your degrees, diplomas, trade certificates, professional membership cards

- any other supporting documents about yourself and your spouse that will be required by Canada Immigration or any other documents that you feel would support your application for permanent residence.

OVERVIEW OF THE PROCESS

After you have considered all the documentation that may be required, you should visit or write to the nearest Canadian immigration office and indicate your desire to receive an **Application for Permanent Residence**.

Interview

You should fill out the Application for Permanent Residence as carefully as possible and submit it along with the necessary documentation. If the application is accepted, you will be called for an interview with a Canadian immigration officer.

You will recall that there are 4 subsections within the Independent Applicant category:

1. Skilled Workers (intending to seek employment in Canada)

2. Entrepreneurs

3. Investors

4. Self-Employed Persons

Depending on your circumstances, and depending on the category in which you have applied, your application will be processed in different ways. These will be outlined later.

There are several possible outcomes to the interview. The immigration officer may refuse to consider your application further and find you not qualified to proceed to Canada. Or, he may approve it for you to go to Canada to seek employment. Or, he may consider your plans to establish or purchase a business in Canada under the Entrepreneur or Self-Employed categories. Or, you may be applying as an Investor. Additional information or documentation may be requested. If your application is approved, the next step for all applicants is to undergo a medical examination and security check.

If you pass the medical and security checks, you will be issued a visa called an **Immigrant Visa and Record of Landing** and may proceed to Canada (Figure 12). After a check at the port of entry, and the completion of certain formalities, you will enter Canada as a permanent resident (landed immigrant).

All this may sound very confusing. However, we will take each step of the process and explain it in much greater detail.

Before doing this and advising you on how to maximize your chances of success in each situation, it is necessary to first evaluate your qualifications.

There is no point in going through the demanding exercise of applying for permanent residence in Canada and paying the substantial Government of Canada processing fee, if you are clearly not qualified.

PROCESSING AND RIGHT OF LANDING FEES

The current processing fee is between Cdn$500 and Cdn$825 depending on the category in which you apply, **plus** Cdn$500 for your spouse, **plus** Cdn$500 for each dependent child over 19 years of age, **plus** Cdn$100 for each child under 19 years of age. Additionally, a Right of Landing fee of Cdn$925 has been imposed for the applicant, his or her spouse and dependent children over 19 years of age. There is no fee for children under the age of 19.

Independent Applicants

The Processing Fee is non-refundable. However, the Right of Landing fee is refunded if an application is refused. Both fees must be submitted along with the Application For Permanent Residence. Please see Appendix D for a more detailed schedule of the Government of Canada fees.

THE POINT SYSTEM—AN OVERVIEW

Up to this point we have only discussed your options and narrowed down the best option for you. We have not examined your situation to see whether or not you have a realistic chance of being successful in your application. The process used to assess the hundreds of thousands of applications received every year is called the **Point System**.

The point system applies to every independent applicant. The norms of assessment do not change by the country of your citizenship, country of your application, officer doing the assessment, or any other special circumstance or situation. The norms of assessment are listed in Figure 2, simplified into non-technical language.

THE POINT SYSTEM IN DETAIL

We will now go through each of the factors listed in Figure 2 to help you evaluate your qualifications. Working charts follow to help you calculate your points.

1. Education
You can be awarded a **maximum of 16 units** for education as follows:

(a) **No units** if secondary (high) school has not been completed.
(b) **Five (5)** units if secondary school has been completed but the Diploma does not provide entrance to university.
(c) **Ten (10)** units if secondary school has been completed and the program provides entry to university.
(d) **Ten (10)** units if secondary school has been completed and the completed program includes trade or occupational cerification.
(e) **Thirteen (13)** units if you have completed a post-secondary program (of at least 1 year) admission to which requires secondary schooling at the level required for entry to univerisity.
(f) **Fifteen (15)** units if you have completed a Bachelor's degree.
(g) **Sixteen (16)** units if you have completed a Master's degree or Ph.D. degree.

Factors	Assessment Criteria	Maximum Points
1. Education	One point is awarded for each year of primary and secondary education you have successfully completed.	16
2. Specific Vocational Preparation (SVP)	The award is measured by the amount of formal professional, vocational, apprenticeship, in-plant or on-the-job training necessary for average performance in the applicant's intended occupation.	18
3. Experience	Points are awarded for the years of experience you have in your occupation or in the business you plan to establish.	8
4. Occupational Demand	Points are awarded on the basis of the demand for the occupation in which you are qualified.	10
5. Arranged Employment (or Designated Occupation)	Points will be awarded to you if you have arranged employment in Canada, provided you have official approval for the job, or if you fall within the current list of Designated Occupations.	10
6. Levels Control (Demographic Factor)	From zero (0) to ten (10) points, depending on predetermined immigration levels.	10
7. Age	If you are between 21 and 44 years old, you will be awarded the maximum points. Two points are subtracted for each full year you are over 44 or under 21.	10

Fig. 2. Assessment under the Point System.

8. Knowledge of French and English	If you are fluent in English and French, the two official languages of Canada, you will receive the maximum points. If you are fluent in one of the two languages you will receive nine (9) points.	15
9. Personal Suitability	An immigration officer will award you up to ten points based on his judgement on whether you will become successfully established in Canada.	10
Total		107
Pass Mark		70

Relatives in Canada
A bonus of five (5) points will be awarded to applicants with eligible relatives in Canada. An eligible relative has to be over 19 years of age and closer than a cousin.

2. Specific Vocational Preparation (SVP)

The points awarded on Specific Vocational Preparation (SVP) are calculated according to the amount of formal professional and other training required for the particular occupation in which you are qualified, and intend to seek in Canada. The Canadian Government has established an SVP code number for each job or occupation and publishes the code numbers in the *Canadian Classification and Dictionary of Occupations (CCDO)*. Those code numbers are then converted into points for immigration purposes. Unfortunately, unless you live in Canada, it is very unlikely you will find these books in your local library.

Since there are seven volumes of the *CCDO* with some 30,000 job titles listed, it would be impossible to reproduce them all in this book. But Appendix E contains a list of all occupations in demand at present with the actual points awarded on the factor of SVP, plus a sampling of job descriptions. Chapter 4 provides more detailed information about SVP.

3. Experience

The number of points you receive for the Experience factor depends not only on the years of experience you have in your occupation, but on the SVP of your occupation as well. Look at the previous section. What is the SVP you have for your occupation? Now use the chart below to find out how many points you can award yourself on the Experience factor.

SVP Points	Experience Points
2 to 3	2 points for each year, to a maximum of 2 points
5 to 7	2 points for each year, to a maximum of 4 points
11 to 15	2 points for each year, to a maximum of 6 points
18	2 points for each year, to a maximum of 8 points

What this means is that, regardless of how many years of experience you have, if your occupational title is Secretary (clerical), which has 11 SVP points, then you will receive a maximum of six (6) points on the experience factor.

- **Regardless of all other factors and considerations, unless you get at least two (2) points on this factor, your application will NOT be approved. In other words, you must have at least one year of experience in your intended occupation.**

4. Occupational Demand

The Occupational Demand factor is essential and usually makes the difference between acceptance or rejection. All applicants, *except* Entrepreneurs, Self-Employed persons and Investors, must receive at least one (1) point on this factor before their application for permanent residence can be approved. If your occupation is not in demand and you receive no points on this factor, your application will almost certainly be refused.

Independent Applicants

Between zero (0) and ten (10) points are awarded, depending on the demand for workers in any particular occupation, as decided by the Immigration Department.

Appendices A, B and C include all occupations currently having some demand and open to independent applicants.

- **Unless you intend to be an Entrepreneur, an Investor, or Self-Employed, you must get AT LEAST ONE POINT on this factor, in order for your application to be approved.**

5. Arranged Employment/Designated Occupation

You will get ten (10) points if you already have a job in Canada. But there is a catch. You must not only have a job waiting for you in Canada, but your employer must have *official sanction* to hire you, a non-resident of Canada, for the job.

You may think it will be rather easy for you to write to a friend or relative and arrange a job in Canada, or employ a third party such as an employment agency in Canada to find you a job. It is not that simple.

In order to obtain official approval to hire a non-resident for a job, a Canadian employer must approach the Canada Employment Centre nearest to the place of employment. The employer must then fill out a form called a Confirmation of Offer of Employment (EMP 5056).

The form requires detailed information about the name, address, and telephone number of the company, details about you, and about the job being offered to you. If the job title is one for which there are many Canadian residents available, the form will not be approved. If a job simply is described as a machine operator, for example, instead of a tool and die maker, although they might both be correct, the job offer may be refused because there are many general machine operators in Canada. The job description should be as detailed and specific as possible.

The employer must state the experience necessary for the job. The job offer must contain details of the related experience needed by anyone to meet the requirements, in addition to language or other skills that may be required.

The job must not be temporary, or only a temporary employment authorization may be issued to you. The employer must state the fringe benefits and salary that will be paid to you, which, of course, must be above the minimum wage.

At this point you might be thinking that your friend or relative in Canada can make up a job offer that is so carefully matched to your situation that no one else can fulfill the requirements. That is not possible. The job has to be matched to your experience and qualifications.

The employer should take this form to the Canada Employment Centre (CEC), along with certain other documents. For example, the employer could advertise the job being offered in Canada, and then take along the advertisements and some proof that there are no persons in Canada suitably qualified for the job.

After the form has been accepted by the Canada Employment Centre, the form will not normally be approved immediately, although that can happen. First, the Canada Employment Centre will usually try to find a Canadian resident for the job. The job title, description, and working conditions might be advertised and circulated to other Canada Employment Centres. Any person found available and qualified will be referred to the employer.

Your friend or relative cannot simply refuse to hire qualified people referred by the Canada Employment Centre, thereby keeping the job open to you. Approval to hire you will not be given in such a case, as officials will know there are qualified Canadian residents available for the job.

If there are no qualified Canadian residents found with the qualifications needed, the job offer may be approved, in which case the approval will be sent to the Canadian High Commission, Embassy or Consulate to which you have applied or will apply, and your application will be processed.

You should note that the process to obtain employment clearance can take weeks or months. Therefore, there are very few employers who will go through this rigorous procedure and wait for a long period of time to hire you, unless they have a very genuine need for your skills.

- **In short, it is not easy to obtain an approved offer of employment in Canada.**

Designated Occupation
You do not necessarily have to have an approved offer of employment to receive 10 points under the Arranged Employment Factor.

Independent Applicants

If you qualify in a Designated Occupation (listed in Appendix A) you will automatically receive the full ten (10) points on this factor.

6. Levels Control (Demographic Factor)
This factor (from 0 to 10 points) is regulated by Immigration to control the overall flow of immigrants. The points may be adjusted upwards or downwards to increase or decrease the number of applicants who would otherwise meet the selection criteria.

- **Eight (8) points are currently awarded to all applicants.**

7. Age
If you are between the ages of twenty-one (21) and forty-four (44), give yourself ten points. Deduct two points for every year you are over 44 or under 21.

8. Knowledge of Canada's Languages—English/French
If you are able to speak, read and write both English and French fluently, award yourself 15 points. (Fluently is defined as not needing language training after arrival in Canada.) If you are able to speak, read and write *either* English or French fluently, award yourself nine (9) points. If your ability is only to speak or to write or to read well either language, the points will be two (2) for each ability, and only one (1) if each ability is demonstrated with difficulty.

9. Personal Suitability
Up to ten (10) points will be awarded by a Canadian immigration officer, based on his assessment of your prospects of becoming successfully established in Canada.

The assessment will be made by the officer at your interview. The number of points he awards you is totally at his discretion, although six (6) or seven (7) out of 10 appears to be about average.

Ask yourself this question: given the Canadian way of life, how sure am I that I can successfully live there and integrate into society? Base your answer on your past experiences in moving, living in another country, on your knowledge of Canada, on your motivation, and so on. Now award yourself points between one and ten, based on your answer.

10. Relatives in Canada

Do you or your spouse have a relative in Canada, **closer** than a cousin, who is willing to help you? To be eligible your relative in Canada must be the mother, father, grandparent, brother, sister, uncle, aunt, nephew or niece of yourself *or* your spouse. If so, you may award yourself an extra five (5) points, provided you can prove the relationship.

We have now completed the point system. You should know that not all applicants have to meet all ten selection criteria.

A SELF-ASSESSMENT

You should now be ready to assess yourself.

Very carefully, you should go back to each factor and assess your points. Do *not* be generous with yourself or give yourself more points than you deserve. It is not in your interest to have anything but a realistic assessment.

You should also do an assessment of your spouse. Canadian law allows either spouse to apply for permanent residence. If your spouse were to apply and be approved, you and your unmarried children, if any, can accompany him or her to Canada. An assessment of your spouse will help you decide which of you should apply as the principal applicant.

SELF-ASSESSMENT CHARTS FOR EMPLOYMENT IN CANADA

Every independent applicant should fill in the table below. Even if you plan to be Self-Employed, an Investor or an Entrepreneur, do the points assessment for employment in Canada, which is based on nine (9) factors of the selection criteria (Figure 3).

If you have 70 or more points, there is a good chance of acceptance, and you should be called to interview.

Now look at your grand total and that of your spouse. First, whose grand total is larger? If it is your spouse's then he or she should probably apply instead of you.

If you have between 65 and 70 points and either you or your spouse have an eligible relative in Canada, you still have a good chance.

Factor	Estimated Assessment of Yourself	Estimated Assessment of Your Spouse	Max.	Min Reqd.
1. Education	( )	( )	16	—
2. SVP	( )	( )	18	—
3. Experience	( )	( )	8	1
4. Occupational Demand	( )	( )	10	1
5. Arranged Employment or Designated Occupation	( )	( )	10	—
6. Levels Control	( )	( )	10	—
7. Age	( )	( )	10	—
8. Knowledge of English/French	( )	( )	15	—
9. Personal Suitability	( )	( )	10	—
TOTAL			107	70

Fig. 3. Self-assessment chart for employment in Canada.

- **Give yourself a bonus of five (5) points if either you *or* your spouse has a relative in Canada over 19 years of age who is closer than a cousin.**

If you have less than 70 points, and no eligible relatives in Canada, you should go back to the section entitled 'How To Narrow Your Options'. Were you qualified to apply as an Entre- preneur or Investor, or a Self-Employed Person? If so, go to the tables below (Figures 4 and 5).

If you have less than 70 points and do not qualify in any of the above categories, then the chances of your application being accepted are not high. But there are always exceptions. For example, if you were educated in Canada and have returned to your home country and now have a year or two of occupational experience, the immigration officer might decide in your favour on a discretionary basis. Canadian immigration officers have the authority to recommend approval in situations where they consider the selection criteria do not accurately reflect your prospects of successful establishment in Canada. Normally, you will be called for interview if you have 60 or more points, before being awarded any points on the factor of Personal Suitability.

You may be able to take certain steps that could increase your qualifications so that you may re-apply at a later date. For example, if you did not receive the maximum points on the Education factor, you might consider going back to school or obtaining more training.

If you did not receive the maximum points on the Experience factor, you might wait a few years until you have more experience in your profession. Or, you might consider learning English or French or both, if you are not fluent in both languages.

As you should know by now, an approved job offer in Canada will dramatically increase the likelihood of your application being approved. So, you might attempt to obtain an approved offer. The procedures discussed above might raise the number of points you will receive, should you decide to postpone your application or re-apply at some later date.

- **If you choose this route, remember to keep abreast of all changes in Canadian immigration procedures and policy, especially changes in the points awarded on the factors of Occupational Demand and Levels Control.**

Factor	Estimated Assessment	Max.	Min Reqd.
1. Education	( )	16	—
2. SVP	( )	18	—
3. Experience	( )	8	1
4. Occupational Demand	Not Assessed	—	—
5. Arranged Employment	Not Assessed	—	—
6. Levels Control	( )	10	—
7. Age	( )	10	—
8. Knowledge of English/French	( )	15	—
9. Personal Suitability	( )	10	—
TOTAL		107	25

Fig. 4. Self-assessment chart for entrepreneur or investor.

Entrepreneur or Investor

If you have business experience and a substantial net worth (see Chapter 5) and are willing and able to transfer your assets to Canada, assess yourself in the table in Figure 4.

Now look at your grand total score. If it is over 25 points, a score which is relatively easy to obtain, then your application may be approved as an Entrepreneur or Investor.

If you have less than 25 points, but a successful background in business I recommend you go ahead and apply anyway. Canada is actively looking for Entrepreneurs and Investors and your application may still be approved at the discretion of the Immigration officer.

Factor	Estimated Assessment	Max.	Min Reqd.
1. Education	( )	16	—
2. SVP	( )	18	—
3. Experience	( )	8	1
4. Occupational Demand	Not Assessed	—	—
5. Arranged Employment	Not Assessed	—	—
6. Levels Control	( )	10	—
7. Age	( )	10	—
8. Knowledge of English/French	( )	15	—
9. Personal Suitability	( )	10	—
TOTAL		107	25
Plus 30 if the officer believes you will become successfully established in you proposed business			
GRAND TOTAL	+30		

Fig. 5. Self-assessment for self-employed persons.

Self-Employed

If you have sufficient funds (see Chapter 5) to transfer to Canada and intend to be self-employed, you should assess yourself using the table in Figure 5.

Now look at your grand total score. If it is over 70 points, your application under the Self-Employed category may be approved.

SUMMARY

You have now assessed your chances of immigrating to Canada. If, after a realistic assessment, your prospects of immigrating to Canada look good, then proceed to the next few chapters dealing with separate stages of the process.

If your prospects do not look good in any category, then you might take some of the steps outlined earlier to improve your chances at some later date. If you cannot apply at this time, do not take it as a personal rejection of your qualifications. It merely means that you cannot meet the requirements Canada has laid down. And remember, Canada receives hundreds of thousands of independent applications each year.

However, it seems certain that over the next few years, increased immigration levels will be encouraged by the Government. It is not unreasonable to expect that in the long term the number of occupations considered in demand will increase and/or the points awarded on occupational demand will rise. Also, the points awarded on Levels Control will probably vary. If you are only a few points short of the requirement, do not become discouraged.

If you keep yourself informed of these changes as they occur, you may very well find that you can meet the requirements over the next year or so.

APPLICANTS DESTINED TO THE PROVINCE OF QUEBEC

The Government of Canada through the Federal Immigration department has exclusive jurisdiction over immigration to Canada. The selection procedures outlined in this chapter are the same for all applicants destined to any Province or Territory of Canada, with the exception of the Province of Quebec.

The Federal Immigration department and the Government of the Province of Quebec have entered into an agreement whereby the Province of Quebec effectively determines who will be selected as immigrants to Quebec. Therefore, there is some variation in the selection procedures of prospective immigrants destined to Quebec. We will outline below the variations you should take into account if you are considering Quebec as your destination in Canada.

- All immigrants to Quebec must be issued with a **Certificat de Sélection de Québec (CSQ)** if they wish to become a permanent resident in that Province.

Generally speaking, applicants submit their applications to the Canadian High Commission, Embassy or Consulate abroad as already indicated. The Immigration office will refer the application to a Quebec Immigration official who will schedule an interview abroad, assess the applicant's qualifications under Quebec's selection criteria, and if approved, issue the CSQ. The application is then referred back to the Canadian Immigration post. Once the CSQ has been issued by Quebec, the Federal Government would only refuse the application if the applicant were unable to meet health and security checks.

Here are the general procedures for applicants destined to Quebec in the various categories already discussed.

Sponsored Applicants to Quebec

The procedure for Sponsored Dependants is virtually the same for Quebec as in other Provinces. A CSQ is required but this is normally only a formality. As in the Federal System, sponsored applicants are not assessed under the point system.

Independent Applicants to Quebec

Independent Applicants to Quebec are assessed under an entirely different point system from the Federal System for the rest of Canada. Here are how the points are awarded in the various categories for Independent Applicants to Quebec (see Figure 6).

Points required for Quebec

(A) *For Employment in Quebec*
This category requires **60 points**.

(B) *Entrepreneurs to Quebec*
Entrepreneurs require **50 points** but are granted a bonus of 25 points. Quebec appears to be quite open to small business ventures. However, it insists on applicants having a knowledge of Quebec through an exploratory visit, a detailed business establishment plan

Factor	Assessment Criteria	Max. Points
1. Education	One point is awarded for each year of successfully completed primary and secondary schooling.	11
2. Specific Vocational Training (SVP)	Points are awarded on the basis of the **amount of training** required in your intended occupation, as follows:	10

Amount of Training	Federal System	Quebec System
Under 6 months	(SVP points 5)	... 2 points
6 to 12 months	(SVP points 7)	... 4 points
1 to 2 years	(SVP points 11)	... 6 points
2 to 4 years	(SVP points 15)	... 8 points
4 or more years	(SVP points 18)	... 10 points

To clarify, look up the SVP points shown for your occupation in Appendices B or C. These are the number of SVP points awarded under the Federal System. Now use the conversion table above to determine the number of points you would receive on this factor under the Quebec system. For example, if you require 1 to 2 years of training in your occupation, you would receive 11 SVP points under the Federal System but only 6 points under the Quebec System.

3. Adaptability	A. Personal Skills	15	22
	B. Motivation	5	
	C. Knowledge of Quebec	2	

A. To establish if an applicant has the personal skills to facilitate his or her integration into Quebec Society, the Quebec Immigration officer asks questions to estimate qualities such as flexibility, sociability, dynamism, initiative, perseverance, self-confidence, realism and maturity, considering the current daily job and social activities of the applicant.

Fig. 6. The Quebec point system.

B. To establish motivation to facilitate his or her integration, the officer asks questions to estimate the motive involved for the applicants emigration and for coming to Quebec specifically.

C. For knowledge of Quebec, the applicant receives:
(i) 1 point if a member of a non-profitable organization or association the purpose of which is to promote cultural exchanges or trade links between his or her country and Quebec.

(ii) 1 point if the applicant has visited at least 2 weeks in Quebec during the 5 years preceding his or her application; and

(iii) 2 points if the applicant has spent at least 2 weeks in Quebec during the last five years working or studying.

15 points at least must be obtained on this factor

4. **Occupational Demand** This factor is similar to the factor of Occupational Demand under the Federal point system but Quebec awards up to 15 points on this factor while the Federal System has a total of 10 points. **At this time, however, all occupations to Quebec which are in demand have only 1 point on this factor.** To determine which occupations are in demand, you may use the lists in Appendices B and C for the rest of Canada, as there are very few variations. 15

It is possible to receive the maximum of 15 points if you can prove that you have a permanent full-time job reserved for you. This is similar to the factor of Arranged Employment under the Federal System and just as difficult to arrange. Here is what you would have to prove in order to receive the full 15 points:

1. You are qualified for the job as defined and described in the *Canadian Classification and Dictionary of Occupations (CCDO)*.

2. You are ready to perform the job immediately you arrive in Quebec.

3. The job is guaranteed by a sincere employer.

4. There is no unrest at the place of employment, i.e. union dispute.

5. Some reasonable actions have been taken by the prospective employer to hire, train or re-train a Quebec resident for the job and especially that the employer has advertised the vacant position in the area or city where the position is to be filled.

1 point at least must be obtained on this factor.

5. Experience Points are awarded for the actual years of full-time experience you have in your intended occupation. 10

Independent Applicants

The apprenticeship, training or specialization period to gain the skills required for the job are *not* taken into consideration in awarding points on this factor.

Also, and this is where it gets a little complicated, if you did *not* receive a certificate or diploma upon the completion of your training period, the points awarded for experience are reduced according to the points received under item 2, Special Vocational Preparation (SVP) as follows:

SVP Points for Quebec	Points to be Deducted
2	-1
4	-2
6	-3
8	-4
10	-5

For example, if you received 6 points on the factor of SVP but are unable to provide proof of your formal vocational training, the points awarded on the factor of experience are to be reduced by 3 points. However, the result of this deduction must not produce a negative total on this factor.

Points are awarded:
½ Yrs. . . . 1 Point   3 Yrs . . . 6 Points
1 Year . . . 2 Points   3½ Yrs . . . 7 Points
1½ Yrs . . . 3 Points   4 Yrs . . . 8 Points
2 Yrs . . . 4 Points   4½ Yrs . . . 9 Points
2½ Yrs . . . 5 Points   5 Yrs . . . 10 Points
1 point must be obtained.

6. **Age**	Up to and including 35 years of age, you are awarded the maximum of 10 points. 36 . . . 9 Points 37 . . . 6 Points 39.. . . 2 Points 40 . . . 1 Point	10
7. **Languages**	French: Up to 15 points. English: Up to 2 points. Points for French language knowledge are awarded as follows: Understanding 6 points Speaking 5 points Reading 3 points Writing 1 point In order to estimate linguistic knowledge of French, the Quebec immigration officer will assess an applicant's ability to: (i) Understand questions of general interest concerning various subjects of daily life. (ii) Provide understandable answers to these questions taking into account pronunciation and grammar. (iii) Read a short text and express the main idea. The same procedure is used in awarding points on English but, as noted above, a maximum of only 2 points are awarded.	15
8. **Relative or Friend**	In area of settlement in Quebec Elsewhere in Quebec	5 2

9. **Bonus Points**	A. Spouse can speak French fluently, i.e. is able to answer questions about daily life in an understandable way taking into account pronunciation and grammar.	5
	B. Spouse is employable, ie has a profession or occupation which is on the list of occupations in demand.	4
	C. Points are also awarded if the applicant has accompanying dependent children, as follows:	
	1 child 1 2 children 2 3 or more children 4	
	Note: The maximum on the Bonus factor is 8 points only, either by adding the points in A and B, or by adding the points in B and C.	

which will employ at least 3 Canadian residents, and being interviewed by a Quebec Business Officer in Montreal. As well, applicants need to have at least 3 years of business experience including at least one year of managerial experience.

(C) *Self-Employed Applicants to Quebec*
This category also requires **50 points** but a bonus of 20 additional points is awarded. Self-employed applicants need experience, money (probably in excess of Cdn$250,000) and a good knowledge of Quebec. Special consideration is given to such applicants who can demonstrate that they will have a positive contribution to make to the cultural and artistic growth of the Province.

(D) *Investors to Quebec*
Once again, the procedure varies only slightly from the Federal system but all investments must be arranged through a broker in

Factor	Estimated Assessment of Yourself	Estimated Assessment of Your Spouse	Max.	Min Reqd.
1. Education	( )	( )	11	—
2. SVP	( )	( )	10	—
3. Experience	( )	( )	22	15
4. Occupational Demand	( )	( )	15	1
5. Arranged Employment or Designated Occupation	( )	( )	10	1
6. Levels Control	( )	( )	10	—
7. Age	( )	( )	15	—
8. Knowledge of English/French	( )	( )	5	—
9. Personal Suitability	( )	( )	8	—
TOTAL			106	

Notes
A. For employment in Quebec — 60 points
B. Entrepreneurs — 50 points
C. Self-employed — 50 points
D. Investors — 50 points

Extra Bonus
—Entrepreneurs — 25 points
—Self-employed — 20 points
—Investors — 25 points

Fig. 7. Self-assessment chart for Quebec.

the Province of Quebec. **50 points** are required but a bonus of 25 is awarded to this category.

Notes

Assessing yourself under the Quebec criteria is somewhat difficult. But, to a large extent, the selection criteria for Quebec appear to be somewhat more of a guideline and Quebec Immigration officers tend to use their positive discretionary powers much more frequently than the Federal Immigration officers.

Independent Applicants

Applicants to Quebec will need to convince the Quebec Immigration officers who interview them that they are deeply interested in Quebec, its French culture and heritage. Applicants must be prepared to show either an ability in the French language or at least a willingness to study and speak French. Also, they must understand that their children will have to attend a French language school.

Applicants approved to the Province of Quebec are quite free to relocate elsewhere in Canada if they should so wish in the future, provided they satisfy any conditions which may be imposed on their visas, such as establishing a business in Quebec.

Now, take a look at the Assessment Chart for Quebec (Figure 7) which will help you to assess your prospects to Quebec compared to the rest of Canada.

Territorial jurisdiction of Quebec immigration offices

For more detailed information about applying to Quebec, you should contact the Service d'Immigration de Québec at one of the following offices, depending where you reside in the world:

Service d'Immigration du Québec, Délégation générale du Québec, 46 avenue des Arts, 7e étage, 1040, Brussels, Belgium. Tel: 011-32-2-512-0036. Fax: 011-32-2-514-2641.
Belgium, Botswana, Burundi, Cape Verde, Comoros, Denmark, Djibouti, Estonia, Ethiopia, Equatorial Guinea, Finland, Gambia, Ghana, Great Britain, Greenland, Guinea-Bissau, Iceland, Ireland, Kenya, Latvia, Lesotho, Liberia, Liechtenstein, Lithuania, Luxembourg, Madagascar, Malawi, Mauritius, Mozambique, Namibia, Netherlands, Nigeria, Norway, Réunion Island, Rwanda, Sao Tomé and Principes, Seychelles, Sierra Leone, Somalia, South Africa, St Helena, Swaziland, Sweden, Switzerland, Tanzania, Uganda, Zambia, Zimbabwe.

Service d'Immigration du Québec, a/s Ambassade du Canada, 4 Latin America, 1er étage, Garden City, P.O. Box 1668, Cairo, Egypt. Tel: 011-202-356-2414/12. Fax: 011-202-356-2408.
Bahrain, Egypt, Kuwait, Oman, Qatar, Saudi Arabia, Sudan, United Arab Emirates, Yemen.

Service d'Immigration du Québec, a/s Ambassade du Canada,

Autostrade Mezzeh, P.O. Box 3394, Damascus, Syria. Tel: 011-852-810-7183. Fax: 011-852-845-3889.
Iraq, Iran, Jordan, Lebanon, Syria.

Service d'Immigration du Québec, Délégation générale du Québec, Lippo Center, Lippo Tower, 19/F, 89 Queensway Central, Hong Kong. Tel: 011-963-11-223-6851/92. Fax: 011-963-11-222-8034.
Afghanistan, Australia, Bangladesh, Bhutan, Brunei, Burma, Cambodia, China, Fiji, Hong Kong, India, Indonesia, Japan, Korea, Laos, Macao, Malaysia, Maldives, Micronesia, Nepal, New Caledonia, New Guinea, New Zealand, Pakistan, Papua, Philippines, French Polynesia, Singapore, Sri Lanka, Taiwan, Thailand, Vietnam.

Service d'Immigration du Québec, Délégation générale du Québec, Avenida Taine 411, Colonia Bosques de Chapultepec, 11580 Mexico City, D.F., Mexico. Tel: 011-52-5-250-8208/22. Fax: 011-52-5-254-4282.
Antigua, Argentina, Barbados, Bolivia, Brazil, Chile, Colombia, Costa Rica, Cuba, Dominica, Ecuador, El Salvador, Falkland Islands, Grenada, Guatemala, Guyana, Honduras, Mexico, Netherlands Antilles and other islands, Nicaragua, Panama, Paraguay, Peru, Puerto Rico, St Lucia, St Vincent and the Grenadines, Surinam, Trinidad and Tobago, Uruguay, Venezuela.

Service d'Immigration du Québec, Délégation générale du Québec, One Rockefeller Plaza, 26th Floor, New York, NY 10020, USA. Tel: (1-212) 843-0960. Fax: (1-212) 376-8984.
United States (States served by CVS Buffalo, Los Angeles, New York and Seattle). Other areas served: Bermuda, St Pierre et Miquelon.

Service d'Immigration du Québec, Délégation générale du Québec, 87/89 rue de La Boétie, 75008 Paris, France. Tel: 011-33-1-42-89-59-19. Fax: 011-33-1-42-89-47-22.
Algeria, Andorra, Angola, Benin, Burkina-Faso, Cameroon, Canary Islands, Central African Republic, Chad, Congo, France, Gabon, Gibraltar, Guinea, Ivory Coast, Mali, Mauritania, Monaco, Morocco, Niger, Senegal, Spain, Togo, Tunisia, Western Sahara, Zaire.

Service d'Immigration du Québec, a/s Ambassade du Canada, Edifice Banque Nova Scotia, B.P. 826, Route de Delmas, Port-au-Prince, Haiti. Tel: 011-509-23-2358. Fax: 011-509-23-8882.
Belize, Dominican Republic, French Guyana, Guadeloupe, Haiti, Jamaica, Martinique.

Service d'Immigration du Québec, Délégation du Québec, XX Settembre 4, 00187 Rome, Italy. Tel: 011-39-6-488-4183. Fax: 011-39-6-488-4205.
Azores, Cyprus, Greece, Holy See, Israel, Italy, Libya, Madeira, Malta, Portugal, San Marino, Turkey.

Service d'Immigration du Québec, a/s Ambassade du Canada, Laurenzerberg, 2, A-1010 Vienna, Austria. Tel: 011-43-1-53138-3005. Fax: 011-43-1-53138-3443.
Albania, Armenia, Austria, Azerbaijan, Belarus, Bosnia-Hercegovina, Bulgaria, Croatia, Czech Republic, Georgia, Germany, Hungary, Kazakhstan, Kyrgyzstan, Moldova, Mongolia, Poland, Romania, Russia, Serbia, Slovakia, Slovenia, Tadjikistan, Turkmenistan, Ukraine, Uzbekistan.

4
Specific Vocational Preparation and Occupational Demand

SPECIFIC VOCATIONAL PREPARATION (SVP)

Specific Vocational Preparation (SVP) points are determined by the government of Canada for each of the over 30,000 job titles in the *Canadian Classification and Dictionary of Occupations (CCDO)*.

Code numbers are allocated in the CCDO for each job classification on a scale of 2 to 9, with 2 being the lowest. The following table illustrates the formal university, college, vocational training, apprenticeship, in-plant training, on-the-job training or experience in other jobs required for each level.

Code numbers	*Training required*	*Points awarded*
1	Up to 30 days	2
3	30 to 90 days	3
4	3 to 6 monts	5
5	6 months to 1 year	7
6	1 to 2 years	11
7	2 to 4 years	15
8	4 to 10 years	18
9	Over 10 years	18

Specific Vocational Preparation

These code numbers on a scale of 1 to 9 are then converted into points for immigration purposes, on a 0 to 18 point scale. **The code numbers in Appendices A, B and C have already been converted to the number of points for your occupation that you should give yourself on the SVP factor.**

OCCUPATIONAL DEMAND

You should go through the list of occupational titles in Appendices A, B and C and find the one best suited to you.

I have deliberately duplicated the occupations in demand in Appendices A, B and C to better help you pin-point your best intended occupation.

- Appendix A (**Designated Occupations List**) contains the designated occupations by province in Canada. This is to help you immediately identify if your occupation may be designated (strongly in demand) in a particular province.

- Appendix B (**General Occupations List**) is broken down into occupational groups. You need to first identify your occupational group and then seek out your specific occupation which is listed in alphabetical order.

- Appendix C (**Alphabetical Listing of Occupations**) contains *all* occupations presently in demand including 'designated occupations'.

The individual job titles are not, it is appreciated, always perfectly clear. You really need access to the CCDO to see the specific job descriptions, but since the CCDO contains some 30,000 job descriptions, that is not possible in this guide. However, Appendix E does provide an example of CCDO job descriptions. The points you will find next to the title are the points awarded on the SVP and Occupational Demand factors for that occupation.

In preparing these lists, I have tried to provide as many alternative job titles as possible in order to help you locate your occupation. For example, let's suppose you are a Secretary. You will find this general occupation also listed as Executive Secretary, Legal Secretary, Medical Secretary and Secretarial Stenographer. Similarly a Court Reporter is also listed as a Law Reporter: both are the identical occupation, but sometimes the SVP and Occupational Demand points may be higher in a closely related occupation. To take the example above of Secretaries, a Legal Secretary is awarded 11 points for SVP, while an Executive Secretary receives 15 points.

This is a big difference! In order to maximize your chances of success, you should use the occupation you are qualified for that has the highest number of points awarded on SVP and Occupational Demand.

This listing of occupations in the Appendices contains only those occupations which are currently 'in demand' and which receive some points on the factor of Occupational Demand. If your occupation is not on these lists, you will almost certainly be refused, since your intended occupation must have at least one (1) point on the Occupational Demand factor in order to be approved.

If your prospects do not look good in any occupation, then you might take some of the steps outlined earlier to improve your chances at some later date. If you cannot comply at this time, do not take it as a personal rejection of your qualifications. It merely means that you cannot meet the requirements Canada has laid down which, quite frankly, do not always make very good sense. And remember, Canada receives hundreds of thousands of independent applications each year.

5
Entrepreneurs, Self-Employed Persons and Investors

Canada is actively seeking immigrants who will either establish or purchase a business interest in Canada. Such persons are called entrepreneurs. An entrepreneur is a person who organizes, manages and assumes the risks of a business or enterprise.

In this chapter we will outline the business categories open to you as an entrepreneur, self-employed person or investor so that you can decide which option best suits your situation.

ENTREPRENEURS

Definition
For Canadian immigration purposes, an entrepreneur means a person who has the ability to establish, purchase or make a substantial investment in a business in Canada that will create or maintain jobs for Canadian residents. As well, it means someone who will take an *active part* in the management of the business. A passive investment will not suffice.

The applicant in this category must show an ability to manage a business based on his or her past experience. This does not mean, necessarily, that the applicant have a background in business, although that generally is the case. For example, a school principal without previous business experience might be approved as an entrepreneur if he or she were purchasing an interest in a private school in Canada, where that applicant had knowledge of educational requirements and was to be involved in the management of the school.

Unconditional visa
There are two ways in which an entrepreneur may apply. Firstly, he or she may apply for an unconditional visa. This usually means

that the applicant must invest in a business before arrival in Canada. The applicant needs to prove that a financial and legal commitment has already been made to establish, purchase or make an investment in a specified business in Canada. Usually the applicant will have visited Canada before applying for permanent residence and thoroughly researched a project.

Conditional visa

The alternative is to apply for a conditional visa. This means that the applicant may receive an immigrant visa but it will contain a condition that the immigrant must establish a business within two years of arrival in Canada. In other words, within a two-year period, the immigrant must approach a Canada Immigration Centre in Canada and provide evidence of having invested and created employment opportunities in a business in which the immigrant is actively involved in the management.

Business proposals

In the past, a detailed business proposal was required of most entrepreneurs. This is no longer a mandatory requirement, although one may be requested by the Immigration authorities during the processing of applicants applying for an unconditional visa. Should you be required to file a detailed business proposal, you would be well advised to seek the assistance of a professional consultant. Unless you have a thorough knowledge of Canadian business procedures and are fully versed in the legal and financial aspects of setting up a business in Canada, it will be difficult for you to successfully write and present a business proposal to the Canadian Immigration authorities without someone in Canada to assist you.

Recommendation

If you are applying as an entrepreneur, you are recommended to apply for a conditional visa. This will eliminate the need for a detailed business proposal. You will only have to prove two things:

- First, that you have a successful business or managerial background, and sincerely intend to live and do business in Canada.

- Secondly, that you have sufficient funds to establish a business in Canada, and provide for your establishment.

No specific amount of money is laid down in the Canadian Immigration Regulations. As a rule of thumb, you would normally have to be in a position to transfer Cdn$250,000 and plan to invest at least Cdn$100,000 in a business in Canada. But there is no hard and fast rule: it depends very much on your business or managerial background and your ability to convince the immigration officer of your prospects of successfully establishing yourself in business in Canada.

On a practical business level, the advantage of applying for a conditional visa is that you give yourself time after arrival in Canada to establish contacts within the business community and familiarize yourself with Canadian business practices, before having to make a financial commitment.

Experience shows that immigrants who rush into a business enterprise before becoming familiar with business conditions often make serious investment mistakes and/or are taken advantage of by unscrupulous individuals, usually within their own ethnic community.

SELF-EMPLOYED

Definition

A self-employed person is an immigrant who has the ability and intends to establish a business in Canada that will create an employment opportunity for himself and will make a significant contribution to the economic, cultural or artistic life of Canada.

Primarily, this refers to farmers, artists, sports personalities and to a lesser extent to the operators of small businesses which certain communities may need.

I find that very few persons are considered in this category. Most businesses, however small, will require at least one employee and the immigration authorities will usually consider even the smallest business enterprise as an entrepreneurial applicant.

However, the successful author, sports or artistic personality who can document his success in his or her own country will usually be favourably considered in this category if he or she appears to have the talent to make a significant cultural or artistic contribution to Canada in the future.

INVESTORS

Definition

An investor is an immigrant who has successfully operated, controlled or directed a financially successful business or commercial undertaking, and who has by his or her own endeavours, accumulated a net worth of at least Cdn$500,000. An investor normally is not actively involved in the project. Usually, he or she is making a passive investment.

It is important to note that this definition of an investor varies in a subtle way from that of an entrepreneur. The definition of entrepreneur refers to the ability to operate a business in Canada. This does not necessarily mean that an entrepreneur must have previous business experience. An investor, however, must have practical business experience. But this does not mean that an investor has to have owned and operated his own business. A senior executive employee whose duties are key to the successful operation of a substantial business and who makes senior management decisions for a company, would meet the criteria.

At the same time, the successful entrepreneur, perhaps someone owning and operating a very small retail outlet, would also meet the definition.

Professional persons

Immigration does not generally consider that self-employed professionals such as doctors, dentists, lawyers, accountants, architects and other professionals qualify under the investor category. In 1986, when the investor program was introduced, the policy was to accept professionals only if they had significant business experience, perhaps being a medical doctor or dentist operating their own clinic and employing other professionals. This policy seems to have eased a little and applicants who are professionals may now find it easier to comply with the definition of an investor.

Still, there remains much confusion as to who can meet the definition of an investor. I would recommend that persons interested in the investor category seek a professional opinion of their eligibility in this category before making an investment.

Investors' options

The investment options open to investors were severely curtailed on 1 July 1996.

Prior to that date, privately administered venture capital funds were approved by the Federal Government in all provinces of Canada. However, all such private funds were allowed to expire on 30 June 1996 and no new private funds will be approved in the foreseeable future. The exception is the Province of Quebec which operates its own immigration investor program.

This leaves only government administered funds open to investors until at least 1 July 1997 at which time a New Immigrant Investor Program may be in place. This means that a person who meets the definition of investor must invest in a fund administered by one of the provincial provinces.

The following government administered funds are being marketed as of 1 July 1996 (Tier 1 funds require a minimum subscription of Cdn$250,000; Tier 2 funds require a minimum subscription of Cdn$350,000):

- British Columbia Investment Fund Ltd. New Escrow. Expiry: 30 June 1997. Tier 2.
  Mr Douglas Alan, BCIF Management Ltd., 712 Yates Street, Victoria, B.C. V8V 1X4. Tel: (604) 356-2246. Fax: (604) 356-8212.

- Nova Scotia Government Fund Limited. New Escrow. Expiry: 30 June 1997. Tier 1.
  Mr C. H. Loveless, Nova Scotia Fund Limited, 1723 Hollis Street, Halifax, Nova Scotia, B3J 2N3. Tel: (902) 424-7698. Fax: (902) 424-0635.

- P.E.I. Government EC. Dev. Fund III Inc. New Escrow. Expiry: 31 December 1996. Tier 1.
  Mr Lennie E. Kelly, Island Investment Development, One First Avenue, Annex I, West Royalty Industrial, Charlottetown, Prince Edward Island, C1E 1␣O. Tel: (902) 368-5957. Fax: (902) 368-5801.

- Sask Govt Growth Fund II. New Escrow. Expiry: 30 June 1997. Tier 1.

Mr Gary K. Benson, 2400 College Ave., Regina, Saskatchewan S4P 3R8. Tel: 306-787-2994. Fax: 306-787-2086.

Advantages of the investor category

The primary attraction and advantage of the investor category is that an unconditional visa is issued to the investor, and he or she need not worry about establishing and operating a business in Canada, nor about encountering the very real aggravation of reporting regularly to Immigration in Canada in order to have conditions removed. An investor is free to work, study, go into business, etc. without any further contact with the Immigration authorities. Also, he or she can reside wherever they wish in Canada, irrespective of the Province in which they invest.

However, an investor must be very cautious. He or she should not think of their investment as the price of admission to Canada. While there is a degree of risk involved in all investments in this category, a few projects and investment funds show good prospects and have a viable track record with competent and honest managers. The problem for the prospective investor is to find a good investment project or fund. Once again, this is where a reputable Canadian consultant can assist you.

RECOMMENDATION

I have not endeavoured to go into any great detail in outlining the procedures for entrepreneurs, self-employed and investor applicants. Processing procedures are too complex to be adequately addressed in a self-help guide as the subject relates more specifically to the wishes and objectives of each individual business applicant.

While the sponsored dependant or skilled immigrant may be fairly confident of submitting his or her application with the advice provided in this guide, the business applicant probably needs professional assistance. This is not only to deal with the immigration process, but more importantly to make sure he or she is not putting hard earned money at unnecessary risk.

This is particularly so in the case of investor applicants, who will be risking a great deal of money.

Unfortunately, there are projects and immigrant investor syndicates on the market which are of very dubious worth. The cost of engaging a professional consultant to assist you in the immigration and investment process may well mean the success of your application for permanent residence and the protection of a very substantial investment.

I also would recommend that all prospective business applicants contact the business development department of the Province in Canada in which they are interested. The Provinces will be able to provide you with valuable information whether you are applying as an entrepreneur or investor.

Provincial government addresses

Director, Immigration Bridging Program, Alberta Career Development and Employment, 11th Floor, City Centre, 10155-102nd Street, Edmonton, **Alberta** T5J 4L5. Tel: (403) 422-6236. Fax: (403) 422-9127.

Manager, Entrepreneur Development Section, Business Immigration Branch, Ministry Responsible for Human Rights and Multiculturalism, 630-999 Canada Place, Vancouver, **British Columbia** V6C 3E1. Tel: (604) 844-1833. Fax: (604) 660-4092.

Senior Development Officer, Investment Promotions Branch, Industry, Trade and Tourism, 410-155 Carlton Street, Winnipeg, **Manitoba** R3C 3H8. Tel: (204) 945-2401. Fax: (204) 945-1193.

Director, Investment and Immigration Department, Economic Development and Tourism, P.O. Box 6000, Fredericton, **New Brunswick** E3B 5H1. Tel: (506) 453-2876. Fax: (506) 453-7904.

Assistant Deputy Minister, Trade and Investment, Department of Industry, Trade and Technology, P.O. Box 8700, St John's, **Newfoundland** A1B 4J6. Tel: (709) 729-2788. Fax: (709) 729-5936.

Director, Business Services, Department of Economic Development and Tourism, P.O. Box 1320, Yellowknife, **Northwest Territories** X1A 2L9. Tel: (403) 873-7388. Fax: (403) 873-0101.

Business Analyst, Investment Promotion Branch, Department of Economic Development, P.O. Box 519, Halifax, **Nova Scotia** B3J 2R7. Tel: (902) 424-5055. Fax: (902) 424-0664.

Business Consultant, Business Immigration Branch, Ministry of Economic Development and Trade, 5th Floor, Hears Block, 900 Bay Street, Toronto, **Ontario** M7A 2E1. Tel: (416) 325-6973. Fax: (416) 325-6653.

Manager, Policy Analysis and Planning, Department of Industry, P.O. Box 200, Charlottetown, **Prince Edward Island** C1A 7N8. Tel: (902) 368-4265. Fax: (902) 368-4224.

Directrice, Direction du support aux opérations, Ministere des Communautés culturelles et de l'immigration, 3e étage, 360 rue McGill, Montréal, **Québec** H2Y 2E9. Tel: (514) 873-2730. Fax: (514) 873-0762.

Manager, Business Immigration Programs, Department of Economic Development, 5th Floor, Office Tower, 1919 Saskatchewan Drive, Regina, **Saskatchewan** S4P 3V7. Tel: (306) 787-8718. Fax: (306) 787-3872.

Director, Industry and Program Development, Department of Economic Development, Mines and Small Businesses, P.O. Box 2703, Whitehorse, **Yukon Territory** Y1Z 2C6. Tel: (403) 667-3014. Fax: (403) 667-8601.

BUSINESS IMMIGRANT COORDINATION CENTRES

In order to provide a better service to business applicants, the Minister of Citizenship and Immigration established Business Immigration Coordination Centres (BICCs) at ten of Canada's missions abroad. The missions designated as BICCs on 1 January 1996 are:

Bonn	London	Seattle
Damascus	Los Angeles	Seoul
Dubai	New York	Singapore
Hong Kong		

These centres specialize in the processing of applications submitted under the business immigration categories: Self-employed, Investor and Entrepreneur. The centres offer a high standard of service from officers with knowledge and expertise in the business program. They seek to ensure efficient and effective processing of applications submitted by persons desiring permanent residence in Canada as business immigrants.

Persons applying as business immigrants are not required to submit their applications to Business Immigrant Coordination Centres, but they are strongly encouraged to do so. While Visa Offices at other Canadian missions have the ability to process business immigration applications, the offices established by the Minister as Business Immigrant Coordination Centres are in a better position to meet the specialized needs of business immigrants.

Anyone wishing to submit an application for permanent residence in Canada as a business immigrant is welcome to apply at one of the Business Immigrant Coordination Centres listed below.

Bonn
The Canadian Embassy, Immigration Section, Godesberger Allee 119, 53175 Bonn, Germany.

Dubai
Consulate of Canada, Juma Al Majid Building, Suite 708, Khalid Ibn Al Waleed Street, Dubai, UAE.

Damascus
The Canadian Embassy, Lot 12, Autostrade Mezzeh, Damascus, Syria.

Hong Kong
Commission for Canada, Immigration Section, 11-13th Floor, Tower 1, Exchange Square, 8 Connaught Place, Hong Kong.

London
The Canadian High Commission, Immigration Division, 38 Grosvenor Street, London W1X 0AA, England.

Los Angeles
The Consulate General of Canada, Immigration Section, 550 South Hope Street, 9th Floor, Los Angeles, California 90071, USA.

New York
The Canadian Consulate General, Immigration Section, 22nd Floor, 1251 Avenue of the Americas, New York, New York 10020-1175, USA.

Seattle
Canadian Consulate General, Immigration Section, 412 Plaza 600, Sixth and Stewart Streets, Seattle, WA 98101-1286, USA.

Seoul
The Canadian Embassy, Immigration Section, Kolon Building, 10th and 11th Floors, 45 Mugyo-dong, Chung-ku, Seoul 100-170, Korea.

Singapore
The Canadian High Commission, Immigration Section, 80 Anson Road, #15-01 IBM Towers, Singapore 0207, Republic of Singapore.

ADDITIONAL DOCUMENTATION—BUSINESS APPLICANTS

Business applicants, i.e. entrepreneurs, self-employed persons and investors, are required to provide much more detailed information than the Independent Applicant coming forward to seek employment. This usually takes the form of a **Business Applicant Summary** and a **Personal Worth Statement**. Samples of these forms follow (Figures 8 and 9). These forms vary somewhat from office to office but they will give you a good idea of the additional information required of business applicants.

Entrepreneurs, Self-Employed Persons and Investors

BUSINESS APPLICANT SUMMARY

If you are applying for permanent residence as an investor, entrepreneur, or self-employed person, the following Business Applicant Summary must be completed. Business immigrants are selected on the basis of proven business background; therefore, it is important that you complete this form fully and accurately, as it will form the basis of our assessment. Do not include attachments or additional documents. Original supporting documents will be required at interview.

PART I

1. Name: _____

2. Date of Birth: _____

3. Category of Application—Check one:

   a). Entrepreneur   _____

   b). Self employed   _____

   c). (i) Investor   _____

      (ii) Name of investment project fund, if known _____

      (iii) Amount of investment to be made C$ _____

Fig. 8. Business applicant summary.

PART II

EXPERIENCE IN BUSINESS MANAGEMENT

1.   On this page tell us, in your own words, about your past and present business management experience. Please include details as to how you started out, the type or nature of businesses in which you have been involved, giving specific details of your responsibilities and duties within the company(ies). Specify your percentage of ownership, if any. Should you require more space than is provided to detail your business experience, you may attach an additional page.

PART III

YOUR BUSINESS PLAN

To be completed by Entrepreneur and Self-employed Applicants

1. Have you decided upon a specific business venture? Yes ____ No ____

a). If yes, please provide details in the space below of the location, type of business, number of employees, amount of capital to be invested, activities of the company, your position and responsibilities.

b). If no, please tell us in your own words in the space below of your plans. Please identify the sector in which you plan to be involved, if known, the amount of capital you have available for investment and outline the nature of the business you plan to establish.

PART IV

1. If your business activity in Canada will not be a sole proprietorship, please indicate your percentage ownership and the share of ownership of the remaining partners. Identify those partners who are not Canadian citizens or permanent residents.

Name: _____ DOB: _____

Name: _____ DOB: _____

2. What steps have you undertaken to research the Canadian business environment to increase the likelihood of success of your plans?

3. Have you ever been involved in a business failure or been associated with a company that went into liquidation, receivership or bankruptcy? Yes ___ No ___
If yes give details.

4. Please detail any formal specialized business training or education you have undertaken.

CONFIDENTIAL
(When completed)

€ommission for €anada   €ommissariat du €anada

PERSONAL WORTH STATEMENT

A complete and current statement of your total personal worth is required. All assets and liabilities, whether located in Hong Kong or elsewhere, should be identified. However, do not include personal items such as jewellery, furniture, etc., due to the difficulty of verifying the ownership of such items.

All assets listed must be your own (or your spouse's) _personal_ holdings and must be documented. The _sources_ of any funds or assets in your possession for less than one year should be identified.

We request and require complete information so that we can better assess your financial background and standing, your personal history, and your experience. This information will be used as a gauge of your ability to meet the requirements of the Canadian Immigration Act and Regulations as it applies to applicants in the Entrepreneur, Investor, Self- Employed and Retired Immigrant Categories.

You will be asked to present original financial documents at the time of your interview to support the information entered into the statement. These documents should also include original property deeds or mortgage argreements and one-year records for fixed deposits and account statements.

In accordance with the Canadian Privacy Act, information presented for immigration purposes cannot be disclosed to Revenue Canada. The Privacy Act also restricts the release of information to other agencies.

Thank you for your co-operation.

Fig. 9. Personal worth statement.

ASSETS

A. BANK DEPOSITS

Current and Savings Accounts
(Specify Currency)

Date Opened	Account Number	Current Balance
	TOTAL CDN$		①

Fixed Deposits
(Specify Currency)

Date of initial Deposit	Maturity Date	Current Balance
	TOTAL CDN$		②

B. PROPERTY

(Specify Currency)

Complete Address	Year Purchased	Mortgaged Yes No	Purchase Price	Estimated Current Market Value
		— —		
		— —		
		— —		
		— —		
		— —		
		— —		
			TOTAL CDN$		③

C. PUBLICLY-TRADED STOCKS AND OTHER PASSIVE INVESTMENTS

(Specify Currency)

Description	Quantity	Estimated Current Market Value
	TOTAL CDN$		④

D. CANADIAN INVESTMENT FUND (INVESTOR APPLICANTS ONLY)

Name of Fund	Date Purchased	Amount Currently Invested
		CDN$	⑤

E. BUSINESS

(Specify Currency)

Name	Percent Owned	Current Book Value (Net Assets)	Estimated Current Market Value
		TOTAL CDN$	⑥

F. PENSION, PROVIDENT FUND AND OTHER ASSETS

(Specify Currency)

Description	Amount
	TOTAL CDN$	⑦

LIABILITIES

G. MORTGAGES

(Specify Currency)

Complete Address	Mortgaged Amount
	TOTAL CDN$	⑧

H. PERSONAL DEBTS (eg. SHAREHOLDER/DIRECTOR'S LOAN, CHILD SUPPORT, ALIMONY)

(Specify Currency)

Nature of Obligation	Amount
	TOTAL CDN$	⑨

NET WORTH

Total Assets (① + ② + ③ + ④ + ⑤ + ⑥ + ⑦) CDN$ _____
Less
Total Liabilities (⑧ + ⑨) — CDN$ _____
Equal

Net Worth CDN$ _____

Which is distributed as follows: (CDN$)

Funds to accompany me to Canada	
Funds to transfer to Canada at a later date	
Funds already in Canada	
Funds remaining abroad	
TOTAL CDN$	

Exchange rate used : CDN$ 1 = HK$ _____

I certify that the above is a complete and true statement of my personal worth, and that this relates specifically to the requirements outlined in Item 22 of the Application for Permanent Residence in Canada (IMM0008IP-P(08-89)E).

Date: _____   Signature: _____

6
The Application Forms and Documents

GATHERING INFORMATION

By now, you should have been able to decide on the best category in which to apply.

The next step in the immigration process is to gather all the necessary documents and information. You will need to provide some of these documents with the **Application for Permanent Residence**, and some for verification at the interview.

Documents generally required

The following are the documents usually needed. Note that this is not an exhaustive list, and that you may need other documents, depending on your particular situation and case. Your spouse must have these documents as well, if applicable.

1. A valid passport.

2. Your national identity card, if applicable.

3. Your birth certificate.

4. Proof of your marital status, such as a marriage certificate, death certificate of spouse, divorce decree, and so on.

5. Proof of your status in the country you will be applying from, if applicable.

6. The birth certificates of all your dependent children whether accompanying you to Canada or not.

7. Proof of all your assets. These might include letters from your

banker, bank statements, certificates of deposit, share certificates, title deeds, business ownership papers, and so on.

8. Proof of any assets you might have in Canada.

9. Court documents as applicable. An example of such a document is a court order granting you custody of your children if you are divorced.

10. Adoption documents, if applicable, relating to any adopted children.

11. All your degrees, diplomas, educational certificates, apprenticeship certificates, professional membership certificates or cards, trade qualification documents, and so on. This is for all levels of education, including elementary and secondary schools and universities.

12. If you are applying as an Independent applicant for employment in Canada and have a relative in Canada, documents showing the relationship of your relative to yourself. These might include copies of marriage and birth certificates of yourself and your relative as well as a copy of your relative's Canadian Citizenship card or Record Of Landing.

13. If you are applying in the Entrepreneur, Investor or Self-Employed categories, business registration certificates, income tax returns, etc.

14. Original letters of employment from past employers stating the duration of employment, the dates of employment, the conditions of employment, salaries and fringe benefits paid, and the exact nature of your duties.

15. Original offers of employment in Canada that you might have, which should contain all the information outlined above.

16. Police clearance certificates for yourself, your spouse, and any dependent children accompanying you to Canada who are over 18. Normally, the Immigration authorities will advise you during the processing of your application if such certificates

are required. There is no need to submit police certificates with your application, unless requested to do so.

Filling in the gaps

Some comments should be made about the documents required above. Make every effort to provide all the documents necessary, but do not be alarmed if you cannot obtain all documents, with certain exceptions. An example of an exception is your passport, which you *must* obtain before leaving for Canada.

However, if, for example, you do not have evidence of a degree you obtained twenty years ago, do not despair. First, write to the college or university you attended and ask for a copy of your degree or other verification. If you are not able to obtain it for whatever reason, simply tell the immigration officer you do not have the degree certificate and your efforts to obtain a copy have failed. The officer will normally continue with the processing of your application.

In some countries birth certificates are not obtained by parents and not usually required in one's life. If you do not have a birth certificate, make sure you have a passport or school-leaving certificate, which might be sufficient.

If, however, you or your spouse have a relative in Canada, then you may have to produce your birth certificate and that of your relative in order to prove your relationship to your relative. But often school certificates or other documentation showing your father or mother's name may be sufficient. If you believe you may have difficulty proving a relationship, an immigration consultant may be able to advise you of the documentation you require, depending on your country of origin.

CONTACTING THE IMMIGRATION OFFICE

Once you have gathered all of the above material, you are ready to contact or write to the nearest Canadian immigration office. Simply write a letter to the Canadian Embassy, High Commission or Consulate nearest you. Appendix F provides the names, addresses, telephone and fax numbers of Canadian Immigration offices overseas.

In the letter state your full name and mailing address and indicate your desire to apply for immigration to Canada. See Figure 10 for a sample letter.

>   (Date)
>
>   (Name)
>   (Address)
>
> Counsellor (Immigration)
> Canadian High Commission
> Immigration Section
> MacDonald House
> 1 Grosvenor Square
> London W1X 0AB
> England, UK
>
>
> Dear Sir:
>
> I wish to apply for permanent residence in Canada.
>
> Kindly send me the appropriate application forms.
>
> Thank you for your attention to this request.
>
> Yours sincerely,
>
> (Signature)
>
> (Name)

Fig. 10. Sample letter to the immigration authorities.

REPLY FROM IMMIGRATION

The reply you receive from Immigration will vary, depending on which office you contact. At the present time, Regional Processing Centres are being established which will process applications from several different areas or countries. For example, the Canadian Consulate in Buffalo, New York, is now processing all applications from within the United States. The Canadian High Commission in London, England, will be handling all applications from the United Kingdom as well as some countries in the Middle East. So don't be surprised if you are asked to submit your application to a quite unexpected location.

The instructions you receive concerning the submission of your application and the documentation required will also vary from office to office. For example, the Canadian High Commission in Singapore requests virtually no supporting documentation while the Canadian High Commission in Hong Kong insists on receiving every conceivable document along with the application for permanent residence.

You must therefore pay particular attention to the instructions you receive with your application forms and follow those instructions carefully. Not to do so can severely delay the processing of your application. For example, certain offices will return your application and all supporting documentation without considering your application if even one document is missing.

However, whatever office you contact, you will receive the basic Application for Permanent Residence in Canada.

THE APPLICATION FOR PERMANENT RESIDENCE

The **Application for Permanent Residence** is known as form IMM 8. It is four pages long and contains 34 questions. It is a standard application form that is used by all Canadian Immigration offices. A sample is reproduced in Figure 11.

You might receive additional forms that are required to complete. For example, all applications in Hong Kong must be accompanied by a complete **Family Composition Information** form. If you receive any such forms, you must fill them in and return them with your Application for Permanent Residence.

First, I suggest you read the form carefully to familiarize yourself with the questions. As you can see, the form is not difficult or complicated and asks simple questions.

- **However, your entire future could be altered by the way you fill in this form.**

Completing the Application for Permanent Residence

The information you provide on the Application for Permanent Residence form will be the main determining factor in the approval or rejection of your application for immigration. Fill it out using

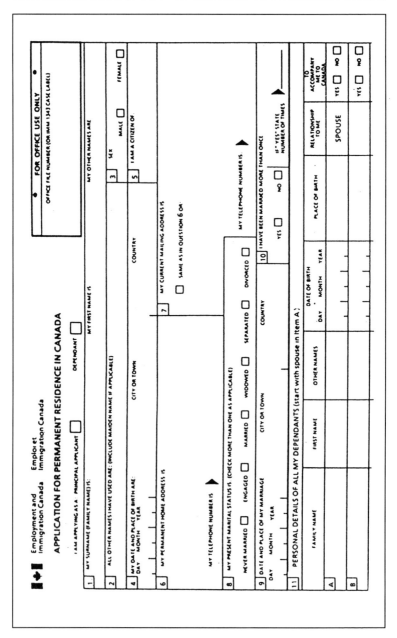

Fig. 11. Application for Permanent Residence in Canada (Form IMM 8).

The Application Forms and Documents 93

12. PASSPORT DETAILS FOR PRINCIPAL APPLICANT AND FOR PERSONS LISTED IN QUESTION 11 (to be completed by principal applicant only)

	FIRST NAME	PASSPORT NUMBER	CITIZEN OF	DATE OF EXPIRY			IDENTITY CARD NO.
				DAY	MO	YR	
	PRINCIPAL APPLICANT						
A	SPOUSE						
B							
C							
D							
E							
F							
G							
H							
I							
J							

C ☐ YES ☐ NO
D ☐ YES ☐ NO
E ☐ YES ☐ NO
F ☐ YES ☐ NO
G ☐ YES ☐ NO
H ☐ YES ☐ NO
I ☐ YES ☐ NO
J ☐ YES ☐ NO

IMM 0008 IP - P (08-89) E

Canada

Migrating To Canada

13.

	ABILITY IN ENGLISH				ABILITY IN FRENCH			
	FLUENTLY	WELL	WITH DIFFICULTY	NOT AT ALL	FLUENTLY	WELL	WITH DIFFICULTY	NOT AT ALL
SPEAK	☐	☐	☐	☐	☐	☐	☐	☐
READ ▶	☐	☐	☐	☐	☐	☐	☐	☐
WRITE	☐	☐	☐	☐	☐	☐	☐	☐

* IF YOU DO NOT SPEAK ENGLISH OR FRENCH, INDICATE THE LANGUAGE OR DIALECT YOU NORMALLY SPEAK

14. MY EDUCATION (INDICATE NUMBER OF YEARS OF SCHOOL SUCCESSFULLY COMPLETED)

YEARS OF ELEMENTARY/PRIMARY SCHOOL	YEARS OF SECONDARY/HIGH SCHOOL	YEARS OF UNIVERSITY/COLLEGE	YEARS OF FORMAL APPRENTICESHIP - TRAINING

15. DETAILS OF MY POST SECONDARY EDUCATION

DATES				NAME OF INSTITUTION (INCLUDING APPRENTICESHIP TRAINING)	CITY AND COUNTRY	TYPE OF CERTIFICATE OR DIPLOMA ISSUED
FROM		TO				
M	Y	M	Y			

16. MY PRESENT OCCUPATION IS

CURRENT GROSS MONTHLY EARNINGS

17. MY INTENDED OCCUPATION IN CANADA IS

MY OCCUPATION

18. MY WORK HISTORY FOR THE PAST 10 YEARS (PROVIDE DETAILS ON A SEPARATE SHEET AS REQUIRED)

DATES				NAME OF EMPLOYER (WRITE NAME IN FULL. DO NOT USE ABBREVIATIONS)	CITY AND COUNTRY	MY OCCUPATION
FROM		TO				
M	Y	M	Y			

The Application Forms and Documents

19 THE FOLLOWING PERSON, EMPLOYER OR ORGANIZATION IN CANADA HAS OFFERED TO ASSIST ME AFTER ARRIVAL (NAME AND ADDRESS AND COPY OF JOB OFFER, IF YOU HAVE ONE)

20 RELATIONSHIP TO ME OF PERSON NAMED IN 19

21 DESTINATION IN CANADA
NAME OF CITY / TOWN — PROVINCE

22 I HAVE THE FOLLOWING ASSETS: (SHOW AMOUNT OR VALUE)

TRANSFERABLE MONEY — PROPERTY — MONTHLY TRANSFERABLE PENSION — OTHER

IF "OTHER", GIVE DETAILS HERE ▲

23 I HAVE THE FOLLOWING DEBTS OR LEGAL OBLIGATIONS (e.g. CHILD SUPPORT PAYMENTS) OWING TO (GIVE NAME OF PERSON (S) OR ORGANIZATION)

TOTAL DEBTS (AMOUNT)

Migrating To Canada

24. During the past 10 years, I have lived at the following addresses

Dates From (M Y)	Dates To (M Y)	Street and Number	City or Town	Country

25. Since my 18th birthday, I have been (or still am) a member of, or associated with the following political, social, youth, student or vocational organizations (including trade unions and professional associations). Include any military service (show rank, unit and location of service in last column)

Dates From (M Y)	Dates To (M Y)	Name and Address of Organization	Type of Organization	Position Held (if any)

26. My Parents

	Date of Birth (D M Y)	City, Town and Country of Birth	Present Address in Full (If deceased give date)
Father's Full Name			
Mother's Full Name Before Marriage			

27. HAVE YOU OR HAS ANY ONE OF THE PERSONS IN QUESTION 11 EVER (ANSWER "YES" OR "NO")

A. HAD ANY SERIOUS DISEASE OR PHYSICAL OR MENTAL DISORDER? ____

D. BEEN REFUSED AN IMMIGRANT OR VISITOR VISA TO CANADA OR ANY OTHER COUNTRY? ____

F. IN PERIODS OF EITHER PEACE OR WAR, HAVE YOU EVER BEEN INVOLVED IN THE COMMISSION OF A WAR CRIME OR CRIME AGAINST HUMANITY, SUCH AS: WILLFUL KILLING, TORTURE, ATTACKS UPON, ENSLAVEMENT, STARVATION OR OTHER INHUMANE ACTS COMMITTED AGAINST CIVILIANS OR PRISONERS OF WAR, OR DEPORTATION OF CIVILIANS? ____

B. BEEN CONVICTED OF OR CURRENTLY CHARGED WITH ANY CRIME OR OFFENCE IN ANY COUNTRY? ____

E. BEEN REFUSED ADMISSION TO, OR ORDERED TO LEAVE CANADA OR ANY OTHER COUNTRY? ____

C. APPLIED PREVIOUSLY FOR AN IMMIGRANT OR VISITOR VISA TO CANADA? ____

IF THE ANSWER TO ANY OF THE ABOVE IS "YES" PROVIDE DETAILS HERE

28. IF MY APPLICATION IS APPROVED, I WISH TO LEAVE FOR CANADA WHEN PROCESSING OF THIS APPLICATION IS COMPLETED ☐ OR IN THE MONTH OF ____

29. PRINCIPAL APPLICANT: ATTACH TWO PASSPORT SIZE PHOTOGRAPHS OF YOURSELF AND EACH PERSON UNDER AGE 18 LISTED IN ITEM 11. SPOUSE OR DEPENDANTS AGE 18 OR OVER ATTACH TWO PHOTOGRAPHS OF YOURSELF ON YOUR SEPARATE APPLICATION FORM

30 AUTHORITY TO DISCLOSE PERSONAL INFORMATION

A I hereby authorize all governmental authorities, including all police, judicial and state authorities in all the countries in which I have resided, to release to the Canadian Government authorities all records and information that they may possess on my behalf concerning any investigations, arrests, charges, trials, convictions and sentences. I understand that this information will be used to assist in evaluating my suitability for admission to Canada, or any other reason, pursuant to Canadian Immigration Legislation

B I understand that, having applied for permanent residence in Canada, I (and my family) may be required to undergo a medical examination, and I therefore consent to the release of specific details concerning the medical condition of myself (and my family if applicable), as may be relevant to my admission to Canada, to the following: Immigration and Visa Officers; authorities of Health & Welfare Canada and the province of my destination; my sponsor in Canada; the Immigration Appeal Division and other judicial bodies

C I also authorize the release of information from my immigration records to: (check one or more)

My Canadian legal representative (if any) ☐   My sponsor / guarantor (if applicable) ☐   I do not authorize the release of any information except to those in A and B above ☐

Signature of applicant: _____   Date: _____

31 DECLARATION OF APPLICANT

- I declare that the information I have given in this application is truthful, complete and correct

- I understand that any false statements or concealment of a material fact may result in my exclusion from Canada, and even though I should be admitted to Canada for permanent residence, a fraudulent entry on this application may be grounds for my prosecution and/or removal.

- Should my answers to questions 8, 11 or 27, change at any time prior to my departure for Canada, I undertake to report such change and delay my departure until I have been informed in writing, by the office dealing with my application, that I may proceed to Canada

- I understand all the foregoing statements, having asked for and obtained an explanation on every point which was not clear to me.

Date: _____   Signature of applicant: _____

The Application Forms and Documents

32 INDIVIDUAL, FIRM OR ORGANIZATION WHO ASSISTED IN THE PREPARATION OF THIS APPLICATION

Name _____ Address _____

Signature of individual or authorized officer _____ Date _____

DO NOT COMPLETE THE FOLLOWING SECTION NOW. YOU WILL BE ASKED TO SIGN IT IN THE PRESENCE OF A REPRESENTATIVE OF THE CANADIAN GOVERNMENT OR OFFICIAL APPOINTED BY THE CANADIAN GOVERNMENT.

33 SOLEMN DECLARATION

I, _____ SOLEMNLY DECLARE THAT THE INFORMATION I HAVE GIVEN IN THE FOREGOING APPLICATION IS TRUTHFUL, COMPLETE AND CORRECT, AND I MAKE THIS SOLEMN DECLARATION CONSCIENTIOUSLY BELIEVING IT TO BE TRUE AND KNOWING THAT IT IS OF THE SAME FORCE AND EFFECT AS IF MADE UNDER OATH

Declared before me at _____ this _____ day of _____ 19____

_____   _____
SIGNATURE OF THE OFFICIAL OF THE GOVERNMENT OF CANADA   SIGNATURE OF THE APPLICANT

34 INTERPRETER DECLARATION

I, _____, do solemnly declare that I have faithfully and accurately interpreted in the _____ language the content of this application and any related forms to the person concerned.

I have been informed by the person concerned, and I do verily believe, that he / she completely understands the nature and effect of these forms, and I make this solemn declaration conscientiously believing it to be true and knowing that it is of the same force and effect as if made under oath.

_____   _____
(SIGNATURE OF INTERPRETER)   (DATE)

the utmost care, providing as much detail as possible and, as always, being absolutely truthful.

We will now go through the form, question by question. You are advised to photocopy the application when you receive it and use the copy to practise on before finalizing the actual application.

You should complete all questions. If any question is not applicable to you, simply insert 'Not Applicable' or 'N/A' in the space provided, but be sure to answer every question.

Firstly, please note that you must tick the appropriate box at the top of the form to indicate if you are the **Principal Applicant** (the person whose qualifications are to be assessed) or if you are a **Dependant** of the Principal Applicant.

Question 1—Name
State your surname (family name), first name and middle name, in that order.

Question 2—Other Names
In this space you should write any other names under which you have been known. If you are a married woman, your maiden name should be included. If you are divorced or have been married more than once, your previous married name(s) should be included. You need not include nicknames, unless people know you only by your nickname and not your real name, or if your nickname is included in any job references.

Question 3—Sex
You should tick the appropriate box.

Question 4—Date of Birth
Insert your date of birth here. Note that in some countries, for example the United States, dates are written differently with the month first, followed by the day and year. You should follow the exact format given in the form, that is, day, month and year. If you do not know your exact date of birth and have no way to find out, insert the word 'about' before the birth date.

Question 5—Citizenship
Insert the name of the country you are a citizen of. If you are not the citizen of any country, you should insert 'Stateless'.

Many people are dual citizens due to naturalization or birth. You may pick one country, usually the country on whose passport you travel, or declare both countries.

Question 6—Present Address
You should give your complete permanent address, including, if applicable, your apartment or house number, apartment or house name, street name, city, state or province, country and postal code. This is the address at which you are presently residing, even if you are a citizen of another country.

Beneath that give your telephone number including the area code.

Question 7—Mailing Address
If your present address and your mailing address are the same, just put an X in the box provided.

If you receive your mail at a different address, perhaps at your place of employment or through a post office box for example, provide that complete mailing address.

Question 8—Marital Status
You should tick the appropriate box for your marital status. Note that 'unmarried (never married)' means that you have not gone through any form of marriage in any country at any time in your life.

Question 9—Date of Marriage
You should state the date and the place you were married, if applicable. You need mention only the city or town and country, not the name of the church in which you were married.

Question 10—Number of Marriages
If you have been married more than once, indicate the number of times. Remember, if you have been married more than once, you should attach copies of your divorce papers or spouses's death certificate to your application.

Question 11—Dependants
Include the names, relationships, dates of birth, places of birth and citizenship of all your children and your spouse's children whether married or single, in descending order of birth and indicate if they intend to accompany you to Canada. You must include the names

of all your unmarried children whether or not they intend to accompany or follow you to Canada.

Question 12—Passport Particulars
Enter the number of your passport or travel document, the date it was issued, the expiration date, and the country it was issued by. Note that this applies not only to you but also to all your unmarried children, whether or not they will accompany you to Canada. The country of issue is the name of the country on whose passport you travel, and not the place where you obtained your passport.

Many countries do not issue identity cards, but some do. If you have one, place the number of your card here.

Question 13—Language Ability
You should indicate your ability to speak, read and write Canada's two official languages, English and French. You may estimate your language skills yourself, and you do not normally have to document your ability. However, if you do have certificates indicating your proficiency in English or French, attach them to the application.

You may be tested in your language abilities, unless you are obviously fluent in either language. You do not have to have any proficiency in either of Canada's official languages in order to have your application approved. Obviously, however, it helps your case if you are fluent in either language, as you will normally need one or the other, or both, to live and work in Canada.

If you speak neither English or French, indicate the language you normally speak. This would normally be your native language. 'Native language' is hard to define, but normally it would mean the language you speak at home or are most proficient in.

Questions 14 and 15—Education
You should fill in the boxes according to the number of years you successfully completed in elementary and secondary school, college and formal training.

It is often difficult to distinguish between secondary schooling and primary schooling. In certain countries primary or elementary schooling is only five years, while in others it might be eight. Similarly, in certain countries secondary or high school is only three years; in others it might be seven.

The breakdown is not important. What is important is that you designate the total number of years you went to school. For example, if you went to school for twelve years, you may break it down into seven years of primary school and five years of high school or six years of primary school and six years of high school, according to the system used in the country of your schooling. However, both must add up to twelve to indicate to the immigration officer you went to school for twelve years.

Similarly, put the total number of years you attended college or university in the appropriate box. You need not break this total down by degrees or levels of college or university.

You should also indicate the number of years you completed in formal training. This does not include training you might have had informally from a friend or taught yourself. Usually, training applies only to occupations in trades, such as mechanics and carpenters. Formal Apprenticeship Training refers to a formal program of instruction which would usually involve both practical and theoretical instruction and the issuance of a certificate or diploma. Informal 'on-the-job training' should be included under Question 18 concerning your work history.

You should remember two points when filling out the section on education. First, you must enter only those years you passed. Failed years of education should not be included, as they are not accepted for the allocation of points.

Second, you will have to prove details of your education, through such documents as copies of your diplomas, degrees, and certificates. You should put down only those years you actually attended a school, college, university or training program. If you attended an institution as a part-time student, you may include it on the form, but should indicate it was for part-time studies only.

Fill in the rest of the question with the months and years you started and finished your post-secondary education at each school, college, university or training program you attended. The name and location of each school, college, university or training program, the type of educational institution it was, and the name and date of any degree, diploma or certificate issued must be included.

In the section on the type of institution, you need not be too specific. If, for example, you attended a four-year affiliated institution granting Bachelor's degrees in liberal arts, you need only put the word 'college' or 'university' in response to this question. If you took a formal training course at a factory or manufacturing plant, or had other on-the-job training, you may put down 'apprenticeship' as the type of institution.

Similarly, you need not be too specific in the type and date of certificate or degree or diploma you received. If, for example, you hold a Doctor of Philosophy in English Literature, you need only put the letters 'Ph.D.' in this section.

Questions 16 and 17—Present and Intended Occupation
Keep in mind that your intended occupation has to appear on either the Designated or General List of Occupations to be approved, unless you are applying within the business categories.

Usually, your present and intended occupation will be the same. However, if you were qualified and employed some years ago in an occupation in demand, while your current occupation is not presently in demand, you should of course apply in your former occupation.

It is very important that you pick your job occupation as carefully as possible. Go back to Chapter 4, Specific Vocational Preparation and Occupational Demand, and also refer to Appendices A, B and C. Go through the lists carefully, checking to see in which occupations you are qualified and in which province you intend to settle in Canada. Then, make a list of all those occupations along with the SVP and Occupational Demand (OD) points indicated. Then choose the occupation that fits your job as closely as possible and indicate it on the form as your present occupation.

Now, go back to the various lists of occupations. Go through the lists once again, choosing those occupations you are qualified for and might work in when you are in Canada. It is extremely important that you pick the occupation that has the highest possible SVP and Occupational Demand, if you want to maximize your chances of success. If you are listing more than one occupation, put the best title first.

You do not have to put down only one occupation. If you are qualified in more than one occupation, such as Accountant or Budget Accountant or Bank Branch Accountant, then put them all down. You should receive consideration for the occupation with the highest SVP and Occupational Demand points.

Be as specific as possible. For example, if you are an Electrical Engineer, do not put down simply 'engineer', as there are chemical, civil, structural, design, electronic, industrial, mechanical, tool, metallurgical, mining, aerospace and other engineers as well. Each of them could have different SVP and Occupational Demand points.

If you are a Sponsored Dependant, simply state your occupation here. Because you are a Sponsored Dependant, your occupation is really not important, since you are not assessed against the point system.

Indicate your monthly salary in your local currency.

Question 18—Work History
List the dates in months and years, the name and address of the employer, your occupation, and your gross monthly earnings for all your jobs over at least the past ten years. You need not limit yourself to only the past ten years, if you have previous relevant experience. In fact, it is recommended that you list your entire work history.

Specify your occupation carefully, as your past experience should be as closely related to your intended occupation in Canada as possible. It is advisable to refer to the occupational demand chart for descriptive names of your previous occupations. You should not put your formal title, such as 'Vice President for Asia, including South East Asia', if that is your title, but rather the descriptive title, 'Manager: Sales'.

Your gross monthly earnings should be stated in your local currency. For the most part, Canadian immigration officers are aware of the significance of the salaries paid in local currencies.

Question 19—Employer or Relatives in Canada
List anyone in Canada who is willing and able to help you get settled in Canada. This person may be either a relative or a friend, or, if you already have arranged employment, your prospective employer. If you are a Sponsored Dependant, list the relative in Canada who is helping you immigrate by sponsoring your application. But only list relatives closer than a cousin who are citizens of Canada or permanent residents.

Question 20—Relationship
You should list the relationship to you of the person named in the previous question, such as brother, friend, prospective employer, etc. If the person is an aunt, uncle, nephew or niece, state clearly the relationship, for example, 'aunt—my father's sister'.

Question 21—Destination
Fill in the place in Canada to which you wish to go. If you have not decided on your destination, write 'Undecided'.

Question 22—Assets
I believe it is best to state your assets in terms of Canadian dollars when completing this question. You should state in the first box, in Canadian dollars, the amount of money you will be able to transfer to Canada. If you already have money in Canada, insert those assets in this box.

In the second box, indicate in Canadian dollars the approximate value of your home and any other real estate you may own.

The third box should show any pension you may receive that can be transferred to Canada.

In the fourth box, 'Other', indicate the value of any other valuables you own, such as stocks, bonds, gold, jewellery, antiques, etc. and provide the details.

Question 23—Debts and Obligations
You are required to provide the details of your debts and legal obligations such as child support payments, etc., if any.

Question 24—Residence Background
You should state all the places you have lived during the past ten years, including dates in months and years, and complete addresses. This is for security checks. Start with your oldest address and work down to your present address. Include your actual residence address, and not mailing addresses such as post office boxes.

Question 25—Clubs/Membership
List all the political, social, student and other groups or organizaions you have belonged to since your eighteenth birthday. Include even service clubs such as Lions, Rotary, etc.

Question 26—Parents' Particulars
You should fill in your father's and mother's *full* names, date of birth, places of birth, and present addresses, as applicable.

Often, prospective immigrants do not have this information. If that is the case, and the information is not available, insert the word 'Unknown' to any question to which you do not know or have the answer, or indicate approximate dates of birth, e.g. 'About 1934'.

You should make every possible effort to obtain this information before filling out this question. If your relative is deceased, write 'Deceased', and give the date on which he or she died, writing the day, month and year in that order, and the city and country where the death occurred.

Question 27—Background
You must answer each question by printing either Yes or No. Again, you are reminded to be entirely truthful in your answers. **Please note that these questions apply to your spouse and any dependants accompanying you to Canada.** Also, you are required to provide details for any question you answer Yes.

Question 27A—Health Questions
If you answer 'yes' to this question, it does not mean your application will be refused. Only Canadian immigration doctors can decide which physical or mental disorders and communicable and chronic diseases are grounds for refusal of an application.

Question 27B—Convictions
If you have been convicted of any crime or offence, you may be refused admission into Canada, and your application may be rejected. There are clearly defined legal rules to judge if a person is inadmissible because of convictions.

First, if you have been convicted of very minor offences, such as parking and speeding offences, you need not tick the 'yes' box.

Second, if you have been convicted of a serious offence, you must tick the 'yes' box and provide details.

If you have a conviction, you may still be allowed to immigrate to Canada under a waiver given by the Minister of Immigration. Generally, these are given only after over five years have passed since you finished your sentence, and are able to demonstrate rehabilitation.

If you have been convicted of offences more serious than driving tickets, we suggest you contact a competent Canadian immigration consultant to advise you before applying.

Question 27C—Previous Applications
If you previously submitted an application for permanent residence

or an application for a visitor's visa, you should indicate 'yes', and indicate below where and when you applied, and the outcome.

A Preliminary Questionnaire is not a formal application. If you have sent in a Preliminary Questionnaire but not sent a formal application, you do not need to answer 'yes'. Immigration does not keep a record of Preliminary Questionnaires.

However, if you have submitted a formal application previously and been refused, you must answer 'yes'. Immigration will probably have a record of your previous application and you might be refused, not because of your previous refusal, but because you have been untruthful on your present application.

Don't worry unduly about previous refusals. Certainly a previous refusal does not help your case, but it does not mean your current application will be refused. You may have applied earlier under an entirely different set of Regulations, or at a time when you were less qualified.

Question 27D—Refused a Visa or Admission to Canada
Question 27E—Or Ordered to Leave Canada, or Any Other Country
A 'Yes' answer does not mean your application will be refused. If you have been ordered to leave or you have been deported from any country, or if you have been refused a visa to enter any country, you are advised to contact a Canadian immigration consultant before submitting a new application.

Question 27F—War Crimes
This question is self-explanatory.

Question 28—Processing Time
You may specify when you would like to leave for Canada after you have your immigrant visa. Normally, you should indicate your desire to leave immediately, since processing times are very lengthy at present.

Question 29—Photographs
If you are the **principal** applicant, *staple*, do not glue, two passport size photographs each of yourself and, if applicable, your spouse and your dependent children *under* the age of 19 in this space. Photos should be from the same negative, taken within the last six months. They should be passport or standard-size, roughly 50 x 70 mm (2 x 2½ inches).

If you are the spouse of the principal applicant or a dependent child of the principal applicant *over* the age of 19, simply staple two photographs of yourself only.

Question 30—Authorization
Read this section carefully. If you are represented by an immigration consultant, you would normally want to tick the first box.

Similarly, if you are applying as a Sponsored Dependant of a relative in Canada, you would probably want to tick the second box as well.

Only if you do *not* want any information released to your representative or to your sponsor in Canada would you tick the third box.

In any event, don't forget to sign and date this section.

Question 31—Declaration
Read this Declaration and Warning very carefully, keeping in mind that all information provided on the application must be complete and factual.

In addition, should your marital status change, your number of dependants change or any of your answers to Question 27 change at any time prior to immigrating to Canada, you must report any such changes to Immigration and perhaps delay your departure. Once again, don't forget to sign and date this section.

Question 32—Consultant's Name and Address
If you are not represented by a consultant in submitting your application, do not complete this section.

If you are represented, your consultant must complete, date and sign this section.

Question 33—Applicant's Declaration
Question 34—Interpreter Declaration
Do *not* complete these Questions. This will be done by the Immigration officer at the time of your interview, if necessary.

SUBMITTING YOUR COMPLETED APPLICATION

Remember, either you or your spouse can apply for permanent residence. Refer back to Chapter 3. Did you decide to have your spouse apply instead of you? If so, then your spouse should fill in the principal Application for Permanent Residence.

Second, do not hesitate to attach additional sheets if necessary. You should put your name on each additional sheet, and indicate the question to which you are referring. Remember to securely fasten the sheets to the form.

Third, I suggest you use a typewriter. The appearance of the application form is important, as you will want to make a favourable first impression on the officer, and it is your application that he will first see.

Fourth, your spouse and unmarried children over 19 years of age must complete separate application forms. If you do not have forms for them, write to the Canadian Embassy, High Commission or Consulate that sent you the Application for Permanent Residence and request additional copies. Or, simply make a good photocopy of your application before completion. This does not mean that your spouse and unmarried children are not being dealt with under your application. However, security checks are conducted on your spouse and your children over 19 accompanying you to Canada.

Documenting the Application

You should also include certain attachments, *even if these have not been specifically requested.* Do not send originals of any documents especially important ones such as your passport and birth certificates. But do attach copies of your degrees, diplomas and educational certificates, letters from past employers, and any offer of employment in Canada.

- *Most important!* be certain to attach a separate sheet of paper providing a complete description of your occupational duties over the years. You are advised to attach a similar job description for your spouse. These job descriptions are essential! Immigration officers have to be satisfied that you are (or your spouse is) qualified in an intended occupation. They do this by considering your practical experience in relation to the thousands of detailed job descriptions listed in the Canadian Classification and Dictionary of Occupations (CCDO) published in Canada.

It is impossible to reproduce these thousands of job descriptions in this book, but to give you an idea of the detail contained in these job descriptions, the CCDO job descriptions of a few occuptions are included under Appendix E. These descriptions should provide you with an idea of the detail you need to go into in preparing the job description for your particular occupation.

When you are satisfied that the Application is properly completed and documented, mail or take it back to the Canadian High Commission, Embassy or Consulate you received it from.

CAUTIONS

1. I will deal with the subject of payment of fees to third parties in Chapter 11. You might want to refer to that chapter before completing the application form. Immigration Canada will warn you that payment to a third party (e.g. an immigration consultant) will not assist or expedite your application. In fact, however, professional advice and a professionally completed application can go a long way in assisting the favourable outcome of your application and often make the difference between acceptance and refusal.

2. You should take no irreversible steps, such as giving up your employment or disposing of your properties, until you have been issued with the **Immigrant Visa and Record of Landing.**

3. I would remind you again to inform the Canadian High Commission, Embassy or Consulate you are applying to if any of the following occur to you before you leave for Canada, but after you have submitted the application form:

- You become engaged, married, widowed, separated or divorced.

- You or your spouse gives birth to a child.

- Any of your answers to question 27 changes from 'no' to 'yes', such as if you are convicted of a serious offence.

Failure to inform the Canadian immigration office dealing with your case could have very serious consequences in the future. For example, if you get married after receiving your Record of Landing and enter Canada without informing immigration officials of your change in marital status, you could be deported from Canada. Deportation would not occur for getting married, but rather for not informing Immigration of the fact.

Once you have mailed in your application, you will have to wait. It will be dealt with according to the established priority system.

Obtaining Visas & Work Permits

How and where to obtain the services of immigration lawyers and consultants worldwide

Roger Jones

This unique guide and directory lists experts in immigration law and procedures who can guide you through the pitfalls and help you obtain the necessary visas. Whether you are planning to settle abroad or have already made the move and now wish to make your residence permanent, their assistance could be crucial in effecting a successful outcome. The entries in the book have been carefully compiled as a result of detailed questionnairing, and provide a valuable new resource for all visa applicants and professional advisers. Roger Jones is a leading writer and broadcaster on international employment matters who has 12 years' experience of living and working overseas.

£9.99, 144 pp illus. paperback. 1 85703 414 7.

Available from How To Books Ltd, Plymbridge House,
Estover Road, Plymouth PL6 7PZ.
Cutomer Services: Tel: (01752) 202301. Fax: (01752) 202331.
Please add postage & packing (£1 UK, £2 Europe, £3 world airmail).

Credit card orders may be faxed or phoned.

7
The Priority System and Interview

THE PRIORITY SYSTEM

Your application will be dealt with according to the following priority system used by all Canadian immigration offices abroad:

1. Sponsored applications for husbands, wives, children under 19 and orphans.

2. Applicants who have a job offer validated in Canada by a Canada Employment Centre.

3. Entrepreneurs, Investors and Self-Employed persons.

4. Persons who are qualified for and willing to work in a Designated Occupation.

5. Sponsored applications for parents and grandparents and all other sponsored applications not listed under priority 1 above.

6. Independent applications for employment, and all others.

The priority system is applied at each individual Canadian immigration office. For example, if you are in priority 6 with the Canadian High Commission in London, England, your application might take only a few months to process. However, if you are in that same priority with the Canadian Embassy in Manila in the Philippines your application may take much longer to process.

To complicate matters, the Government is now assigning annual quotas to all offices abroad, so it is difficult to know if the prescribed priority system really has much meaning.

Please note that you can apply to any Canadian Immigration

office, even if you do not live in that area of the world. You must, however, be able to provide a mailing address within the processing area of the office to which you apply. The exception is individuals legally but temporarily residing in Canada as a visitor, student or under an employment authorization who can use their Canadian address if applying through a Canadian Immigration Office in the United States. Normally, you are best advised to apply to the office in your own area, as that office has a better appreciation of local customs, and will probably be better able to fairly assess your qualifications.

However, many months of processing time can sometimes be saved by applying at a less busy office in the world, provided you are prepared to meet the expenses involved in travelling elsewhere for interview and medical examination.

After your application has been reviewed and provisionally approved, you should be called for an interview. The Canadian Immigration office to which you sent your application will send you a letter indicating where and when you should present yourself for an interview, or, more probably, you will receive a letter stating you will be contacted at a later date.

The 'call-in-letter' when received will state all the additional documentation required.

PREPARING FOR THE INTERVIEW

You will meet a Canadian immigration officer for an interview, which may last from 30 minutes to 2 hours. It all depends on your situation. The officer will ask you a series of questions after he or she has examined your application. *Go prepared.*

Typical questions asked

There is no standard list of questions Canadian immigration officers use. Each officer may ask any question he or she wishes to ask, so long as it pertains to your application. However, there are certain questions most officers ask prospective immigrants.

Accompanying persons
The officer will ask your name and who the people are accompanying you, if there are any. Your family accompanying you to the interview might also be asked questions. The officer will then

normally ask for verification of all the information you gave in the application form starting with your passport.

Documents

He will want to see your birth certificate to verify your place and date of birth. The officer will want your marriage or divorce papers to verify your marital status. You will have to produce your identity card, if you have one.

The officer will want to see proof of all your assets, such as bank statements and other documents. If you have a job offer in Canada, he will want to see some proof of that, such as a letter offering employment. He will want to see all your diplomas, degrees and certificates. The officer will also want to see proof of your work history and past earnings.

You will then be asked to sign the last page of the Application for Permanent Residence in front of the officer.

General questions

Then the officer will begin the questioning. Probably the most frequently asked question is 'Why do you want to immigrate to Canada?' You should, as in all your answers, be truthful and detailed.

You are not advised to answer by saying simply 'because I want to join my brother'. Indeed, you should tell the officer this if this is your motivation. But do not stop there. If, for example, you have visited Canada and liked Canada, tell the officer that. Tell the officer what you know about Canada, about its culture, way of life, and so on. If you believe Canada would be a good place to live and work, say so.

You can also answer the question by pointing out the lack of opportunities in your home country, if it is appropriate. If your home country is undergoing particular economic or political instability, you can point this out to the officer.

The officer will probably ask you about employment opportunities for you in Canada. He will want to know where in Canada you intend to go, how you will look for a job, and so on. You should have some knowledge of employment opportunities in your occupation in Canada to respond to these questions.

If you know there are good opportunities for you in Canada, tell the officer so. And tell him how you found out. Suggested methods to find out include going to your local library and reading a

Canadian newspaper, which should also be available at all Canadian Embassies, High Commissions and Consulates. Or contact a relative or friend in Canada and ask him or her to find out about job opportunities for you.

The officer will want to know about your financial resources. How much money do you have to transfer to Canada? How much will you have with you when you arrive? You will have to show the officer that you have enough money immediately on hand to live on until you find a job or set up in business.

The officer might want to know what you know about Canada. For example, what is the weather like in the place you intend to reside? How much does a two bedroom apartment or flat cost there? Do you have some knowledge about life in Canada? Again, you might ask a friend or relative in Canada to find out this information for you.

The above questions are meant only as guidelines for you to prepare for the interview. Your interview with a Canadian immigration officer is the most important stage in the process with regard to the number of points you will receive on the Personal Suitability factor.

OUTCOME OF THE INTERVIEW

Your application may be provisionally approved on the basis of your coming to Canada for employment or as an entrepreneur, investor or self-employed person. You will then be issued medical examination instructions. Or your application may be refused at this point. The immigration officer may not give you his decision at the interview, but he will write to you later sending medical examination papers or stating that your application has been rejected.

If you are refused, there is unfortunately no formal avenue of appealing against the decision, unless you have been 'sponsored' by a close relative in Canada. However, if you truly believe you meet the requirements, you do have the right to argue the decision or to hire a consultant to argue for you. Such representations are sometimes successful as immigration officers do make mistakes.

More likely, however, you are going to have to take steps to improve your chances with a new application. Take a look again at the suggestions in this regard in Chapter 3.

8
The Clearance Checks

YOUR SECURITY CHECK

Unless you have any of the convictions outlined previously, or you have engaged in terrorist or subversive activities, you should have no difficulty passing the security check.

YOUR MEDICAL CHECK

Once you receive a letter from a Canadian immigration office informing you that a medical examination is required, you may indulge in a little rejoicing! **This letter is an indication that your application for Permanent Residence has been provisionally approved, and that you are well on your way to becoming an immigrant to Canada.**

The letter will come attached to a set of medical instructions and medical examination forms for yourself and your dependants. You and the physician examining you should carefully follow the instructions.

You should take the letter to the examining physician. You will also have to take your passport and/or identity card for identification.

The examining physician

You may be able to complete the examination with any physician of your choice, including your own doctor. However, in certain countries the Canadian government has designated certain doctors to examine prospective immigrants. If this is the case, a list of designated doctors will be given to you or you may be directed to a specific doctor.

It is up to you to make an appointment with the examining physician. Normally, you should undergo the examination within

60 or 90 days of the date the Canadian immigration office writes to you. You will have to pay the costs of the medical examination and any further tests or treatment which may be required.

You or the examining physician will send the medical forms to the appropriate address provided on the medical examination forms. Canadian immigration doctors will examine the results and forward their recommendations to the immigration office you are dealing with.

Results

If you have failed the medical examination outright, there is no formal appeal, unless you fall within the Sponsored Dependant category. However, you should be able to ask why you failed the medical examination so that you may be treated and cured and re-examined for immigration purposes.

If you pass the medical examination, a letter will be sent to you, usually within four (4) months, indicating your immigrant visa (Record of Landing) is ready and that you may present your passport to the immigration office to receive the visa, or the visa itself will be mailed to you.

The results of the medical examination are valid for one year from the date of examination. You must proceed to Canada as an immigrant within this time period. **Canadian Immigrant Visas will not be extended for any reason.**

WHEN TO DEPART

You will have to immigrate to Canada within one year of your medical examination, even if it is a few months after the medical examination that you receive your visa. If you fail to immigrate within the validity of your visa, you must reapply and go through the whole process again, under whatever regulations are in effect at that time. In other words, if you fail to exercise your visa, there is no guarantee that a subsequent application will succeed.

9
What is an Immigrant Visa?

THE RECORD OF LANDING

Congratulations! The envelope you received to present to an immigration officer at the Canadian border or port of entry contains an immigrant visa called an **Immigrant Visa and Record of Landing** (see Figure 12). There is no Canadian immigrant visa attached to or impressed in your passport, unlike the procedure in many other countries.

The Immigrant Visa will contain the following information:

- your name
- date and place of birth
- country of citizenship
- accompanying family members
- passport particulars
- intended occupation
- other administrative details.

The Visa will also contain two details of immediate importance to you. First, the expiration date. You *must* bring the Immigrant Visa and Record of Landing and enter Canada as an immigrant before that date. Secondly, it will contain the terms and conditions attached to your status, if any. For example, the visa might state that you must establish a business within a specified period of time, usually within 2 years of your arrival. Whatever the terms and conditions set forth in the visa, you must fulfil them.

You may travel to Canada by any route you wish and enter through any Canadian port of entry, unless you are specifically instructed otherwise by the Canadian High Commission, Embassy or Consulate processing your application.

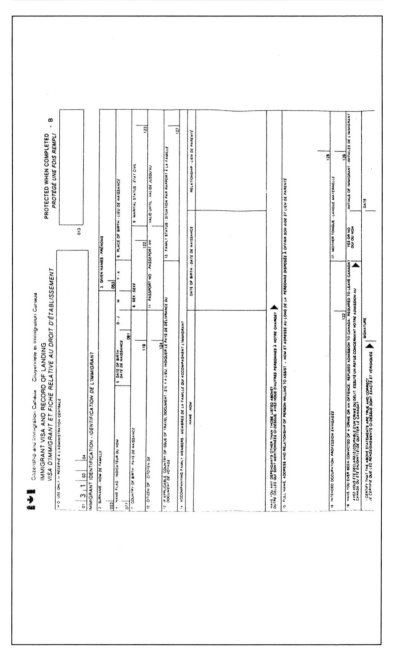

Fig. 12. Record of Landing (Form IMM 1000).

What is an Immigrant Visa?

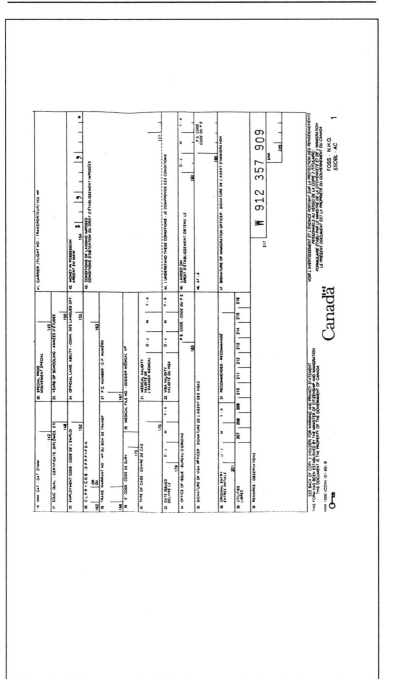

THE PORT OF ENTRY CHECK

Immigration

You should give the immigration officer the envelope containing your Immigrant Visa and Record of Landing. The officer will then complete certain formalities, such as asking you to sign it. The officer will then sign and attach a copy of the Record of Landing to your passport, and stamp your passport with a '**Permanent Resident**' stamp.

Customs

You will then have to proceed through Canadian Customs. You may enter Canada with all your household and personal goods without paying any duty provided they have been in your use prior to migrating. This includes such items as your furniture, automobiles, jewellery, and so on. Customs regulations are beyond the scope of this book, and you should check with the nearest Canadian High Commission, Embassy or Consulate if you have any questions before leaving your home country.

- **After you have cleared Canadian Customs, you will enter Canada as a permanent resident (landed immigrant).**

WHAT IS A LANDED IMMIGRANT OR PERMANENT RESIDENT?

A **Landed Immigrant** or **Permanent Resident** enjoys most of the rights of a Canadian citizen.

You may, as an immigrant, engage in any activity, work in any employment, and live wherever in Canada you would like to. You are under no obligation to register with the police or immigration as in many other countries. However, remember that there might be certain conditions attached to your immigrant visa that you must fulfil. Also, you will want to register yourself and your dependants in the Government sponsored medical care plan of the Province in which you are going to live as soon as possible after arrival. Also you will need to apply for a **Social Insurance Number** (SIN card) in order to take up employment in Canada.

Permanent residence confers on you all the legal rights of

Canadian citizenship, with a few minor exceptions. You are guaranteed fundamental rights of all Canadians.

Restrictions

You may not vote, however, in any federal election or be eligible to run as a candidate in any election. You may not be able to engage in certain professions, such as practising law or medicine, unless you are a Canadian citizen, depending on the regulations of the province in which you reside. There are also certain restrictions on drawing old age pensions or general welfare payments. For the most part, however, you will be free to do anything you want.

APPLYING FOR CANADIAN CITIZENSHIP

After three years of residency in Canada as a permanent resident (or less if you resided in Canada previously as a non-immigrant, perhaps as a student or under an employment visa) you will be eligible to apply for Canadian citizenship.

HOW NOT TO LOSE YOUR IMMIGRANT STATUS

Before you arrive . . .

There are several ways you could lose your immigrant visa **before you arrive in Canada, but after your immigrant visa has been issued**. If you are convicted of serious offences, have engaged in or might engage in espionage or terrorism, you might be excluded from entering into Canada.

After you arrive . . .

You can lose your immigrant status even once you are in Canada. If you received your visa by means of false documents or misleading statements; if you wilfully fail to support yourself or your family; if you have broken some condition of your visa such as failing to establish a business you said you would; if you are convicted of a serious offence in Canada prior to becoming a citizen, you may be forced to leave.

Returning Resident Permits

You may also lose your immigrant status if you are outside Canada for over 183 days in any twelve month period, unless you have a

Returning Resident Permit. You should note that you should not be out of Canada for more than 183 days in *any* twelve month period, not just the calendar year from January to December.

If you intend to be out of Canada for a prolonged period of time, you should apply for a Returning Resident Permit, before leaving. If you are outside Canada and find for some unforeseen reason that you have to remain outside Canada for over 183 days or you simply did not obtain a Returning Resident Permit before leaving Canada, you may apply for one at any Canadian Immigration office outside Canada.

A Returning Resident Permit is usually valid for one year only, but it may be issued or extended for up to two years. You should return to Canada before the permit expires, in order to protect your immigrant status.

There are no standard reasons why a Returning Resident Permit may be issued. You might be going abroad to study, to work, or to go on a long trip. But if you are planning to set up your family in Canada, and then return to your former employment abroad, you probably will not be issued a Returning Resident Visa. Your principal place of residence has to be in Canada. There has to be some extraordinary reason why you have to be outside Canada for a prolonged period, such as being employed in Canada by an international Canadian firm which decides to transfer you to a position abroad. Of course, once you acquire Canadian citizenship, you may leave Canada for as long as you want. A Canadian citizen always has the right to enter Canada.

10
Conclusion

I have tried to explain Canadian immigration procedures and policy clearly and concisely. Perhaps you will now be able to proceed with your application without any further assistance from anyone except a Canadian immigration office.

You should, at this point, have gained a good overall understanding regarding immigrating to Canada and know the different application methods. You should also know which category to apply in, how to apply as a Sponsored Dependant or an Independent Applicant, how to determine your chances of succeeding, and how to fill in and document the application forms.

You should have some knowledge about what to do once you obtain your visa, and how not to lose your immigrant status once in Canada.

APPEALS

I have deliberately left out certain parts of the overall immigration process, such as those that relate to visitors and students to Canada and refugees, since this book is primarily designed to aid applicants for permanent residence who are outside Canada. I have also left out the appeal process and procedure. It is not possible to rely on any guide such as this to appeal against a refused application. Instead, you should contact a competent immigration consultant to help you. In short, this book covers the most usual situations and procedures. There are many exceptions made in immigration procedures, usually for humanitarian and compassionate reasons. Also, procedures and policies may exist which have limited application but which could help you. This is where a competent and experienced immigration consultant can particularly help you.

FAMILY BUSINESSES

For example, one such exception concerns *Family Businesses and the Processing of Job Offers to Relatives*. Independent applicants who have a relative in Canada but who cannot meet the point system may nevertheless comply if coming forward to join an existing family oriented business in Canada, provided the relative already in Canada can, among other things, demonstrate a genuine need to employ a relative in the business, rather than someone already resident in Canada.

If you have reason to believe your particular situation warrants special consideration or is unique in some way, then you should seek professional assistance.

OBTAINING PROFESSIONAL HELP

This brings me to the final point: that of third-party involvement in the Canadian immigration process. Unfortunately, there are persons within and outside Canada who offer incompetent, misleading and inaccurate advice to prospective immigrants for exorbitant fees.

By the very fact that you have read this book and have gained a knowledge of Canada's immigration procedures and policies, you should be able to judge the competency of any such adviser and be able to pinpoint any inaccurate counsel you receive.

You are strongly advised to ask yourself certain questions about any such adviser before proceeding. What, for example, are the adviser's credentials in Canadian immigration matters? What are the services the adviser offers? Does he make claims he cannot possibly fulfill, such as assurances or guarantees you will be granted an immigrant visa? What is his track record? How many years has he been in business? How many cases has he dealt with, and what percentage of his cases succeed? You should also ask a friend or relative in Canada to check out him or her for you.

That is not to say, however, that there are not reputable, experienced and competent Canadian immigration consultants who genuinely aid prospective immigrants. Indeed, there are many instances, such as business establishment cases, where the assistance of consultants is recommended, and appeals to the Immigration Appeal Board or the Federal Court of Appeals where counsel is essential.

Conclusion

M. J. Bjarnason & Associates Ltd has assisted several thousand individuals and families to immigrate to Canada from all over the world who are now successfully settled from coast to coast. Should you require more specific assistance concerning your individual situation, please contact this service (for address please see the useful addresses section on page 218).

Appendix A
Designated Occupations List

As outlined in the text, applicants qualified in a Designated Occupation receive ten (10) points on the factor of Occupational Demand, **plus** ten (10) points on the factor of Pre-Arranged Employment. Here is the current list of Designated Occupations by Province in Canada (effective from 1 November 1994).

Province	*Occupation*	CCDO	SVP	OD
Newfoundland	Consultations not complete			
Prince Edward Island	No designations			
Nova Scotia	No designations			
New Brunswick	Consultations not complete			
Quebec	Exclusive provincial selection of independent immigrants			
Ontario	Occupational Therapist*	3137.118	15	10
Manitoba	No designations			
Saskatchewan	No designations			

Alberta	Occupational Therapist*	3137.118	15	10
British Colombia	No designations			
North West Territories	No designations			
Yukon	No designations			

Notes:
Applicants in designated occupations destined to the designating region will be awarded:

(a) 10 units of assessment for the occupation factor

(b) 10 units of assessment for designated occupation under the arranged employment factor

(c) processing priority for designated occupations as defined in the Regulations.

*Applicants in these occupations will probably be required to obtain evidence from the authorities of the province in which they intend to settle that they will be able to meet licensing requirements. While it is not an explicit requirement of the Immigration Act and Regulations, applicants who are professional Accountants, Dental Hygienists, Engineers, Engineering Technologists, Nurses, Occupational Therapists and Physiotherapists may expect that they will have to provide some evidence that they will be able to meet licensing requirements upon arrival in Canada or shortly thereafter. This applies as well to applicants in these occupations who come under the General Occupations List, Appendices B and C.

Appendix B
General Occupations List

**OCCUPATIONS OPEN TO PROSPECTIVE IMMIGRANTS—
effective 1 November 1994**

This is a duplication of the official listing issued by Canadian Immigration. It provides a general listing of occupations in demand under major occupational groupings. However, when you see only 4 digits for the CCDO (rather than 7), it means that all occupations under that Occupational Category are in demand. For example, CCDO 5131 (Technical Sales Occupations) encompasses no less than 36 different occupational titles such as Salesmen, Feed Products Salesman, Broadcasting Equipment Salesman, Dental Equipment, etc.

In addition, this official listing of occupations in demand provides only the points awarded on the factor of Occupational Demand and not on the factor of Specific Vocational Preparation (SVP).

You should refer to Appendix C, an Alphabetical Listing of Occupations, for a more detailed listing of occupations in demand, and the points awarded on the factors of Specific Vocational Preparation (SVP) and Occupational Demand (OD) in each occupation.

CCDO Code	Occupational title	Points
1171	ACCOUNTANTS, AUDITORS AND OTHER FINANCIAL OFFICERS	3
1173	ORGANIZATION AND METHODS ANALYSTS	3
1174	PERSONNEL AND RELATED OFFICERS	
1174-110	Labour-Relations Specialist	3

Appendix B 131

1174-118	Personnel Officer	3
1174-119	Employment Recruiter	3
1174-121	Outplacement Relocation Specialist	3
1174-122	Occupational Analyst	3
1174-126	Financial-Aids Officer	3
1174-132	Counsellor, Pre-Retirement	3
1174-134	Employment Interviewer	3
1175	PURCHASING OFFICERS AND BUYERS, EXCEPT WHOLESALE AND RETAIL TRADE	1
1176	INSPECTORS AND REGULATORY OFFICERS, NON-GOVERNMENT	
1176-110	Safety Inspector	5
1176-114	Insurance Inspector, Loss-Prevention	5
1176-122	Safety Coordinator	5
1176-126	Traffic Inspector	5
1176-130	Radiation-Contamination Monitor	5
1176-134	Service-Station Inspector	5
1176-138	Acreage-Quota-Assignment Officer	5
1176-142	Dining-Service Inspector	5
1176-146	Inspector, Travel Accommodation	5
1176-150	Gas-Customer-Liaison Agent	5
1176-154	Ammunition-Safety Inspector	
1179	OCCUPATIONS RELATED TO MANAGEMENT AND ADMINISTRATION	
1179-118	Agent	1
1179-138	Campaign Consultant	1
1179-139	Tour Operator	1
1179-140	Travel Agent	1
1179-142	Coordinator, Tourism	1
1179-146	Public-Relations Agent	1
1179-148	Interpretation-Visitor Services Coordinator	1
1179-149	Community Arts Coordinator	1
1179-150	Industrial-Development Representative	1
1179-154	Sales-Promotion Administrator	1
1179-158	Technical-Service Consultant	1
1179-174	Management-Seminar Leader	1
1179-178	Corporate Secretary	1
1179-180	Quantity Surveyor	1
1179-182	Administrative Officer	1
1179-186	Corporate Planner	1
1179-190	Contracts Administrator	1
1179-192	Conference and Meeting Planner	1
1179-194	Stations-Relations Administrator	1

1179-198	Property Administrator	1
1179-200	Food-And-Beverage Controller	1
1179-202	Freight-Traffic Consultant	1
1179-204	Cost Estimator	1
1179-205	Graphoanalyst	1
2111	CHEMISTS	1
2112	GEOLOGISTS AND RELATED OCCUPATIONS	1
2113	PHYSICISTS	1
2114	METEOROLOGISTS	1
2117	PHYSICAL SCIENCES TECHNOLOGISTS AND TECHNICIANS	
2117-110	Chemical Technologist	1
2117-114	Forest-Products Technologist	1
2117-118	Geological Technologist	1
2117-122	Geophysical Technologist	1
2117-126	Laboratory Physical Sciences Technologist	1
2117-130	Textile Technologist	1
2117-232	Holographic Technician	1
2117-240	Assayer	1
2117-244	Water-Purification Technician	1
2117-246	Chemical Technician, Heavy Water Plant and Nuclear Generation Station	1
2117-248	Chemical Technician	1
2117-252	Geological Technician	1
2117-256	Hydrology Technician	1
2117-260	Meteorological Technician	1
2117-264	Laboratory Physical Sciences Technician	1
2117-268	Textile Technician	1
2117-272	Geophysical-Equipment Operator, Airborne	1
2117-276	Geophysical Technician	1
2119	OCCUPATIONS IN PHYSICAL SCIENCES	
2119-110	Metallurgist, Physical	1
2119-112	Crime Detection Lab Analyst	1
2119-116	Hair and Fibre Examiner	1
2119-118	Prospector	1
2119-120	Alcohol Examiner	1
2131	AGRICULTURIST AND RELATED SCIENTISTS	1
2133	BIOLOGISTS AND RELATED SCIENTISTS	1

2135	LIFE SCIENCES TECHNOLOGISTS AND TECHNICIANS	1
2139	OCCUPATIONS IN LIFE SCIENCES	
2139-110	Forester	1
2141	ARCHITECTS	1
2142	CHEMICAL ENGINEERS	5
2143	CIVIL ENGINEERS	
2143-110	Materials And Testing Engineer	5
2143-114	Structural-Design Engineer	5
2143-118	Civil Engineer, General	5
2143-122	Airport Engineer	5
2143-126	Buildings And Bridge Engineer	5
2143-127	Coastal Engineer	5
2143-128	Ocean Engineer	5
2143-130	Environmental Engineer	5
2143-134	Highway Engineer	5
2143-138	Irrigation And Drainage Engineer	5
2143-142	Pipeline Engineer	5
2143-146	Railway Engineer	5
2143-150	Soil Engineer	5
2143-154	Water-Resources Engineer	5
2144	ELECTRICAL ENGINEERS	
2144-110	Design and Development Engineer, Electrical and Electronic	5
2144-114	Research Engineer, Electrical and Electronic	5
2144-118	Electrical Engineer, General	5
2144-122	Electronic Engineer, General	5
2144-126	Audio Engineer	5
2144-130	Distribution Engineer	5
2144-134	Electrical and Electronic Aerospace Engineer	5
2144-138	Electrical-Equipment Engineer	5
2144-142	Electrical-Systems-Planning Engineer	5
2144-146	Illuminating Engineer	5
2144-150	Plant Engineer, Electrical	5
2144-154	Signal Engineer	5
2144-158	Telephone Engineer	5
2144-162	Transmission Engineer	5
2145	INDUSTRIAL ENGINEERS	5
2147	MECHANICAL ENGINEERS	

2147-110	Power Engineer, Mechanical	5
2147-114	Tool Engineer	5
2147-118	Mechanical Engineer, General	5
2147-122	Automotive Engineer	5
2147-126	Heating-Ventilating And Air-Conditioning Engineer	5
2147-130	Lubrication Engineer	5
2147-134	Mechanical Engineer, Gas Utilization	5
2147-138	Propulsion Engineer, Aerospace Vehicles	5
2147-142	Refrigeration Engineer	5
2151	METALLURGICAL ENGINEERS	5
2153	MINING ENGINEERS	5
2154	PETROLEUM ENGINEERS	5
2155	AEROSPACE ENGINEERS	
2155-110	Aerospace Engineer, Design and Development	5
2155-114	Aerospace Engineer, Mass properties	5
2155-118	Aerospace Engineer, General	5
2155-122	Aerospace Engineer, Flight-Test	5
2155-126	Aerospace Engineer, Materials and Processes	5
2155-130	Aerospace Engineer, Flight Operations	5
2155-134	Aerospace Engineer, Flight Support	5
2157	NUCLEAR ENGINEERS	5
2159	ARCHITECTS AND ENGINEERS	
2159-110	Agricultural Engineer	5
2159-114	Ceramics Engineer	5
2159-118	Marine Engineer	5
2159-122	Ship-Construction Engineer	5
2159-123	Biomedical Engineer, Research and Development	5
2159-124	Biomedical Engineer, Clinical	5
2159-126	Gas and Steam-Distribution Engineer	5
2159-130	Cryogenics Engineer	5
2159-134	Geological Engineer	5
2159-138	Forest Engineer	5
2159-142	Welding Engineer	5
2159-146	Fire-Prevention Engineer	5
2159-150	Traffic Engineer	5
2159-154	Corrosion Engineer	5
2159-158	Logging Engineer, Oil Well	5
2161	SURVEYORS	
2161-110	Hydrographic Surveyor	1

Appendix B

2161-114	Surveyor	1
2161-118	Instrument Man/Woman	1
2163	**DRAUGHTING OCCUPATIONS**	
2163-110	Draughtsperson, General	1
2163-114	Cartographer	1
2163-116	Computer-assisted Design Draughtsperson	1
2163-118	Design Checker	1
2163-122	Detail Draughtsperson	1
2163-126	Draughtsperson, Architectural	1
2163-130	Draughtsperson, Civil	1
2163-134	Draughtsperson, Commercial	1
2163-138	Draughtsperson, Electrical	1
2163-140	Draughtsperson, Electro-mechanical	1
2163-142	Draughtsperson, Electronic	1
2163-146	Draughtsperson, Heating and Ventilating	1
2163-150	Draughtsperson, Marine	1
2163-154	Draughtsperson, Mechanical	1
2163-158	Draughtsperson, Mine	1
2163-162	Draughtsperson, One-tenth Scale	1
2163-164	Draughtsperson, Petroleum Exploration	1
2163-168	Draughtsperson, Pipe Organ	1
2163-170	Draughtsperson, Process Piping	1
2163-172	Editor, Map	1
2163-176	Technical Illustrator	1
2163-177	CAD Designer, Printed Circuit Boards	1
2165	**ARCHITECTURAL AND ENGINEERING TECHNOLOGISTS AND TECHNICIANS**	
2165-110	Aerospace-Engineering Technologist	1
2165-122	Civil-Engineering Technologist	1
2165-126	Electrical-Engineering Technologist	1
2165-130	Electronic-Engineering Technologist	1
2165-134	Industrial-Engineering Technologist	1
2165-142	Mechanical-Engineering Technologist	1
2165-150	Mining-Engineering Technologist	1
2165-154	Nuclear-Engineering Technologist	1
2165-160	Manufacturing Cost Estimator	1
2165-162	Mould Designer	1
2165-210	Aerospace-Engineering Technician	1
2165-222	Civil-Engineering Technician	1
2165-225	Drilling-Fluid Technician, Offshore Drilling Rig	1
2165-226	Electrical-Engineering Technician	1
2165-228	Metrology Technician	1
2165-230	Electronic-Engineering Technician	1
2165-234	Geological-Engineering Technician	1
2165-238	Industrial-Engineering Technician	1

2165-246	Mechanical-Engineering Technician	1
2165-250	Metallurgical-Engineering Technician	1
2165-254	Mining-Engineering Technician	1
2165-258	Nuclear-Engineering Technician	1
2165-262	Petrochemical-Engineering Technician	1
2165-270	Pollution Control Technician	1
2169	OTHER OCCUPATIONS IN ARCHITECTURE AND ENGINEERING	
2169-110	Photogrammetrist	5
2169-112	Remote Sensing Technician	5
2169-118	Stereoplotter	5
2181	MATHEMATICIANS, STATISTICIANS AND ACTUARIES	1
2183	SYSTEMS ANALYSTS, COMPUTER PROGRAMMERS AND RELATED OCCUPATIONS	10
2189	OCCUPATIONS IN MATHEMATICS, STATISTICS, SYSTEMS ANALYSIS AND RELATED FIELDS	
2189-114	Statistical Technician	1
2311	ECONOMISTS	1
2313	SOCIOLOGISTS, ANTHROPOLOGISTS AND RELATED SOCIAL SCIENTISTS	1
2315	PSYCHOLOGISTS	3
2319	OCCUPATIONS IN SOCIAL SCIENCES	1
2331	SOCIAL WORKERS	
2331-110	Social-Work Supervisor	5
2331-114	Community-Organization Worker	5
2331-118	Parole Officer	5
2331-122	Probation Officer	5
2331-124	Social Worker	5
2331-126	Social Worker, Case Work	5
2331-130	Social Worker, Group	5
2331-134	Counsellor, Addiction	5
2333	OCCUPATIONS IN WELFARE AND COMMUNITY SERVICES	5
2333-115	Child-Care Worker	5

Appendix B

2333-116	Community-Development Worker	5
2333-117	Teaching Homemaker	5
2333-119	Half-Way House Supervisor	5
2333-120	Geriatric-Activities Aide	5
2333-124	Detention-Home Worker	5
2339	OCCUPATIONS IN SOCIAL WORK AND RELATED FIELDS	
2339-110	Research Officer, Social Welfare	5
2339-114	Student-Activities Adviser	5
2349	OCCUPATIONS IN LAW AND JURISPRUDENCE	
2349-110	Patent Agent	1
2349-114	Law Clerk	1
2349-115	Trade Mark Agent	1
2349-117	Patent Searcher	1
2349-118	Contract Clerk	1
2349-122	Land-Titles Clerk	1
2349-126	Title Examiner	1
2351	LIBRARIANS, ARCHIVISTS AND CONSERVATORS	3
2353	TECHNICIANS IN LIBRARY, MUSEUM AND ARCHIVAL SCIENCES	1
2359	OCCUPATIONS IN LIBRARY, MUSEUM AND ARCHIVAL SCIENCES	1
2391	EDUCATIONAL AND VOCATIONAL COUNSELLORS	1
2399	OTHER OCCUPATIONS IN SOCIAL SCIENCES AND RELATED FIELDS	
2399-110	Rehabilitation Specialist	5
2399-114	Counsellor, Rehabilitation	5
2399-122	Counsellor, Marriage	5
2399-126	Counsellor, Attendance	5
2399-130	Hypnotherapist	5
2797	INSTRUCTORS AND TRAINING OFFICERS	
2797-118	Instructor, Airline Pilot	1
2797-120	Training Specialist, Computers	1
2797-122	Flying Instructor	1
2797-126	Flying Instructor, Helicopter	1

2797-128	Sewing Instructor	1
2797-130	Ground-School Instructor	1
2797-134	Instructor, Police	1
2797-138	Instructor, Flight Attendant	1
2797-142	Training Representative	1
2797-146	Instructor, Auto Driving	1
3115	**VETERINARIANS**	1
3137	**PHYSIOTHERAPISTS, OCCUPATIONAL AND OTHER THERAPISTS**	
3137-110	Audiologist	10
3137-114	Speech Pathologist	10
3137-116	Clinical Occupational Therapy Specialist	10
3137-117	Community Occupational Therapist	10
3137-118	Occupational Therapist	10
3137-122	Physiotherapist	10
3137-130	Remedial Gymnast	10
3139	**NURSING, THERAPY AND RELATED ASSISTING OCCUPATIONS**	
3139-110	Surgical Assistant	1
3139-111	Operating Room Assistant	1
3139-113	Music Therapist	1
3139-114	Recreational Therapist	1
3139-115	Art Therapist	1
3139-116	Dance Therapist	1
3151	**PHARMACISTS**	1
3152	**DIETITIANS AND NUTRITIONISTS**	1
3155	**RADIOLOGICAL TECHNICIANS**	
3155-108	Diagnostic Medical Sonographer	5
3155-110	Nuclear-Medicine Technician	5
3155-114	Diagnostic-Radiological Technician	5
3155-118	Radiotherapy Technician	10
3156	**MEDICAL LABORATORY TECHNOLOGISTS AND TECHNICIANS**	
3156-110	Biochemistry Technologist	5
3156-112	Cytogenetics Technologist	5
3156-114	Cytotechnologist	5
3156-116	Electron Microscopy Technologist	5
3156-118	Histology Technologist	5

3156-122	Medical-Laboratory Technologist	5
3156-123	Immunology Technologist	5
3156-124	Immunohematology Technologist	5
3156-126	Microbiology Technologist	5
3156-130	Laboratory Technician, Veterinary	5
3157	DENTURISTS, DENTAL HYGIENISTS, DENTAL ASSISTANTS AND DENTAL TECHNICIANS	
3157-110	Dental Hygienist	5
3157-126	Denturist	1
3157-138	Dental Technician, General	1
3157-142	Dental Ceramist	1
3157-146	Dental Technician, Crown and Bridge	1
3157-150	Dental Technician, Metal	1
3157-154	Orthodontic Technician	1
3157-158	Denture Setter	1
3157-162	Framework Finisher, Dentures	1
3157-166	Moulder, Bench	1
3157-170	Orthodontic-Band Maker	1
3159	OTHER OCCUPATIONS IN MEDICINE AND HEALTH	
3159-110	Prosthetist-Orthotist	10
3159-134	Respiratory Technologist	10
3159-138	Electroencephalographic Technician	10
3313	PRODUCT AND INTERIOR DESIGNERS	
3313-110	Exhibition and Display Designer	1
3313-114	Interior Designer and Decorator	1
3313-118	Furniture Designer	1
3313-122	Set Designer	1
3313-126	Stained-Glass Artist	1
3313-130	Fur Designer	1
3313-134	Garment Designer	1
3313-138	Industrial-Products Designer	1
3313-142	Shoe Designer	1
3313-146	Textile Designer	1
3313-150	Commercial-Design Artist	1
3313-154	Package Designer	1
3313-158	Pottery Designer	1
3313-162	Women's Fashion Designer	1
3313-166	Designer, Paper Securities	1
3313-174	Embroidery Designer	1
3313-178	Handbag Designer	1
3313-182	Sign Designer	1
3313-184	Office-Space Planner	1

140 Migrating To Canada

3314	ADVERTISING AND ILLUSTRATING ARTISTS	3
3315	PHOTOGRAPHERS AND CAMERA OPERATORS	
3315-110	Photographer, General	1
3315-114	Scientific Photographer	1
3315-116	Forensic Photographer	1
3315-118	Commercial Photographer	1
3315-120	Photographic Technician	1
3315-122	Chief Photographer	1
3315-126	Portrait Photographer	1
3315-130	News Photographer	1
3315-134	Animation-Camera Operator	1
3315-138	Aerial Photographer	1
3315-170	Camera Operator, Senior Motion Picture	1
3315-172	Camera Operator, Motion Picture	1
3315-174	News-Camera Operator	1
3315-178	Television-Camera Operator	1
3319	OCCUPATIONS IN FINE AND COMMERCIAL ART, PHOTOGRAPHY AND RELATED FIELDS	
3319-110	Scenery Artist	1
3319-114	Sign Painter	1
3319-118	Airbrush Artist	1
3319-122	Artist, Positive	1
3319-126	Photograph Retoucher	1
3319-130	Mannequin Artist	1
3319-134	Colourist, Photography	1
3319-162	Paster, Graphics	1
3319-166	Copy Stylist	1
3319-170	Sign-Layout Detailer	1
3319-202	Display Designer	1
3319-206	Diorama Maker	1
3319-226	Silhouette Artist	1
3319-228	Carver, Reproduction	1
3319-230	Floral Arranger	1
3330	PRODUCERS AND DIRECTORS, PERFORMING AND AUDIOVISUAL ARTS	3
3337	RADIO AND TELEVISION ANNOUNCERS	
3337-110	Announcer-Producer International Service	1
3337-114	Announcer	1
3337-116	Broadcast Journalist	1
3337-118	Sports Announcer	1
3337-122	Master of Ceremonies	1
3337-126	Public-Address Announcer	1

3339	OCCUPATIONS IN PERFORMING AND AUDIOVISUAL ARTS	
3339-110	Property Master	1
3339-114	Wardrobe Supervisor	1
3339-116	Special-Effects Technician	1
3339-118	Chief-Stage Electrician	1
3339-120	Light Technician	1
3339-122	Program Planner, Music	1
3339-124	Stage Production Technician	1
3339-126	Production Assistant	1
3339-130	Script Assistant	1
3351	WRITERS AND EDITORS, PUBLICATION	3
3353	WRITERS AND EDITORS: RADIO, TELEVISION, THEATRE AND MOTION PICTURES	1
3355	TRANSLATORS AND INTERPRETERS	1
3359	OCCUPATIONS IN WRITING	
3359-110	Humorist	1
3359-114	Reader, First	1
3359-122	Cross-Word-Puzzle Maker	1
4111	SECRETARIES AND STENOGRAPHERS	
4111-110	Secretary	5
4111-111	Executive Secretary	5
4111-112	Legal Secretary	5
4111-113	Medical Secretary	5
4111-114	Court Reporter	5
4111-115	Technical Secretary	5
4131	BOOKKEEPERS AND ACCOUNTING CLERKS	
4131-114	Bookkeeper	1
4135	INSURANCE, BANK AND OTHER FINANCE CLERKS	
4135-110	General Clerk, Insurance	1
4135-114	Policy-Change Clerk	1
4135-118	Property and Equipment Insurance Clerk	1
4135-122	Special-Endorsement Clerk	1
4135-182	Utility Clerk, Bank	1
4135-186	Foreign-Remittance Clerk	1
4135-190	Reserves Clerk	1

4139	BOOKKEEPING, ACCOUNT-RECORDING AND RELATED OCCUPATIONS	
4139-110	Contract Clerk	1
4139-114	Rate Reviewer	1
4143	ELECTRONIC DATA-PROCESSING EQUIPMENT OPERATORS	
4143-110	Computer Operator	1
4143-112	Computerized-Information Processor	1
4151	PRODUCTION CLERKS	
4151-110	Production Co-ordinator	1
4151-114	Material Co-ordinator	1
4151-118	Motor Vehicle Repair Co-ordinator	1
4151-122	Control Clerk, Advertising	1
4155	STOCK CLERKS AND RELATED OCCUPATIONS	
4155-110	Production-Supply Clerk	3
4155-111	Storekeeper, Drilling Rig	3
4159	MATERIAL RECORDING, SCHEDULING AND DISTRIBUTING OCCUPATIONS	
4159-110	Estimator, Jewellery	1
4169	LIBRARY, FILE AND CORRESPONDENCE CLERKS AND RELATED OCCUPATIONS	
4169-114	Credits-Assessment Clerk	1
4192	ADJUSTERS, CLAIM	
4192-110	Claim Adjuster	3
4192-114	Service Representative	3
4192-118	Claim Examiner	3
4192-120	Marine-Cargo Surveyor	3
4199	OTHER CLERICAL AND RELATED OCCUPATIONS	
4199-150	Copy Cutter	3
4199-154	Bus-Transportation-Service Co-ordinator	3
4199-162	Suggestion-Program Clerk	3
4199-164	Engineering Clerk	3

Appendix B

5131	TECHNICAL SALES OCCUPATIONS AND RELATED ADVISERS	1
5133	COMMERCIAL TRAVELLERS	
5133-110	Manufacturers' Agent	1
5133-114	Pharmaceutical Representative	1
5133-118	Sales Representative, Textbooks	1
5133-122	Sales Representative, Canvas Products	1
5133-126	Sales Representative, Commercial and Industrial Equipment and Supplies	1
5133-130	Sales Representative, Food Products	1
5133-132	Sales Representative, Wine, Beer and Spirits	1
5133-134	Sales Representative, Garments and Other Textile Products	1
5133-138	Sales Representative, Motor Vehicles and Equipment	1
5133-142	Sales Representative, Petroleum Products	1
5133-146	Sales Representative, Plastic Products	1
5133-150	Sales Representative, Pulp and Paper Products	1
5133-154	Sales Representative, Rubber Products	1
5135	SALES WORKERS, COMMODITIES	
5135-110	Salesperson, Motor Vehicles	3
5135-111	Leasing Representative, Motor Vehicles	3
5135-114	Salesperson, Sewing Machines	3
5135-116	Salesperson, Computers	3
5135-118	Salesperson, Hearing Aids	3
5135-120	Salesperson, Livestock	3
5135-121	Salesperson, Art	3
5135-122	Salesperson, Musical Instruments and Supplies	3
5135-123	Automotive Partsperson	3
5135-124	Salesperson, Wood Burning Appliances	3
5135-125	Industrial Engines and Equipment Partsperson	3
5135-126	Salesperson, Parts	3
5149	SALES OCCUPATIONS, COMMODITIES	
5149-110	Auctioneer	1
5174	ADVERTISING SALES OCCUPATIONS	3
5177	BUSINESS SERVICES SALES OCCUPATIONS	
5177-110	Sales Engineer, Oil-Well Services	1
5177-114	Sales Representative, Hotel Services	1
5177-118	Sales Representative, Telecommunications	1
5177-120	Sales Representative, Employment Services	1
5177-121	Sales Representative, Freight Forwarding Services	1

144   Migrating To Canada

5177-122	Sales Representative, Freight Service	1
5177-126	Membership Promotion Officer	1
5177-130	Sales Representative, Financial Services	1
5177-134	Sales Representative, Printing	1
5191	**BUYERS, WHOLESALE AND RETAIL TRADE**	
5191-110	Buyer	1
5191-112	Grain-Elevator Manager	1
5199	**OTHER SALES OCCUPATIONS**	
5199-110	Appraiser	1
5199-112	Antique Dealer	1
5199-114	Pawnbroker	1
5199-118	Appraiser, Automobile	1
6111	**FIRE-FIGHTING OCCUPATIONS**	
6111-122	Fire-Fighter, Crash	3
6111-126	Fire-Fighter	3
6119	**PROTECTIVE SERVICE OCCUPATIONS**	
6119-110	Conservation Officer	3
6121	**CHEFS AND COOKS**	
6121-111	Chef-Cook, General	10
6121-112	Head Chef	10
6121-113	Banquet Chef	10
6121-114	Cook, Small Establishment	10
6121-115	Chef, Patissier	10
6121-116	Chef, Saucier	10
6121-117	Chef, Rotisseur	10
6121-118	Cook, Domestic	10
6121-119	Chef, Garde-Manger	10
6121-120	Chef, Entremetier	10
6121-121	Caterer	10
6121-122	Cook, Institution	10
6121-123	Working Sous-Chef	10
6121-124	Cook, Kosher Foods	10
6121-126	Cook, Foreign Foods	10
6121-127	Cook, First	10
6121-129	Cook, Therapeutic Diet	10
6121-132	Cook, Camp	10
6141	**FUNERAL DIRECTORS, EMBALMERS AND RELATED OCCUPATIONS**	

Appendix B

6141-110	Funeral Director	1
6141-112	Cemetery Manager	1
6141-114	Embalmer	1
6143	BARBERS, HAIRDRESSERS AND RELATED OCCUPATIONS	
6143-110	Make-Up Artist	1
6143-112	Image Consultant	1
6143-114	Barber	1
6143-118	Hairdresser	1
6169	APPAREL AND FURNISHING SERVICE OCCUPATIONS	
6169-110	Dyer	1
6199	OTHER SERVICE OCCUPATIONS	
6199-110	Diver	1
7195	NURSERY AND RELATED WORKERS	
7195-110	Tree Surgeon	1
7195-112	Plant Doctor	1
8137	MOULDING, COREMAKING AND METAL CASTING OCCUPATIONS	
8137-130	Moulder, Bench	10
8143	PLATING, METAL SPRAYING AND RELATED OCCUPATIONS	
8143-110	Jewellery Coverer	1
8155	FORMING OCCUPATIONS: CLAY, GLASS AND STONE	
8155-114	Potter	1
8155-210	Master-Glass Blower	1
8155-212	Scientific-Glass-Apparatus Blower	1
8155-218	Undermaster Glass Blower	1
8155-230	Glass Blower	1
8155-234	Glass-Novelty Maker	1
8213	BAKING, CONFECTIONERY MAKING AND RELATED OCCUPATIONS	

8213-110	Cake Decorator	1
8213-114	Baker	1
8213-122	Bench Hand	1
8226	INSPECTING, TESTING, GRADING AND SAMPLING OCCUPATIONS: FOOD, BEVERAGE AND RELATED PROCESSING	
8226-110	Food Tester	1
8226-111	Fish-Roe Technician	1
8226-120	Inspector-Grader, Fish	1
8226-194	Taster and Buyer, Beverages	1
8226-198	Beer Tester	1
8256	INSPECTING, TESTING, GRADING AND SAMPLING OCCUPATIONS: PULP AND PAPERMAKING	
8256-110	Laboratory Tester	1
8263	TEXTILE SPINNING AND TWISTING OCCUPATIONS	
8263-110	Rope-machine Setter	1
8267	TEXTILE WEAVING OCCUPATIONS	
8267-110	Braid-Pattern Setter	1
8267-114	Loom-Pattern Changer	1
8271	KNITTING OCCUPATIONS	
8271-110	Knitting-Pattern Setter	1
8271-114	Knitting-Machine Fixer	1
8271-118	Looper Fixer	1
8273	TEXTILE BLEACHING AND DYEING OCCUPATIONS	
8273-110	Master Dyer	1
8275	TEXTILE FINISHING AND CALENDERING OCCUPATIONS	
8275-110	Fixer, Boarding Room	1
8296	INSPECTING, TESTING, GRADING AND SAMPLING OCCUPATIONS: PROCESSING	

Appendix B

8296-110	Inspector, Pharmaceuticals and Toiletries	1
8311	TOOL-AND-DIE-MAKING OCCUPATIONS	
8311-110	Tool and Die Maker	5
8311-112	Mould Maker	5
8311-114	Diamond-Tool Maker	5
8311-118	Die Maker, Bench, Stamping	5
8311-122	Die Maker, Wire-Drawing	5
8311-126	Die Sinker, Bench	5
8311-130	Tool Maker, Bench	5
8311-134	Carbide-Tool Maker	5
8311-138	Die Finisher	5
8311-142	Die Maker, Jewellery	5
8311-146	Extrusion-Die Template Maker	5
8313	MACHINIST AND MACHINING-TOOL SETTING-UP OCCUPATIONS	
8313-110	Machinist, Experimental	1
8313-114	Patternmaker, Metal	1
8313-118	Turbine-Blade Fitter	1
8313-122	Machinist, Ballistics Laboratory	1
8313-126	Machinist, Model Maker	1
8313-130	Pinion-and-wheel-cutting Set-up Operator	1
8313-134	Grinder Set-up Operator, Jig	1
8313-138	Instrument Maker	1
8313-142	Machine-tool Setter	1
8313-146	Machine-Tool Set-Up Operator	1
8313-150	Machinist, Automotive	1
8313-153	Machinist, Numerical	1
8313-154	Machinist, General	1
8313-158	Machinist, Motion-picture Equipment	
8313-162	Machinist, Maintenance	1
8313-166	Sample Maker Household Appliances	1
8313-174	Rotary-head-milling-machine Set-Up Operator	1
8316	INSPECTING AND TESTING OCCUPATIONS, METAL MACHINING	
8316-110	Inspector, Tool and Gauge	5
8316-114	Inspector, Machine Shop	5
8316-118	Gear Inspector	5
8316-122	Propeller Inspector	5
8331	FORGING OCCUPATIONS	
8331-110	Die Setter	5
8331-114	Blacksmith	5

8333	SHEET-METAL WORKERS	
8333-110	Model Maker, Heating Apparatus	1
8333-114	Coppersmith	1
8333-116	Precision Sheet-metal Fabricator	1
8333-118	Sheet-metal Worker	1
8333-122	Model Maker, Fluorescent Lightings	1
8333-126	Model Maker, Metal Furniture	1
8333-130	Sheet-metal Layout Detailer	1
8335	WELDING AND FLAME CUTTING OCCUPATIONS	
8335-110	Welder Setter, Resistance	
8335-112	Welder, Drilling Rig	1
8335-114	Welder-Fitter	1
8335-118	Welder, Tool & Die	1
8335-119	Welder, Laser-beam	1
8335-120	Welder, Pipeline	1
8335-122	Welder, Pressure Vessels	1
8335-126	Welder, Combination	1
8335-130	Welding-machine Operator, Gas-shielded Arc	1
8335-134	Welding-machine Operator, Submerged Arc	1
8335-138	Welder, Arc	1
8335-142	Welder, Gas	1
8335-334	Welding Technician	1
8336	INSPECTING OCCUPATIONS, WOOD MACHINING	
8336-110	Weld Inspector	1
8337	BOILERMAKERS, PLATERS AND STRUCTURAL-METAL WORKERS	
8337-110	Boilermaker	1
8337-114	Structural-metal Fabricator	1
8337-118	Boilermaker, Erection and Repair	1
8337-122	Fitter, Structural Metal	1
8337-126	Layout Marker, Structural Metal	1
8337-130	Metal Former, Hand	1
8337-150	Steel-Plate Shaper	1
8339	METAL SHAPING AND FORMING OCCUPATIONS: EXCEPT MACHINING	
8339-110	Art-metal Worker	1
8339-130	Metal-can Machine Setter	1
8351	WOOD PATTTERNMAKING OCCUPATIONS	

Appendix B

8351-110	Patternmaker, Wood	5
8351-114	Model Maker, Wood	5
8351-118	Model Maker, Last	5
8373	ABRADING AND POLISHING OCCUPATIONS: CLAY, GLASS, STONE AND RELATED MATERIALS	
8373-206	Lens-grinder-polisher Setter	1
8373-210	Optician	1
8379	CLAY, GLASS, STONE AND RELATED MATERIALS MACHINING OCCUPATIONS	
8379-150	Lens Marker	1
8391	ENGRAVING, ETCHERS AND RELATED OCCUPATIONS	
8391-110	Engraver, Hand	1
8391-114	Roller repairer, Textile	1
8391-118	Engraver, Decorative	1
8391-122	Design Cutter, Jewellery	1
8391-126	Glass Engraver	1
8391-130	Engraver, Pantograph	1
8391-190	Chaser	1
8395	PATTERNMAKERS AND MOULDMAKERS	
8395-114	Sample Maker, Jewellery	5
8395-118	Model Maker	5
8395-126	Patternmaker, Metal	5
8395-130	Loftsman/Woman	5
8395-134	Model Maker, Jewellery	5
8395-138	Patternmaker, Metal Furniture	5
8395-142	Patternmaker, Pantograph Machine	5
8395-146	Patternmaker, Envelopes	5
8395-150	Template maker	5
8395-154	Patternmaker, Hat	5
8395-158	Patternmaker, Plaster	5
8395-200	Model-And-Mould Maker, Concrete Products	5
8395-204	Mould Maker	5
8395-208	Tire-Mould Repairer	5
8395-244	Jig-And-Form Maker	5
8396	INSPECTING AND TESTING OCCUPATIONS, MACHINING	
8396-110	Balancing-machine Operator	1

8399	OTHER MACHINING AND RELATED OCCUPATIONS	
8399-110	Aircraft Mechanic, Experimental	1
8399-114	Model and Mock-up Maker	1
8399-116	Die Maker, Paperboard	1
8511	ENGINE AND RELATED EQUIPMENT FABRICATING AND ASSEMBLING OCCUPATIONS	
8511-110	Turbine Fitter	1
8523	INDUSTRIAL FARM, CONSTRUCTION AND OTHER MECHANIZED EQUIPMENT AND MACHINERY FABRICATING AND ASSEMBLING OCCUPATIONS	
8523-110	Prototype Builder	1
8523-114	Locomotive Builder	1
8523-118	Machine Builder	1
8523-122	Pipe Fitter, Turbines	1
8523-130	Pipe Fitter, Railway Car and Locomotive	1
8526	INSPECTING AND TESTING OCCUPATIONS, FABRICATING AND ASSEMBLING METAL PRODUCTS	
8526-154	Firearms Inspector	1
8526-246	Instrument Inspector and Tester	1
8526-250	Major-assembly Inspector	1
8526-258	Hydraulic Tester	1
8526-274	Tensile-strength Tester	1
8527	PRECISION INSTRUMENTS AND RELATED EQUIPMENT FABRICATING AND ASSEMBLING OCCUPATIONS	
8527-110	Scale Calibrator	1
8529	OTHER FABRICATING AND ASSEMBLING OCCUPATIONS, METAL PRODUCTS	
8529-178	Diamond-saw Maker	1
8533	ELECTRICAL AND RELATED EQUIPMENT INSTALLING AND REPAIRING OCCUPATIONS	
8533-110	Electrical Repairer	1
8533-114	Electrical, Automotive	1

Appendix B

8533-118	Refrigeration Mechanic	1
8533-122	Repairer, Electric Motor	1
8533-124	Rig Electrician	1
8533-126	Repairman, Major Appliance	1
8533-130	Electrician, Aircraft	1
8533-134	Electrician, Marine Equipment	1
8533-138	Electrician, Rail Transport	1
8533-142	Repairer, Electrical Instruments	1
8533-146	Wirer and Repairer, Office Machines	1
8533-150	Repairer, Refrigeration Unit	1
8533-154	Installer and Repairer, Automatic-Pinsetting Machine	1
8533-158	Installer-Servicer, Dental Equipment	1
8533-162	Repairer, Air-Conditioner	1
8533-166	Repairer, Electric Tool	1
8533-170	Repairman, Portable Appliance	1
8533-174	Repairer, Storage Battery	1
8533-178	Installation Man, Household Appliance	1
8535	ELECTRONIC AND RELATED EQUIPMENT INSTALLING AND REPAIRING OCCUPATIONS	
8535-105	Electronic Technician, Drilling Rig	1
8535-106	CADD/CAM Repair Technician	1
8535-107	Robotics Technician	1
8535-108	Computer Equipment Repair Technician	1
8535-109	Process-Control Equipment Repairer	1
8535-110	Installer, Aircraft-Electronic-Equipment	1
8535-114	Repairer, Electronic-Equipment	1
8535-118	Installer and Repairer, Audio-Visual Equipment	1
8535-122	Repairer, Radio-Communication Equipment	1
8535-123	Video Equipment Repairer	1
8535-124	Electronic Music Equipment Repairer	1
8535-125	Cellular Telephone Installer	1
8535-126	Repairer, Television-Studio Equipment	1
8535-127	Security Alarm Installer	1
8535-130	Installer and Repairer, Public-Address System	1
8535-134	Repairer, Nucleonic-Controller	1
8535-136	Electronic Games Repairer	1
8335-138	Repairer, Automated-Processing Equipment	1
8535-140	Satellite Antenna Installer	1
8535-142	Hearing-Aid Repairer	1
8535-146	Production Repairer	1
8536	INSPECTING AND TESTING OCCUPATIONS: FABRICATING, ASSEMBLING, INSTALLING AND REPAIRING ELECTRICAL, ELECTRONIC AND RELATED EQUIPMENT	
8536-110	Tester, Control-panel	1

8536-122	Tester, Systems	1
8536-130	Inspector and Tester, Aircraft-electrical Equipment	1
8536-134	Inspector and Tester, Aircraft-electronic Equipment	1

8537	RADIO AND TELEVISION SERVICE REPAIRERS	
8537-110	Television Repair Servicer	1
8537-112	Consumer Products Service Technician	1
8537-114	Radio Servicer	1

8539	FABRICATING, ASSEMBLING, INSTALLING AND REPAIRING OCCUPATIONS: ELECTRICAL, ELECTRONIC AND RELATED EQUIPMENT	
8539-114	Test-equipment Repairer, Oil Exploration	1
9539-118	Photoelectric-sorting-machine Repairer	1

8541	CABINET AND WOOD FURNITURE MAKERS	
8541-110	Cabinetmaker	1
8541-114	Lay-out Marker	1
8541-118	Assembler, Frame and Mirror	1

8549	FABRICATING, ASSEMBLING AND REPAIRING OCCUPATIONS, WOOD PRODUCTS	
8549-222	Stringed-instrument Maker	1
8549-226	Stringed-instrument Repairer	1
8549-246	Wood Carver	1
8549-302	Jib Builder	1

8551	PATTERNMAKING, MARKING AND CUTTING OCCUPATIONS: TEXTILE, FUR AND LEATHER PRODUCTS	
8551-110	Sailmaker	1
8551-114	Design-and-pattern maker, Canvas Goods	1
8551-118	Patternmaker	1
8551-122	Patternmaker, Shoe	1
8551-126	Pattern Modifier	1

8553	TAILORS AND DRESSMAKERS	
8553-110	Tailor, Made-to-measure Garments	1
8553-114	Tailor, Ready-to-wear Garments	1
8553-118	Tailor, Men's Garment Alterations	1
8553-142	Dressmaker	1
8553-146	Sewer	1
8553-150	Sewer, Women's Garment Alterations	1

Appendix B

8553-174	Costumer	1
8553-178	Sample-garment Maker	1
8555	**FURRIERS**	
8555-110	Furrier, All Round	1
8555-118	Fur-Repair Estimator	1
8557	**MILLINERS, HAT AND CAP MAKERS**	
8557-110	Milliner	1
8561	**SHOEMAKING AND REPAIRING OCCUPATIONS**	
8561-110	Shoemaker, Custom	1
8561-114	Shoe Repairer	1
8562	**UPHOLSTERERS**	
8562-110	Upholsterer, All Around	1
8562-111	Custom Upholsterer	1
8562-112	Patternmaker-And-Upholsterer, Aircraft	1
8562-114	Vehicle-Upholstery Repairer	1
8569	**FABRICATING, ASSEMBLING AND REPAIRING OCCUPATIONS: TEXTILE, FUR AND LEATHER PRODUCTS**	
8569-110	Canvas Worker	1
8569-114	Rug Repairer	1
8573	**MOULDING OCCUPATIONS: RUBBER, PLASTIC AND RELATED PRODUCTS**	
8573-108	Plastics Moulding, Technician	1
8579	**FABRICATING, ASSEMBLING AND REPAIRING OCCUPATIONS: RUBBER, PLASTIC AND RELATED PRODUCTS**	
8579-110	Rubberizing Mechanic	1
8579-114	Roller Repairer	1
8581	**MOTOR-VEHICLE MECHANICS AND REPAIRERS**	
8581-110	Motor-vehicle Mechanic	1
8581-111	Antique-car Restorer	1
8581-114	Engine Repairer	1
8581-115	Fuel System Conversion Installer	1

8581-116	Commercial Transport Vehicle Mechanic	1
8581-118	Industrial-truck Mechanic	1
8581-119	Automotive Technician, Engine Fuel System Repairs	1
8581-120	Automotive Technician, Front-end Systems	1
8581-121	Automotive Technician – Automatic Transmissions	1
8581-122	Transmission Mechanic	1
8581-126	Trolley-coach Mechanic	1
8581-130	Shop Estimator	1
8581-132	Recreation-vehicle Repairer	1
8581-134	Tune-up Specialist	1
8581-138	Mechanical-unit Repairer	1
8581-140	Truck-trailer Repairer	1
8581-142	Body Repairer	1
8581-146	Automotive-air conditioning Mechanic	1
8581-150	Carburetor Repairer	1
8581-154	Front-end Aligner	1
8581-158	Motorcycle Repairer	1
8581-162	New-car Preparer	1
8581-166	Automotive-brake Repairer	1
8581-170	Automotive-radiator Repairer	1
8582	AIRCRAFT MECHANICS AND REPAIRERS	
8582-108	Aircraft Maintenance Engineer	1
8582-110	Aircraft Mechanic	1
8582-114	Aircraft-Accessories Mechanic	1
8583	RAIL TRANSPORT EQUIPMENT MECHANICS AND REPAIRERS	
8583-110	Car Repairer	1
8583-114	Streetcar and Subway-car Mechanic	1
8584	INDUSTRIAL FARM AND CONSTRUCTION MACHINERY MECHANICS AND REPAIRERS	
8584-110	Printing-Machinery Mechanic	10
8584-112	Heavy-Duty-Equipment Mechanic	10
8584-114	Loom Fixer	10
8584-118	Machine Fixer, Textile	10
8584-122	Millwright	10
8584-126	Ore-Processing-Equipment Repairer	10
8584-130	Powerhouse Repairer	10
8584-132	Mechanical Maintainer, Nuclear-Generating Station and Heavy Water Plant	10
8584-134	Metalworking-Machinery Mechanic	10
8584-138	Chemical-Process-Equipment Mechanic	10
8584-139	Open-End Technician	10
8584-140	Plastics Processing Equipment Mechanic	10

Appendix B 155

8584-142	Bakery-Machinery Mechanic	10
8584-146	Boilerhouse Repairer	10
8584-150	Forge-Shop-Machinery Repairer	10
8584-154	Gum-Wrapping-Machine Mechanic	10
8584-158	Tannery-Machinery Repairer	10
8584-162	Packaging-Machine Mechanic	10
8584-166	Quilting-Machine Fixer	10
8584-170	Maintenance Mechanic, Compressed-Gas-Plant	10
8584-174	Mining-Machinery Mechanic	10
8584-178	Oil-tool Repairer	10
8584-182	Powder-Line Repairer	10
8584-186	Treatment-Plant Mechanic	10
8584-188	Farm-Equipment Installer	10
8584-190	Welding-Equipment Repairer	10
8584-194	Oven-Equipment Repairer	10
8584-198	Sewing-Machine Mechanic	10
8584-202	Ammunition-Assembling-Machine Adjuster	10
8584-206	Carton-Forming-Machine Repairer	10
8584-210	Fibreglass-Forming-Machine Repairer	10
8584-214	Laundry-Machine Mechanic	10
8584-218	Record-Process-Equipment Repairer	10
8584-222	Seamer-Machine Repairer	10
8584-226	Tobacco-Machine Adjuster	10
8584-230	Card Grinder	10
8584-234	Shearing-Machine Fixer	10
8584-238	Machine-Clothing Replacer	10
8584-242	Roll Builder	10
8584-326	Dairy-Equipment Repairer	10
8584-330	Farm-Equipment Mechanic	10
8584-350	Mine Hoist Repairer	10
8584-354	Crane repairer	10
8584-358	Conveyor Repairer	10
8584-378	Construction-Equipment Mechanic	10
8584-382	Diesel Mechanic	10
8585	BUSINESS AND COMMERCIAL MACHINE MECHANICS AND REPAIRERS	
8585-110	Mail-Processing-Equipment Mechanic	1
8585-114	Repairer, Punched-card Machines	1
8585-118	Office-Machine Repairer	1
8585-120	Photocopying-Machine Servicer	1
8585-121	Word and Information Processing Equipment Servicer	1
8585-122	Dictating and Transcribing Machines Servicer	1
8585-124	Electronic Cash Register Servicer	1
8586	INSPECTING AND TESTING OCCUPATIONS, EQUIPMENT REPAIR	

8586-110	Aircraft Inspector, Repair	3
8586-114	Locomotive Inspector	3
8586-118	Inspector, Heavy Equipment	3
8586-122	Inspector and Tester, Meteorological Equipment	3
8586-126	Tester, Automotive Vehicle	3
8586-130	Aircraft-Engine Tester	3
8586-134	Aircraft-Hydraulics Tester	3
8586-138	Maintenance Analyst	3
8586-142	Railway-Car Inspector	3
8586-150	Wheel-And-Axle Inspector	3
8586-154	Gas-Meter Tester	3
8587	WATCH AND CLOCK REPAIRERS	
8587-110	Watch Repairer	1
8587-114	Taximeter Repairer	1
8588	PRECISION-INSTRUMENT MECHANICS AND REPAIRERS	
8588-110	Aircraft-Instrument Mechanic	5
8588-112	Control Technician, Nuclear-Generating Station and Heavy Water Plant	5
8588-114	Instrument Mechanic, Utilities	5
8588-115	Biomedical and Laboratory Equipment repairer	5
8588-118	Instrument Repairer	5
8588-122	Surveying-And-Optical-Instrument Repairer	5
8588-126	Camera Repairer	5
8588-130	Photo-Finishing-Equipment Repairer	5
8588-134	Gas-Meter Repairer	5
8588-138	Gyroscope Repairer	5
8588-146	Speedometer Repairer	5
8589	MECHANICS AND REPAIRERS, EXCEPT ELECTRICAL	
8589-110	Filed-service Representative	5
8589-114	Automotive-maintenance-equipment Servicer	5
8589-118	Dredge Mechanic	5
8589-122	Gunsmith	5
8589-126	Pump Installer and Repairer	5
8589-130	Fuel-Injection-Unit Servicer	5
8589-134	Pump Repairer	5
8589-138	Airport maintenance Worker	5
8589-142	Safe-and-vault Servicer	5
8589-144	Repairer, Small Engines	5
8589-146	Locksmith	5
8589-150	Pneumatic-Tool Repairer	5
8589-154	Pneumatic-tube Repairer	5

Appendix B 157

8589-158	Salvager, Machinery	5
8589-162	Hydraulic-unit Repairer	5
8589-166	Pneumatic-Unit Tester and Repairer	5
8589-170	Scale Mechanic	5
8589-178	Air-Compressor Repairer	5
8591	JEWELLERY AND SILVERWARE FABRICATING, ASSEMBLING AND REPAIRING OCCUPATIONS	
8591-110	Diamond Cutter	1
8591-114	Lapidary	1
8591-118	Gemmologist	1
8591-122	Jeweller	1
8591-126	Precious Stone Setter	1
8591-210	Silversmith	1
8591-214	Hammersmith	1
8592	MARINE CRAFT FABRICATING, ASSEMBLING AND REPAIRING	
8592-110	Loftsperson	1
8592-114	Shipwright, Metal	1
8592-118	Shipwright, Wood	1
8592-122	Pipe Fitter	1
8592-126	Ship Fitter	1
8592-130	Rigger	1
8592-134	Engine Fitter	1
8592-138	Joiner	1
8592-201	Rig Mechanic	1
8592-202	Marine-Engine Mechanic	1
8592-206	Outboard-motor Mechanic	1
8595	PAINTING AND DECORATING OCCUPATIONS, EXCEPT CONSTRUCTION	
8594-114	Painter	1
8596	INSPECTING, TESTING AND GRADING OCCUPATIONS: PRODUCT FABRICATING, ASSEMBLING AND REPAIRING	
8596-180	Inspector, Returned Materials	1
8596-184	Materials and Parts Inspector	1
8599	OTHER PRODUCT FABRICATING, ASSEMBLING AND REPAIRING OCCUPATIONS	
8599-214	Harpischord Builder	1
8599-218	Musical-instrument repairer	1

8599-222	Pipe-organ Tuner and Repairer	1
8599-226	Accordion Repairer	1
8599-230	Piano Repairer	1
8599-234	Pipe-organ Builder	1
8599-238	Wind-instrument Repairer	1
8599-242	Organ-pipe Voicer	1
8599-246	Pipe-organ Erector	1
8599-250	Piano-tone Regulator	1
8731	ELECTRICAL POWER LINE WORKERS AND RELATED OCCUPATIONS	
8731-110	Line Maintainer, Emergency Service	5
8731-114	Line Repairer	5
8731-118	Line Maintainer	5
8731-122	Cable Installer-Repairer	5
8731-126	Line Maintainer, Street railway	5
8735	WIRE COMMUNICATIONS AND RELATED EQUIPMENT INSTALLING AND REPAIRING OCCUPATIONS	
8735-110	Central-Office-Equipment Repairer	3
8735-114	Rural-Telephone Maintainer	3
8735-118	Electrician, Communications Equipment	3
8735-122	Private-Branch-Exchange Repairer	3
8735-126	Station Repairer	3
8735-130	Signal Maintainer	3
8735-134	Telegraph-Equipment Repairer	3
8735-136	Cable Installer	3
8735-138	Line Installer-Repairer	3
8735-142	Protective-Signal servicer	3
8735-146	Repairer, Shop	3
8735-154	Central-Office-Equipment Installer	3
8735-158	Private-Branch-Exchange Installer	3
8735-162	Telephone Station Installer	3
8735-166	Telecommunications-Equipment Installer	3
8735-170	Cable-Television Installer	3
8736	INSPECTING AND TESTING OCCUPATIONS: ELECTRICAL POWER, LIGHTING AND WIRE COMMUNICATIONS EQUIPMENT ERECTING, INSTALLING AND REPAIRING	
8736-110	Electrical-Wiring Inspector	5
8736-114	Cable Tester	5
8736-122	Meter Tester	5
8736-126	Tester and Regulator	5
8736-130	Exchange Tester	5

Appendix B

8736-134	Electrical-Testing Technician	5
8736-138	Terminal and Repeater Tester	5
8736-142	Transmission Tester	5
8736-160	Powerline Patroller	5
8739	ELECTRICAL POWER, LIGHTING AND WIRE COMMUNICATIONS EQUIPMENT ERECTING, INSTALLING AND REPAIRING OCCUPATIONS	
8739-110	Electrician, Powerhouse	1
8739-114	Circuit-breaker Mechanic	1
8739-118	Electrician, Substation	1
8739-122	Electric-meter Repairer	1
8739-126	Relay tester-repairer	1
8739-130	Cable Splicer	1
8739-134	Power-transformer Repairer	1
8739-138	Transformer Repairer	1
8739-146	Salvage Repairer	1
8739-150	Neon-sign Erector	1
8739-152	Traffic-light Installer	1
8739-154	Voltage-regulator Maintainer	1
9111	AIR PILOTS, FLIGHT OFFICERS AND FLIGHT ENGINEERS	
9111-110	Test Pilot	1
9111-112	Pilot, General Aviation	1
9111-114	Patrol Pilot	1
9111-118	Airline Captain	1
9111-119	First Officer	1
9111-122	Executive Pilot	1
9111-126	Helicopter Pilot	1
9111-130	Aerial Survey Pilot	1
9111-134	Spray Pilot	1
9111-136	Second Officer	1
9113	AIR TRANSPORT OPERATING SUPPORT OCCUPATIONS	
9113-114	Flight Dispatcher	1
9113-118	Air-Traffic Controller	1
9113-120	Air-Traffic Control Officer	1
9113-124	Station Agent	1
9113-126	Schedule Analyst	1
9113-128	Traffic Technician	1
9113-129	Air-Traffic Control Assistant	1
9131	LOCOMOTIVE OPERATING OCCUPATIONS	

9131-110	Locomotive Engineer	1
9131-114	Yard Engineer	1
9135	RAILWAY TRANSPORT OPERATING SUPPORT OCCUPATIONS	
9135-110	Train Dispatcher	1
9135-114	Car Assignments Clerk	1
9179	MOTOR TRANSPORT OPERATING OCCUPATIONS	
9197-114	Route Planning Analyst	1
9179-142	Mobile-Support-Equipment Operator	1
9199	OTHER TRANSPORT AND RELATED EQUIPMENT OPERATING OCCUPATIONS	
9199-112	Subway-traffic Controller	1
9311	HOISTING OCCUPATIONS	
9311-106	Crane Operator, Drilling Rig	1
9531	POWER STATION OPERATORS	
9531-110	Load Dispatcher	1
9531-114	Substation Inspector	1
9531-118	Diesel-Plant Operator	1
9531-122	Power-Switchboard Operator	1
9531-130	Power-Control-Room Operator	1
9531-134	Nuclear-Reaction Operator	1
9531-138	Hydro-Electric-Station Operator	1
9531-142	Turbine Operator, Steam	1
9531-144	Field Operator, Nuclear-Generating Station	1
9531-146	Central Office Power-Room Operator	1
9531-154	Feeder Switchboard Operator	1
9533	STATIONARY ENGINE AND AUXILIARY EQUIPMENT OPERATING AND MAINTAINING OCCUPATIONS	
9533-110	Boiler Operator	1
9533-111	Power Engineer, Automated Control	1
9533-113	Energy-From-Waste Plant Operator	1
9533-114	Refrigeration Operator	1
9533-118	Diesel Engine Operator, Stationary	1
9533-122	Power Engineer, General	1
9533-124	Steam Operator	1

Appendix B

9533-126	Boiler Operator, Pulverized Coal	1
9533-128	Building Systems Technician	1
9533-134	Compressor Operator, Caisson	1
9551	RADIO AND TELEVISION BROADCASTING EQUIPMENT OPERATORS	5
9555	SOUND AND VIDEO RECORDING AND REPRODUCTION EQUIPMENT OPERATORS	
9555-110	Sound Mixer	5
9555-114	Stereo-Tape Editor	5
9555-118	Re-Recording Mixer	5
9555-126	Video-And Sound Recorder	5
9555-130	Sound-Effects Technician	5
9557	MOTION PICTURE PROJECTIONISTS	1
9599	MISCELLANEOUS CRAFTS AND EQUIPMENT OPERATING OCCUPATIONS	
9599-110	Totalizator-systems analyst	1
9599-114	Model Maker	1
9599-118	Prop Maker	1
9916	INSPECTING, TESTING, GRADING AND SAMPLING OCCUPATIONS	
9916-110	Radiographer, Industrial	3
9916-114	Tester, Ultrasonic	3
9919	OTHER OCCUPATIONS	
9919-108	Research Assistant	1

Appendix C
Alphabetical Listing of Occupations Open to Prospective Immigrants

EFFECTIVE 1 NOVEMBER 1994

OCCUPATIONS	CCDO	SVP	OD
Accountant, Tax	1171.134	18	3
Accountant, Machine Processing	1171.126	18	3
Accountant, Professional	1171.114	18	3
Accountant, Property	1171.130	18	3
Accountant, Cost	1171.122	18	3
Accountant, Budget	1171.118	18	3
Actuary	2181.118	18	1
Administrative Officer	1179.182	15	1
Advertising Representative	5174.118	11	3
Advertising Copywriter	3351.162	15	3
Aerial-Survey Operator	2117.272	11	1
Aerial-Photograph Analyst	2169.114	11	5
Aerodynamicist, Physical	2113.138	18	1
Aerodynamicist	2113.138	18	1
Aeronautical Engineer	2155.118	18	5
Aerospace-Engineering Technologist	2165.110	15	1
Aerospace Engineer, Design and Development	2155.110	18	5
Aerospace-Engineering Technician	2165.210	11	1
Aerospace Engineer, Flight-Test	2155.122	18	5
Aerospace Engineer, Flight Operations	2155.130	18	5
Aerospace Engineer, Materials and Processes	2155.126	18	5
Aerospace Engineer, General	2155.118	18	5
Aerospace Engineer, Flight Support	2155.134	18	5
Aerospace Engineer, Mass Properties	2155.114	18	5
Agent, Entertainment	1179.118	11	1
Agricultural Chemist	2111.110	18	1
Agricultural Research Chemist	2111.110	18	1
Agricultural-Engineering Technician	2165.214	11	1
Agricultural Economist	2311.118	18	1
Agricultural Engineer	2159.110	18	5
Agricultural Scientist	2131.110	18	1
Agriculturist	2131.110	18	1

Agrologist	2131.110	18	1
Agronomist	2131.122	18	1
Air-Compressor Repairman	8589.178	11	5
Air-Compressor Mechanic	8589.178	11	5
Air-Traffic Control Assistant	9113.129	11	1
Air-Traffic Controller	9113.118	15	1
Air-Traffic Control Officer	9113.130	15	1
Aircraft, Hydraulics Tester	8586.134	15	3
Aircraft Inspector, Repair	8586.110	18	3
Airline Captain	9111.118	18	1
Airport Engineer	2143.122	18	5
Aligner Front-end	8581.154	11	1
Ammunition Assembling Machine Adjuster	8584.202	11	10
Ammunition-Safety Inspector	1176.154	11	5
Analyst, Route Planning	9179.114	11	1
Analyst, Schedule	9113.126	11	1
Analyst, Political (broadcasting)	3353.118	18	1
Analyst, News Broadcasting	3353.118	18	1
Analyst, Totalizator-systems	9599.110	18	1
Analyst, Stock Market (broadcasting)	3353.118	18	1
Analytical-Research Chemist	2111.114	18	1
Analytical Chemist	2111.114	18	1
Anatomist	2133.194	18	1
Animal Scientist	2131.114	18	1
Animation Artist	3314.114	15	3
Animator	3314.114	15	3
Announcer, Sports	3337.118	11	1
Announcer, Public-address	3337.126	11	1
Announcer	3337.114	15	1
Announcer-producer Int'l Service	3337.110	15	1
Anthropologist	2313.110	18	1
Antique Dealer	5199.112	11	1
Anvilsmith	8331.114	15	5
Apiculturist	2133.118	18	1
Appliance Serviceman and Repairman	8533.126	15	1
Application Programmer	2183.124	11	10
Appraiser, Automobile	5199.118	11	1
Appraiser	5199.110	15	1
Appraiser, Insurance	5199.110	15	1
Appraiser, Furniture	5199.110	15	1
Archaeologist	2313.118	18	1
Architect	2141.110	18	1
Architectural Technologist	2165.114	15	1
Archivist	2351.146	15	3
Art Director	3330.170	15	3
Art Layout Man	3314.136	15	3
Art Work, Assembler	3319.162	11	1
Artist, Background and Title	3314.130	15	3
Artist, Commercial	3314.118	15	3

Artist, Animation	3314.114	15	3
Artist, Airbrush Photography	3319.118	11	1
Artist, Mannequin	3319.130	11	1
Artist, Positive	3319.122	11	1
Artist, Silhouette	3319.226	11	1
Artist, Wallpaper	3319.122	11	1
Artist, Scenery	3319.110	11	1
Artist, Airbrush	3319.118	11	1
Artist, glass	3319.122	11	1
Assayer	2117.240	11	1
Assembler, Grader	8523.118	15	1
Assembler, Crane	8523.118	15	1
Assembler, Compressor	8523.118	15	1
Assembler, Frame and Mirror	8541.118	11	1
Assembler-Fitter Machine	8523.118	15	1
Assistant, Script	3339.130	11	1
Assistant, Production	3339.126	11	1
Astronomer	2113.114	18	1
Astronomer, Celestial Mechanisms	2113.114	18	1
Astrometrist	2113.114	18	1
Astrophysicist	2113.114	18	1
Auctioneer	5149.110	11	1
Audio Engineer	2144.126	18	5
Audiologist	3137.110	15	10
Auditor	1171.162	18	3
Author	3351.154	18	3
Automotive Engineer	2147.122	18	5
Automotive Partsperson	5135.123	11	3
Background-and-Title Artist	3314.130	15	3
Bacteriologist, Public-Health	2133.146	18	1
Bacteriologist, Industrial	2133.158	18	1
Bacteriologist, Food	2133.154	18	1
Bacteriologist, Dairy	2133.154	18	1
Bacteriologist, Veterinary	2133.146	18	1
Bacteriologist, Pharmaceutical	2133.170	18	1
Bacteriologist	2133.146	18	1
Bacteriologist, Soil	2133.174	18	1
Bacteriologist, Fishery	2133.150	18	1
Bacteriologist, Medical	2133.162	18	1
Baker	8213.114	11	1
Baker, Speciality Foods	8213.114	11	1
Bakery-Machinery Mechanic	8584.142	11	10
Ballistician	2113.138	18	1
Bank Branch Accountant	1171.138	15	1
Banquet Chef	6121.113	18	10
Barber	6143.114	11	1
Bench Hand (Bake. prod.)	8213.122	11	1
Bibliographer	2351.122	15	3
Biologist, Aquatic	2133.110	18	1

Biochemist, Analytical	2133.146	18	1
Biochemist	2133.234	18	1
Biochemist, Cellular	2133.242	18	1
Biologist, Marine	2133.110	18	1
Biologist, Molecular	2133.254	18	1
Biologist, Development	2133.254	18	1
Biologist, Cell	2133.242	18	1
Biomedical Engineer, Research and Development	2159.123	18	5
Biomedical Engineer, Clinical	2159.124	18	5
Biophysicist, Radiation	2133.238	18	1
Biophysicist, Medical	2133.238	18	1
Biophysicist, Mathematical	2133.238	18	1
Biophysicist, Physiological	2133.238	18	1
Biophysicist, Molecular	2133.238	18	1
Biophysicist, Medical-Engineering	2133.238	18	1
Biophysicist	2133.238	18	1
Blacksmith	8331.114	15	5
Blower, Glass-Master	8155.210	18	1
Blower, Glass Undermaster	8155.218	18	1
Blower, Bottle	8155.230	15	1
Blower, Glass	8155.230	15	1
Blower, Glass-Apparatus Scientific	8155.212	18	1
Boiler Tender, Low Pressure	9533.150	5	1
Boiler Operator, Pulverized Coal	9533.126	15	5
Boiler Operator	9533.110	15	5
Boiler Maker	8337.110	15	1
Boiler Maker, Erection and Repair	8337.118	15	1
Boilerhouse Repairman	8584.146	11	10
Bookkeeper	4131.114	11	1
Bookmobile Librarian	2351.120	11	3
Botanist	2133.114	18	1
Botanist, Economic	2133.114	18	1
Branch Accountant, Bank	1171.138	15	1
Broadcast Transmitter Operator	9551.114	15	5
Broadcast Journalist	3337.116	15	1
Builder, Machine	8523.118	15	1
Builder, Locomotive	8523.114	15	1
Builder, Prototype	8523.110	18	1
Builder, Pipe-organ	8599.234	15	1
Builder, Harpsichord	8599.214	18	1
Building Systems Technician	9533.128	11	5
Buildings and Bridge Engineer	2143.126	18	5
Bursar	1171.186	15	3
Bus-Transportation-Service Coordinator	4199.154	11	3
Business Editor	3351.126	18	3
Business Manager	1179.110	11	1
Buyer, Time and Space	1175.110	15	1
Buyer, Material	1175.118	15	1
Buyer	5191.110	15	1

Buyer, Food and Related Products	1175.114	15	1
Cabinetmaker	8541.110	15	1
Cable Installer-Repairer	8731.122	15	5
Cable Tester	8736.114	15	5
Cable-Television Installer	8735.170	11	3
Cable Installer	8735.136	15	3
Cable Splicer	8739.130	15	1
Cake Decorator	8213.110	11	1
Calibrator, Scale	8527.110	15	1
Camera Repairman	8588.126	15	5
Camera-Operator, Television	3315.178	15	1
Camera-Operator, Motion Picture	3315.172	15	1
Camera-Operator, Animation	3315.134	15	1
Camera-Operator, News	3315.174	15	1
Camera-Operator, Senior Motion Picture	3315.170	15	1
Cameraman, Second	3315.172	15	1
Campaign Consultant	1179.138	15	1
Carbide Tool Maker	8311.134	15	1
Card Grinder	8584.230	11	10
Card Setter	8584.230	11	10
Carding Machine Fixer	8584.230	11	10
Cartographer	2163.110	15	1
Cartographic Technician	2163.110	15	1
Cartographic Draughtsman	2163.110	15	1
Cartographic Compiler	2163.110	15	1
Carton-Forming-Machine Repairman	8584.206	11	10
Cartoon-Background Artist	3314.140	15	3
Cartoonist	3314.134	15	3
Cartoonist, Motion Picture	3314.114	15	3
Carver, Native Art	3319.228	15	1
Carver, Reproduction	3319.228	15	1
Carver Wood, Reproduction	3319.228	15	1
Casting Officer	3330.130	15	3
Cataloguer	2351.126	15	3
Caterer	6121.121	18	10
Cemetery Manager	6141.112	15	1
Central Office Power Room Operator	9531.146	15	1
Central-Office-Equipment Installer	8735.154	15	3
Central-Office-Equipment Repairer	8735.110	18	3
Ceramics Engineer	2159.114	18	5
Chaser (Jewellery)	8391.190	11	1
Chef, Patissier	6121.115	18	10
Chef, Garde-Manger	6121.119	18	10
Chef, Rotisseur	6121.117	18	10
Chef, Banquet	6121.113	18	10
Chef, Saucier	6121.116	18	10
Chef-Cook, General	6121.111	18	10
Chef, Entremetier	6121.120	18	10
Chef, Pastry	8213.114	11	1

Chemical-Process-Equipment Mechanic	8584.138	15	10
Chemical Technician	2117.248	11	1
Chemical Engineer, Production	2142.118	18	5
Chemical-Engineering Technologist	2165.118	15	1
Chemical Analyst	2111.114	18	1
Chemical Oceanographer	2111.118	18	1
Chemical Technician Heavy Water Plant	2117.246	11	1
Chemical Technologist	2117.110	15	1
Chemical-Engineering Technician	2165.218	11	1
Chemical Engineer, Design and Development	2142.110	18	5
Chemical Engineer, Research	2142.114	18	5
Chemist, Analytical-Research	2111.114	18	1
Chemist, Enzyme	2133.234	18	1
Chemist, Clinical	2133.246	18	1
Chemist, Biological	2133.234	18	1
Chemist, Agricultural Research	2111.110	18	1
Chemist, Agricultural	2111.110	18	1
Chemist, Medicinal	2133.234	18	1
Chief-Petroleum Engineer	2154.110	18	5
Chief Conservator, Art Gallery	2359.114	18	1
Child-Care Worker	2333.115	11	5
Civil Engineer, General	2143.118	18	5
Claim Adjuster	4192.110	15	3
Claim Examiner	4192.118	15	3
Clerk, Car Assignment	9135.114	11	1
Clerk, Contract	4139.110	15	1
Clerk, Credit-Assessments	4169.114	11	1
Climatologist	2114.114	18	1
Clinical Chemist	2133.246	18	1
Clinical Occupational Therapy Specialist	3137.116	15	10
Clock Repairman	8587.110	15	1
Cloth Designer	3313.146	18	1
Clothes Designer	3313.134	18	1
Co-ordinator, Tourism	1179.142	15	1
Co-ordinator, Material	4151.114	11	1
Co-ordinator, Motor-Vehicle Repair	4151.118	11	1
Co-ordinator, Production	4151.110	15	1
Coastal Engineer	2143.127	18	5
Cobbler	8561.114	15	1
Columnist	3351.166	15	3
Commercial-Systems Analyst	2183.110	18	10
Commercial Artist	3314.118	15	3
Commercial-Design Artist	3313.150	15	1
Community-Development Worker	2333.116	11	5
Community Occupational Therapist	3137.117	15	10
Community Arts Coordinator	1179.149	15	1
Community-Organization Worker	2331.114	18	5
Compressor Operator, Caisson	9533.134	11	5
Computer Graphics Specialist	2183.150	15	10

Computer Operator	4143.110	11	1
Computer-Search Librarian	2351.121	15	3
Computer Consultant, Market Support	5131.116	15	1
Computer Hardware Specialist	2183.154	15	10
Computerized-Information Processor	4143.112	11	1
Conference and Meeting Planner	1179.192	15	1
Conservation Officer	6119.110	11	3
Conservator	2351.166	18	3
Construction Equipment Mechanic	8584.378	15	10
Continuous-Mining-Machine Operator	7717.118	11	1
Contract Clerk	2349.118	11	1
Contracts Administrator	1179.190	15	1
Control Chemist	2111.134	18	1
Control Clerk, Advertising	4151.122	11	1
Controller, Air-Traffic	9113.118	15	1
Controller Subway traffic	9199.112	11	1
Conveyor Repairman	8584.358	11	10
Cook, Domestic	6121.118	15	10
Cook, Therapeutic Diet	6121.129	15	10
Cook, Institution	6121.122	15	10
Cook, Small Establishment	6121.114	15	10
Cook, First	6121.127	15	10
Cook, Camp	6121.132	15	10
Cook, Foreign Foods	6121.126	15	10
Cook, Kosher Foods	6121.124	15	10
Coppersmith	8333.114	18	1
Copy Cutter	4199.150	18	3
Copywriter	3351.162	15	3
Corporate Planner	1179.186	15	1
Corporate Secretary	1179.178	18	1
Corrosion Engineer	2159.154	18	5
Cosmetician, Mannequin	3319.130	11	1
Cosmologist	2113.114	18	1
Cost Engineer, Retirements	1171.202	15	3
Cost Estimator	1179.204	15	1
Costumer	8553.174	15	1
Counsellor, Addiction	2331.134	15	5
Counsellor, Attendance	2399.126	11	5
Counsellor, Rehabilitation	2399.114	15	5
Counsellor, Marriage	2399.122	15	5
Counsellor, Preretirement	1174.132	11	3
Counsellor, Vocational	2391.122	15	1
Counsellor, Educational	2391.118	15	1
Counsellor, General (educ.)	2391.114	15	1
Court Reporter	4111.114	11	5
Crane Repairman	8584.354	15	10
Credit Officer	1171.210	11	3
Critic	3351.150	18	3
Critic, Book	3351.110	18	3

Cryogenics Engineer	2159.130	18	5
Custom Upholsterer	8562.111	15	1
Cutter Diamond	8591.110	18	1
Cutting-Machine Operator	7717.122	11	1
Cytologist	2133.242	18	1
Cytotechnologist	3156.114	15	5
Dairy Bacteriologist	2133.154	18	1
Dairy Equipment Repairman	8584.326	15	10
Data-Processing-Sales Representative	5131.114	18	1
Delineator	3319.170	15	1
Demographer	2181.126	18	1
Dental Technician, General	3157.138	11	1
Dental Ceramist	3157.142	15	1
Dental Technician, Crown and Bridge	3157.146	15	1
Dental Hygienist	3157.110	11	5
Dental Technician, Metal	3157.150	15	1
Denture Setter	3157.158	15	1
Denturist	3157.126	15	1
Design and Development Engineer, Electrical/Electronic	2144.110	18	5
Design and Pattern Maker, Canvas Goods	8551.114	11	1
Design Detailer, Auto-body	2163.122	15	1
Design Checker	2163.118	15	1
Design-Cutter, Jewellery	8391.122	11	1
Designer, Shows and Demonstrations	3313.110	18	1
Designer, Clothes	3313.134	18	1
Designer, Paper Securities	3313.166	18	1
Designer, Embroidery	3313.174	15	1
Designer, Highways	2163.126	15	1
Designer Cad, Printer Circuit Boards	2163.177	15	1
Designer, Office-layout	2163.134	15	1
Designer, Display	3319.202	11	1
Deskman, Sports	3351.202	15	3
Detail Man, Furniture	2163.122	15	1
Detailer, Sign-Layout	3319.170	15	1
Detention-Home Worker	2333.124	11	5
Development Economist	2311.122	18	1
Diagnostic Medical Sonographer	3155.108	15	5
Diagnostic-Radiological Technician	3155.114	11	5
Diamond Tool Maker	8311.114	15	1
Diamond-saw Maker	8529.178	15	1
Die Barber	8311.138	15	1
Die Fitter	8311.138	15	1
Die Maker, Wire Drawing	8311.122	15	1
Die Finisher	8311.138	15	1
Die Maker Bench Stamping	8311.118	15	1
Die Maker Jewellery	8311.142	11	1
Die Setter	8331.110	15	5
Die Sinker, Bench	8311.126	15	1

Die Maker, Paperboard	8399.116	15	1
Diesel-Plant Operator	9531.118	15	1
Diesel Mechanic	8584.382	15	10
Diesel Engine Operator, Stationary	9533.118	15	5
Dietitian, Consultant	3152.114	15	1
Dietitian	3152.122	15	1
Dietitian, Therapeutic	3152.126	15	1
Dining-Service, Inspector	1176.142	11	5
Diorama Maker	3319.206	11	1
Director, Casting	3330.130	15	3
Director, Art	3330.170	15	3
Director, Broadcasting	3330.158	15	3
Director, Motion Picture	3330.150	18	3
Director, State	3330.162	15	3
Dispatcher, Flight	9113.114	18	1
Display Maker	3319.206	11	1
Distribution Engineer	2144.130	18	5
Diver	6199.110	11	1
Doctor, Plant	7195.112	11	1
Draughting Clerk, Transit	2169.126	11	5
Draughtsman, Relay (elec. equip)	2163.138	15	1
Draughtsman, Structural Steel	2163.126	15	1
Draughtsman, Directional Survey (oil and nat. gas)	2163.164	15	1
Draughtsman, Hydraulic Machinery (ship and boat bldg.)	2163.150	15	1
Draughtsman, Radio	2163.142	15	1
Draughtsman, Geophysical	2163.164	15	1
Draughtsman/Woman, Computer-assisted Design	2163.116	15	1
Draughtsman, Air-Conditioning Systems	2163.146	15	1
Draughtsman Optical	2163.162	15	1
Draughtsman, Monopol	2163.162	15	1
Draughtsman, Refrigeration Systems	2163.146	15	1
Draughtsman, Hull (ship and boat bldg.)	2163.150	15	1
Draughtsman, Tool Design	2163.154	15	1
Draughtsman, Geological	2163.164	15	1
Draughtsman Marine, Electrical (ship and boat bldg)	2163.138	15	1
Draughtsman, Communications (Elec. power)	2163.138	15	1
Draughtsman, Ship Detail (ship and boat bldg.)	2163.150	15	1
Draughtsperson, Civil	2163.126	15	1
Draughtsperson, Detail	2163.122	15	1
Draughtsperson, Architectural	2163.126	15	1
Draughtsperson, Petroleum Exploration	2163.164	15	1
Draughtsperson, Electronic	2163.142	15	1
Draughtsperson, Process Piping	2163.170	15	1
Draughtsperson, Mine	2163.158	15	1
Draughtsperson, Mechanical	2163.154	15	1
Draughtsperson, Electro-Mechanical	2163.140	15	1

Draughtsperson, Commercial	2163.134	15	1
Draughtsperson, Heating and Ventilating	2163.146	15	1
Draughtsperson, One-tenth Scale	2163.162	15	1
Draughtsperson, Pipe Organ	2163.168	15	1
Draughtsperson, General	2163.110	15	1
Draughtsperson, Electrical	2163.138	15	1
Draughtsperson, Marine	2163.150	15	1
Drawing-Detail Man, Sheet Metal	2163.122	15	1
Dressmaker	8553.142	18	1
Dyer	6169.110	11	1
Dyer, Master (knitting)	8273.110	15	1
Ecologist	2133.130	18	1
Ecologist, Plant	2133.114	18	1
Ecologist, Animal	2133.126	18	1
Econometrician	2311.126	18	1
Economic-Development Officer	1179.150	15	1
Economist, Agricultural	2311.118	18	1
Economist, General	2311.114	18	1
Economist, Home	2319.126	18	1
Editor, Sports	3351.158	15	3
Editor, Advertising	3351.114	18	3
Editor, Financial	3351.126	18	3
Editor, Magazine	3351.130	18	3
Editor, Special Features	3351.198	15	3
Editor, Make-Up	3351.206	11	3
Editor Telecommunications	3351.186	15	3
Editor, Picture	3351.210	11	3
Editor, News	3351.134	18	3
Editor, Trade or Technical Journal	3351.142	18	3
Editor, Book	3351.110	18	3
Editor, City	3351.118	18	3
Editor, Editorial Page	3351.122	18	3
Editor, Copy	3351.190	11	3
Editor, Technical Publication	3351.138	18	3
Editor, Map	2163.172	15	1
Editor, News Broadcasting	3353.110	18	1
Editor, News, Special Events and Public Affairs	3353.110	18	1
Editor, Film and Script Television News	3353.110	18	1
Editor, Foreign-News Broadcasting	3353.110	18	1
Editor, Continuity and Script	3353.114	18	1
Editorial Writer	3351.170	15	3
Editorial Assistant	3351.194	11	3
Electrical Engineering Technologist	2165.126	15	1
Electrical and Electronic Aerospace Engineer	2144.134	18	5
Electrical-Equipment Engineer	2144.138	18	5
Electrical Repairman	8533.110	15	1
Electrical-Engineering Technician	2165.226	11	1
Electrical Engineer, General	2144.118	18	5
Electrical-Systems-Planning Engineer	2144.142	18	5

Electrician, Communications Equipment	8735.118	15	3
Electrician Rail Transport	8531.138	15	1
Electrician Aircraft	8533.130	15	1
Electrician Marine Equipment	8533.134	15	1
Electrician, Powerhouse	8739.110	15	1
Electrician, Chief-Stage	3339.118	15	1
Electrician, Substation	8739.118	15	1
Electroencephalographic Technician	3159.138	11	10
Electronic Engineering Technologist	2165.130	15	1
Electronic-Engineering Technician	2165.230	11	1
Electronic Engineer, General	2144.122	18	5
Embalmer	6141.114	11	1
Embroidery Designer	3313.174	15	1
Embryologist	2133.194	18	1
Employment Interviewer	1174.134	11	3
Employment Recruiter	1174.119	15	3
Engineer, Airport	2143.122	18	5
Engineer, Cryogenics	2159.130	18	5
Engineer, Electrical	2144.118	18	5
Engineer, Aeronautical	2155.118	18	5
Engineer, Aerospace	2155.118	18	5
Engineer, Agricultural	2159.110	18	5
Engineer, Audio	2144.126	18	5
Engineer, Electrical Equipment	2144.138	18	5
Engineer, Automotive	2147.122	18	5
Engineer, Locomotive	9131.110	15	1
Engineer, Yard	9131.114	11	1
Engineering-Depreciation Evaluator	1171.202	15	3
Engineering Clerk	4199.164	11	3
Engraver, Hand	8391.110	15	1
Engraver, Glass	8391.126	11	1
Engraver, Decorative	8391.118	15	1
Engraver, Pantograph	8391.130	11	1
Entomologist	2133.118	18	1
Environmental Engineer	2143.130	18	5
Enzymologist	2133.254	18	1
Epidemiologist	2181.136	18	1
Erector, Neon-sign	8739.150	11	1
Erector, Pipe-organ	8599.246	15	1
Estimator, Shop (motor vehicle)	8591.130	15	1
Estimator, Jewellery	4159.110	11	1
Estimator, Crating and Moving	5177.122	11	1
Examiner, Alcohol	2119.120	15	1
Examiner, Firearms	2119.114	15	1
Examiner, Hair and Fibre	2119.116	15	1
Exchange Tester	8736.130	11	5
Executive Secretary (Clerical)	4111.111	15	5
Exhibition and Display Designer	3313.110	18	1
Experimentalist, Elementary-particle	2114.126	18	1

Exploration Geophysicist	2112.110	18	1
Extrusion Die Template Maker	8311.146	11	1
Fabrictor, Structural-Metal	8337.114	15	1
Fabricator, Precision Sheet Metal	8333.116	15	1
Farm Equipment Mechanic	8584.330	15	10
Farm Equipment Installer	8584.188	11	10
Feeder-Switchboard Operator	9531.154	11	1
Feltman	8584.238	11	10
Fermentologist	2133.234	18	1
Fibreglass Forming Machine Repairman	8584.210	11	10
Field Operator, Nuclear-Generating Station	9531.144	15	1
Field Service Man	2131.134	18	1
File-Systems Analyst	1173.126	11	3
Film Editor	3330.174	15	3
Financial Economist	2311.130	18	1
Financial Analyst	1171.184	18	3
Financial-Aids Officer	1174.126	15	3
Fire Fighter	6111.126	11	3
Fire Fighter, Crash	6111.122	11	3
Fire-Prevention Engineer	2159.146	18	1
Fitter, Ship	8592.126	15	1
Fitter, Pipe (ship and boat bldg.)	8592.122	15	1
Fitter, Engine (ship and boat bldg.)	8592.134	15	1
Fitter, Turbine	8511.110	18	1
Fitter, Turbine-blade	8313.118	18	1
Fitter, Structural Metal	8337.122	15	1
Fixer, Cutting Machine	8584.234	11	10
Fixer	8584.114	15	10
Fixer, Boarding Room	8275.110	11	1
Floral Arranger	3319.230	11	1
Florist	3319.230	11	1
Flying Instructor, Helicopter	2797.126	15	1
Flying Instructor	2797.122	15	1
Food Scientist	2131.118	18	1
Food Bacteriologist	2133.154	18	1
Food Tester	8226.110	11	1
Food-And-Beverage Controller	1179.200	11	1
Foreign Exchange Trader	1171.206	15	3
Foreign Banking Arrangements Officer	1171.188	15	3
Foreign-Broadcast Translator	3355.118	11	1
Foreign-Remittance Clerk	4135.186	11	1
Foreman, Stage-property	3339.110	15	1
Forest Products Technologist	2117.114	15	1
Forest Engineer	2159.138	18	5
Forester	2139.110	18	1
Forge Shop Machinery Repairman	8584.150	11	10
Forging Die Maker	8311.126	15	1
Forging Machine Set-Up Man	8331.110	15	5
Forms Management Analyst	1173.118	11	3

Forms Designer	2169.130	11	5
Forms Analyst-And-Designer	1173.118	11	3
Forms-layout Man	2169.130	11	1
Frame Wirer, Telephones	8735.182	11	3
Framework Finisher, Dentures	3157.162	11	1
Freight-Traffic Consultant	1179.202	11	1
Funeral Director	6141.110	15	1
Fur Designer	3313.130	18	1
Fur-Repair Estimator	8555.118	11	1
Furniture Designer	3313.118	18	1
Furrier, All Round	8555.110	15	1
Garment Designer	3313.134	18	1
Garment Maker, Sample	8553.178	11	1
Gas-Customer-Liaison Man	1176.150	11	5
Gas Meter Repairman	8588.134	11	5
Gas And Steam-Distribution Engineer	2159.126	18	5
Gauge Checker	8316.110	15	5
Gear Inspector	8316.118	15	5
Gemmologist	8591.118	15	1
General Clerk, Insurance	4135.110	11	1
Geneticist	2133.250	18	1
Geodetic Computer	2161.114	15	1
Geographer	2319.110	18	1
Geological Technician	2117.252	11	1
Geological Technologist	2117.118	15	1
Geological Engineer	2159.134	18	5
Geological-Engineering Technician	2165.234	11	1
Geologist	2112.114	18	1
Geophysical Technician	2117.276	11	1
Geophysical Technologist	2117.122	15	1
Geophysicist	2112.118	18	1
Geriatric-Activities Aide	2333.120	11	5
Glass Blower	8155.230	15	1
Glass-Novelty Maker	8155.234	15	1
Grain-Elevator Manager	5191.112	11	1
Graphic Artist	3314.118	15	3
Graphoanalyst	1179.205	15	1
Ground-School Instructor	2797.130	15	1
Guidance Head (educ.)	2391.110	18	1
Gum Wrapping Machine Mechanic	8584.154	11	10
Gunsmith	8589.122	15	5
Hairdresser	6143.118	11	1
Half-Way House Supervisor	2333.119	11	5
Hammersmith	8591.214	11	1
Handbag Designer	3313.178	15	1
Head Office Underwriter	1171.194	15	3
Head Chef	6121.112	18	10
Heating, Ventilating/Air-Conditioning Engineer	2147.126	18	5
Heavy Forger	8331.118	15	5

Heavy Duty Equipment Mechanic	8584.112	18	10
Helminthologist, Wildlife	2133.258	18	1
Herpetologist	2133.126	18	1
Highway Engineer	2143.134	18	5
Histologist	2133.194	18	1
Histopathologist	2133.202	18	1
Historian	2319.114	18	1
Holographic Technician	2117.232	15	1
Home-Decorating Consultant	3313.114	18	1
Horticulturist	2131.130	18	1
Humorist	3359.110	15	1
Hydraulic Tester	8586.134	15	3
Hydraulic-Unit Repairman	8589.162	11	5
Hydro-Electric-Station Operator	9531.138	15	1
Hydrologist	2112.122	18	1
Hydrology Technician	2117.256	11	1
Hypnotherapist	2399.130	11	5
Ichthyologist	2133.126	18	1
Illuminating Engineer	2144.146	18	5
Image Consultant	6143.112	11	1
Immunologist	2133.168	18	1
Industrial Engineer, General	2145.110	18	5
Industrial Economist	2311.134	18	1
Industrial Products Designer	3313.138	18	1
Industrial-Efficiency Engineer	2145.110	18	5
Industrial-Engineering Technician	2165.238	11	1
Industrial-Engineering Analyst	2145.122	18	5
Industrial Engines and Equipment Partsperson	5135.125	11	3
Industrial Hygienist	2145.114	18	5
Industrial-Safety Engineer	2145,118	18	5
Industrial Diamond Cutter and Polisher	8311.114	15	1
Industrial Engineering Technologist	2165.134	15	1
Industrial Representative	5131.110	18	1
Industrial-Development Representative	1179.150	15	1
Information Service Worker, Encyclopedia	2359.118	11	1
Inorganic-Research Chemist	2111.122	18	1
Inorganic Chemist	2111.122	18	1
Inspector Machine Shop	8316.114	15	5
Inspector Tool and Gauge	8316.110	15	5
Inspector, Ammunition-Safety	1176.154	11	5
Inspector, Travel Accommodation	1176.146	11	5
Inspector, Returned materials	8596.180	11	1
Inspector and Tester, Instruments	8526.246	15	1
Inspector, Materials and Parts	8596.184	11	1
Inspector and Tester, Aircraft-Electronic Equipment	8536.134	15	1
Inspector, Major-Assembly	8526.250	11	1
Inspector, Firearms	8526.154	11	1
Inspector, Pharmaceuticals and Toiletries	8296.110	15	1

Inspector and Tester, Aircraft-Electrical Equipment	8536.130	15	1
Inspector-Grader, Fish	8226.120	11	1
Installation Man, Household Appliance	8533.178	11	1
Installer, Cellular Telephone	8535.125	11	1
Installer, Security Alarm	8535.127	11	1
Installer, Satellite Antenna	8535.140	11	1
Installer and Repairer, Audio-Visual Equipment	8535.118	11	1
Installer and Repairer, Public-Address System	8535.130	11	1
Installer, Aircraft-Electronic-Equipment	8535.110	15	1
Installer, Closed-Circuit Television	8535.118	11	1
Installer, Fuel System Conversion (motor vehicle)	8581.115	15	1
Installer, Traffic-light	8739.152	11	1
Instructor, Police	2797.134	15	1
Instructor, Flight Attendant	2797.138	15	1
Instructor, Airline Pilot	2797.118	18	1
Instructor, Auto Driving	2797.146	11	1
Instrument Man	8588.118	15	5
Instrument Technician, Aircraft	8588.110	15	5
Instrument Man/Woman	2161.118	15	1
Instrument Maker	8313.138	15	1
Insurance Inspector, Loss-Prevention	1176.114	15	5
Inter-Bank Arrangements Officer	1171.188	15	3
Interior Decorator	3313.114	18	1
Interior Designer and Decorator	3313.114	18	1
International-Trade Economist	2311.138	18	1
Interpretation-Visitor Services Coordinator	1179.148	15	1
Interpreter	3355.110	15	1
Inventory and Cost Engineer	1171.202	15	3
Investment Analyst	1171.184	18	3
Irrigation and Drainage Engineer	2143.138	18	5
Jeweller	8591.122	15	1
Jewellery Coverer	8143.110	11	1
Jig Builder	8549.302	11	1
Joiner (ship and boat bldg.)	8592.138	15	1
Journalist	3351.166	15	3
Knitting, Machine-Fixer	8271.114	11	1
Knitting, Pattern Setter	8271.110	15	1
Lab Analyst, Crime Detection	2119.112	15	1
Laboratory Chemist	2111.134	18	1
Laboratory Physical Science Technician	2117.264	11	1
Laboratory Physical Science Technologist	2117.126	15	1
Labour Economist	2311.142	18	1
Labour-Relations Specialist	1174.110	18	3
Land-Titles Clerk	2349.122	11	1
Landscape Architect	2141.114	18	1
Lapidary (gem cutter)	8591.114	18	1
Laundry Machine Mechanic	8584.214	11	10

Law Reporter	4111.114	11	5
Law Clerk	2349.114	15	1
Lay-out Marker, Structural Metal	8337.126	15	1
Lay-out Marker	8541.114	15	1
Layout Man, Art	3314.136	15	3
Layout Detailer, Sheet Metal	8333.130	11	1
Leasing Representative, Motor Vehicles	5135.111	11	3
Legal Secretary	4111.112	11	5
Lens Marker	8379.150	11	1
Lettering Artist	3314.146	11	3
Level Man	2161.118	15	1
Lexicographer	3351.146	18	3
Librarian	2351.114	15	3
Lightkeeper, Triangulation	2161.118	15	1
Limnologist	2133.110	18	1
Line Maintainer, Emergency Service	8731.110	18	5
Line Installer-Repairer	8735.138	15	3
Line Repairer	8731.114	15	5
Line Maintainer	8731.118	15	5
Linguist	2319.118	18	1
Literary Writer	3351.154	18	1
Load Dispatcher	9531.110	18	1
Loan Analyst	1171.210	11	3
Locksmith	8589.146	11	5
Locomotive Inspector	8586.114	18	3
Locomotive Builder	8523.114	15	1
Loftsperson (ship and boat bldg.)	8592.110	18	1
Logging Engineer	2159.158	18	5
Loom Fixer	8584.114	15	10
Loom Repairman	8584.114	15	10
Looper Fixer (knitting)	8271.118	11	1
Lubrication Engineer	2147.130	18	5
Machine Clothing Man	8584.238	11	10
Machine Fixer Textile	8584.118	15	10
Machine-Tool Designer	2147.114	18	5
Machine Builder	8523.118	15	1
Machinist, General	8313.154	15	1
Machinist, Precision	8313.154	15	1
Machinist, All-Round	8313.154	15	1
Machinist, Fitter	8313.154	15	1
Machinist, Motion-Picture Equipment	8313.158	15	1
Machinist, Research	8313.110	18	1
Machinist, Experimental	8313.110	18	1
Machinist, Maintenance	8313.162	15	1
Machinist, NC	8313.153	15	1
Machinist, Model Maker	8313.126	15	1
Machinist, Ballistics Laboratory	8313.122	15	1
Machinist, Automotive	8313.150	15	1
Maintainer Line, Street Railway	8731.126	15	1

Maintainer, Voltage-regulator	8739.154	11	1
Maintenance Mechanic Compressed Gas Plant	8584.170	11	10
Maintenance Engineer, Aircraft	8582.108	18	1
Maintenance Mechanic Laundry	8584.214	11	10
Make-up Artist	6143.110	11	1
Maker, Stringed-instrument	8549.222	18	1
Mammalogist	2133.126	18	1
Management Analyst	1173.114	15	3
Management Engineer	1173.114	15	3
Management-Seminar Leader	1179.174	18	1
Manufacturers' Agent	5133.110	15	1
Manufacturers' Representative	5133.110	15	1
Manufacturing Engineer	2145.126	18	5
Manufacturing Cost Estimator	2165.160	15	1
Maple-Syrup Maker	7199.182	11	1
Marine-Cargo Surveyor	4192.120	11	3
Marine-Engineering Technician	2165.242	11	1
Marine Engineer	2159.118	18	5
Marine-Engineering Technologist	2165.138	15	1
Market-Research Analyst	2311.158	15	1
Master-Control-Equipment Operator	9551.110	15	5
Master of Ceremonies	3337.122	11	1
Materials and Testing Engineer	2143.110	18	5
Mathematical Economist	2311.146	18	1
Mathematician, Applied	2181.130	18	1
Mathematician, Research	2181.110	18	1
Mathematician, Pure Mathematics	2181.110	18	1
Mechanic, Bakery Machinery	8584.142	11	10
Mechanic, Diesel	8584.382	15	10
Mechanic, Construction Equipment	8584.378	15	10
Mechanic, Mail-Processing-Equipment	8585.110	15	1
Mechanic, Process-Control Equipment	8535.114	15	1
Mechanic, Air-Compressor	8589.178	11	5
Mechanic, Electronics	8535.114	15	1
Mechanic, Aircraft	8582.110	15	1
Mechanic, Turbine-Engine	8582.110	15	1
Mechanic, Radar	8535.114	15	1
Mechanic, Helicopter	8582.110	15	1
Mechanic, Aircraft and Engine	8582.110	15	1
Mechanic, Vibrating Equipment	8523.118	15	1
Mechanic, Piston-Engine	8582.110	15	1
Mechanic, Aircraft-Accessories	8582.114	11	1
Mechanic,Outboard-motor (ship and boat bldg.)	8592.206	11	1
Mechanic, Industrial Truck	8581.118	15	1
Mechanic, Trolley-Coach	8581.126	15	1
Mechanic, Dredger	8589.118	15	5
Mechanic, Automotive-air-conditioning	8581.146	11	1
Mechanic, Rubberizing	8579.110	11	1

Mechanic Aircraft, Experimental	8399.110	18	1
Mechanic, Marine-engine	8592.202	15	1
Mechanic, Transmission	8581.122	15	1
Mechanic, Motor-Vehicle	8581.110	15	1
Mechanic, Rig	8592.201	15	1
Mechanic, Streetcar and Subway-car	8583.114	15	1
Mechanic, Circuit-breaker	8739.114	15	1
Mechanic, Commercial Transport Vehicle	8581.116	15	1
Mechanical-Engineering Technician	2165.246	11	1
Mechanical Engineer, Gas Utilization	2147.134	18	5
Mechanical Maintainer, Nuc, Gen. Stn. and Heavy Water Plant	8584.132	15	10
Mechanical-Engineering Technologist	2165.142	15	1
Mechanical Engineer, General	2147.118	18	5
Medical Bacteriologist	2133.162	18	1
Medical Secretary	4111.113	11	5
Medical Illustrator	3314.122	15	3
Metal Working Machiner Mechanic	8584.134	15	10
Metal Former, Hand	8337.130	11	1
Metallographer	2119.110	18	1
Metallurgical Engineer	2151.110	18	5
Metallurgical-Engineering Technician	2165.250	11	1
Metallurgical-Engineering Technologist	2165.146	15	1
Metallurgist, Extractive	2151.110	18	5
Metallurgist, Physical	2119.110	18	1
Metallurgist, Research	2119.110	18	1
Meteorologist, Dynamic	2114.110	18	1
Meteorological Technician	2117.260	11	1
Meteorologist, Physical	2114.110	18	1
Meteorologist	2114.110	18	1
Meteorologist, Applications and Impact	2114.118	18	1
Meteorologist, Industrial	2114.110	18	1
Meteorologist, Synoptic	2114.110	18	1
Methods and Procedures Analyst	1173.114	15	3
Methods Designer	2145.130	18	5
Microbiologist	2133.166	18	1
Milliner (hats)	8557.110	15	1
Millwright	8584.122	15	10
Mine Hoist Repairman	8584.350	15	10
Mineral Engineer	2153.110	18	5
Mineralogist	2112.126	18	1
Minicomputer/Microcomputer Specialist	2183.158	15	10
Mining-Engineering Technologist	2165.150	15	1
Mining Engineer	2153.110	18	1
Mining-Engineering Technician	2165.254	11	1
Mobile-Broadcast-Equipment Installer	9551.122	15	5
Mobile Equipment Repairman	8584.378	15	10
Model and Mock-Up Maker	8399.114	18	1
Model Maker, Metal Furniture	8333.126	11	1

Model Maker	9599.114	15	1
Model Maker, Fluorescent Lighting	8333.122	15	1
Model Maker, Heating Apparatus	8333.110	18	1
Morphologist	3351.147	18	3
Mosaicer	2169.122	15	5
Motor-Vehicle Mechanic	8581.110	15	5
Mould Maker	8311.112	15	1
Mould Designer	2165.162	15	1
Moulder, Bench	3157.166	11	5
Music, Program-Planner	3339.122	15	1
Musical Director	3330.154	18	3
Musical-program Director	3339.122	15	1
Museum, Cataloguer	2353.130	11	1
Museum, Exhibit Designer	2359.110	18	1
Museum, Extension Officer	2359.115	15	1
Museum Educator	2359.116	15	1
Mycologist	2133.122	18	1
Nematologist, Plant	2133.206	18	1
Neuropathologist	2133.202	18	1
Nuclear-medicine Technician	3155.110	15	5
Nuclear-Reactor Operator	9531.134	15	1
Nuclear Engineer	2157.110	18	5
Nuclear-Operations Engineer	2157.114	18	1
Nuclear-Engineering Technician	2165.258	11	1
Nuclear Technologist	2165.156	15	1
Nuclear-Engineering Technologist	2165.154	15	1
Numerical Control Machinist	8313.153	15	1
Nutritionist	3152.118	15	1
Occupational Therapist	3137.118	15	10
Occupational Analyst	1174.122	15	3
Ocean Engineer	2143.128	18	5
Office-Space Planner	3313.184	15	1
Officer, Second (air)	9111.136	15	1
Officer, First (air)	9111.119	15	1
Oil Tool Maintenance Man	8584.178	15	10
Operations-Research Analyst	2181.122	18	1
Operator, Boiler	9533.110	15	5
Operator, Mobile-Support-Equipment	9179.142	11	1
Operator Set-up, Pinion and Wheel Cutting	8313.130	15	1
Operator Grinder Set-Up, Jig	8313.134	15	1
Operator, Balancing-Machine	8396.110	11	1
Operator-crane, Drilling Rig	9311.106	11	1
Optician	8373.210	15	1
Ore Processing Equipment Repairman	8584.126	15	10
Organic-Research Chemist	2111.126	18	1
Organic Chemist	2111.126	18	1
Organizational Analyst	1173.122	15	3
Ornithologist	2133.126	18	1
Orthodontic-Band Maker	3157.170	11	1

Orthodontic Technician	3157.154	15	1
Outplacement Relocation Specialist	1174.121	15	3
Oven Equipment Repairman	8584.194	11	10
Package Designer	3313.154	15	1
Packaging Machine Mechanic	8584.162	11	10
Painter, Glass	3313.126	18	1
Painter, Sign	3319.114	15	1
Painter, Mannequin	3319.130	11	1
Painter (motor vehicle)	8595.114	11	1
Paleontologist	2112.130	18	1
Parasitologist, Medical	2133.258	18	1
Parasitologist, Veterinary	2133.258	18	1
Parasitologist	2133.258	18	1
Parole Officer	2331.118	15	5
Partsperson, Automotive	5135.123	11	3
Passenger and Freight Rates Analyst	1171.198	15	3
Paster, Graphics	3319.162	11	1
Patent Searcher	2349.117	11	1
Pathologist, Surgical	2133.202	18	1
Pathologist, Haematological	2133.202	18	1
Pathologist, Medical	2133.202	18	1
Pathologist, Plant	2133.206	18	1
Pathologist, Animal	2133.198	18	1
Pathologist, Veterinary	2133.198	18	1
Pathologist, Oral	2133.202	18	1
Pathologist, Forensic	2133.202	18	1
Pathologist, Research-Plant	2133.206	18	1
Pathologist, Clinical	2133.202	18	1
Pattern Moulder	8137.110	15	10
Pattern Setter, Braid	8267.110	15	1
Pattern Modified	8551.126	11	1
Pattern Changer, Loom	8267.114	15	1
Patternmaker and Upholsterer Aircraft	8562.112	15	5
Patternmaker, Wood	8351.110	18	5
Patternmaker, Metal	8395.126	15	5
Patternmaker, Shoe	8551.122	11	1
Patternmaker, Metal	8313.114	18	1
Patternmaker (Furn. and Fabric)	8551.118	11	1
Pawnbroker	5199.114	11	1
Personal Financial Planner	1171.196	15	3
Personnel Administrator	1174.118	15	3
Personnel Officer	1174.118	15	3
Petrochemical-Engineering Technologist	2165.158	15	1
Petrochemical-Engineering Technician	2165.262	11	1
Petroleum Engineer	2154.114	18	5
Petroleum Geologist	2112.134	18	1
Petroleum-Engineering Technician	2165.266	11	1
Pharmaceutical-Detail Man	5133.114	15	1
Pharmaceutical Representative	5133.114	15	1

Pharmacist, Hospital	3151.110	18	1
Pharmacist, Industrial	3151.114	18	1
Pharmacist, Retail	3151.118	18	1
Pharmacologist	2133.210	18	1
Pharmacologist, Clinical	2133.212	18	1
Photo Finishing Equipment Repairman	8588.130	15	5
Photogrammetrist	2169.110	15	5
Photograph Retoucher	3319.126	11	1
Photographer, Portrait	3315.126	15	1
Photographer, Scientific	3315.114	15	1
Photographer, Medical	3315.114	15	1
Photographer, Chief	3315.122	15	1
Photographer, Commercial	3315.120	15	1
Photographer, Aerial	3315.138	15	1
Photographer, Forensic	3315.116	15	1
Photographer, General	3315.110	15	1
Photographer, News	3315.130	15	1
Photographer, Biological	3315.114	15	1
Photography, Colourist	3319.134	11	1
Photomicrographer	3315.114	15	1
Physical-Research Chemist	2111.130	18	1
Physical Chemist	2111.130	18	1
Physical Oceanographer	2113.150	18	1
Physicist, Nuclear	2113.142	18	1
Physicist, Theoretical-Nuclear	2113.142	18	1
Physicist, Optics	2113.142	18	1
Physicist, Plasma	2113.154	18	1
Physicist, Microwave	2113.122	18	1
Physicist, Other	2113.199	18	1
Physicist, Crystal	2113.158	18	1
Physicist, Mechanics	2113.138	18	1
Physicist, Nuclear-Reactor	2113.142	18	1
Physicist, Acoustics	2113.110	18	1
Physicist, Fluids	2113.130	18	1
Physicist, Metal	2113.158	18	1
Physicist, Cosmic-Ray	2113.142	18	1
Physicist, Atomic and Molecular	2113.118	18	1
Physicist, High-temperature	2113.162	18	1
Physicist, Health	2113.134	18	1
Physicist, Solid-State	2113.158	18	1
Physicist, Magnetism	2113.122	18	1
Physicist, Cryogenics	2113.162	18	1
Physicist, Elementary-particle	2113.126	18	1
Physicist, Semi-Conductor	2113.158	18	1
Physicist, Chemical	2113.118	18	1
Physicist, Electricity and Magnetism	2113.122	18	1
Physicist, Relativity	2113.199	18	1
Physicist, Beta-Spectroscopy	2113.142	18	1
Physicist, Thermal	2113.162	18	1

Physicist, Accelerator	2113.142	18	1
Physicist, Alpha-Spectroscopy	2113.142	18	1
Physiologist, Molecular	2133.254	18	1
Physiologist, Insect	2133.214	18	1
Physiologist, Plant	2133,214	18	1
Physiologist, Cellular	2133.214	18	1
Physiologist, Veterinary	2133.214	18	1
Physiologist	2133.214	18	1
Physiologist, Human (Medical)	2133.214	18	1
Physiotherapist	3137.122	15	10
Phytopathologist	2133.206	18	1
Pilot, Aerial Survey	9111.130	15	1
Pilot, Executive	9111.122	15	1
Pilot, Helicopter	9111.126	15	1
Pilot, General Aviation	9111.112	15	1
Pilot, Spray	9111.134	15	1
Pilot, Patrol	9111.114	15	1
Pilot-test	9111.110	18	1
Pipe Fitter, Railway Car and Locomotive	8523.130	11	1
Pipe Fitter, Turbines	8523.122	15	1
Pipeline Engineer	2143.142	18	5
Placement Officer	1174.134	11	3
Plane-Table Man	2161.118	15	1
Planner, Conference and Meeting	1179.192	15	1
Planner, Urban and Regional	2319.130	18	1
Planner, Community Recreation	2319.132	15	1
Plant Scientist	2131.122	18	1
Plant Engineer, Electrical	2144.150	18	5
Plastics Processing Equipment Mechanic	8584.140	11	10
Pneumatic-Tool Repairman	8589.150	11	5
Pneumatic-Tube Repairman	8589.154	11	5
Pneumatic-Unit Tester and Repairer	8589.166	11	5
Policy-Change Clerk	4135.114	11	1
Political Scientist	2319.122	18	1
Pollution Control Technician	2165.270	11	1
Poster Layout Man	3319.170	15	1
Potter	8155.114	15	1
Pottery Designer	3313.158	15	1
Powder Line Repairman	8584.182	11	10
Power Engineer, Mechanical	2147.110	15	5
Power-Switchboard Operator	9531.122	15	1
Power-Control-Room Operator	9531.130	15	1
Power Engineer, General	9533.122	15	5
Power-Plant Engineer	2147.110	18	5
Powerhouse Repairman	8584.130	15	10
Powerline Patroller	8736.160	11	5
Preparator	2353.127	11	1
Pressure-Vessel Welder	8335.122	15	1
Price Economist	2311.150	18	1

Printing Machinery Mechanic	8584.110	18	10
Private-Branch-Exchange Repairer	8735.122	15	3
Private-Branch-Exchange Installer	8735.158	11	3
Probation Officer	2331.122	15	5
Producer, Stage	3330.114	18	3
Producer, Motion Picture	3330.110	18	3
Producer, Broadcasting	3330.118	15	3
Production, Audio-Amplifier Repairer	8535.146	11	1
Production, Repairman	8535.146	11	1
Production, Television Repairman	8535.146	11	1
Production Engineer	2145.134	18	5
Production Planner	2145.134	18	5
Production-Supply Clerk	4155.110	11	3
Program Director	3330.158	15	3
Program Co-ordinator, Broadcasting	3330.126	15	3
Programmer, Business	2183.118	15	10
Programmer, Engineering and Scientific	2183.122	15	10
Programmer, Detail	2183.130	11	10
Projection Illustrator	3319.170	15	1
Projectionist Motion Picture	9557.110	11	1
Promotion Officer, Membership	5177.126	11	1
Prop Maker (broadcast)	9599.118	15	1
Propeller Inspector	8316.122	11	5
Property Master (broadcast)	3339.110	15	1
Property And Equipment Insurance Clerk	4135.118	11	1
Property Administrator	1179,198	11	1
Property Manager	1179.198	11	1
Propulsion Engineer, Aerospace Vehicles	2147.138	18	5
Prospector (Mining and Quarrying)	2119.118	15	1
Prosthetist-Orthotist	3159.110	15	10
Protozoologist	2133.258	18	1
Psychologist, Counselling	2315.138	18	3
Psychologist, Developmental	2315.118	18	3
Psychologist, Engineering	2315.126	18	3
Psychologist, Educational	2315.122	18	3
Psychologist, General	2315.110	18	3
Psychologist, Clinical	2315.134	18	3
Psychologist, Social	2315.130	18	3
Psychologist, School	2315.146	18	3
Psychologist, Industrial	2315.142	18	3
Psychologist, Experimental	2315.114	18	3
Psychometrist	2315.150	15	3
Public Adjuster	4192.110	15	3
Public-Relations Man	1179.146	15	1
Publicity Director	1179.146	15	1
Publisher's Representative	5133.118	11	1
Purchasing Officer, Food and Related Products	1175.114	15	1
Purchasing Officer, Business Services	1175.110	15	1

Purchasing Officer, Material	1175.118	15	1
Puzzle Maker, Cross-Word	3359.122	11	1
Puzzle Maker, Bilingual	3359.122	11	1
Quality Surveyor	1179.180	18	1
Quality-Control Engineer	2145.138	18	5
Quality-Control Chemist	2111.134	18	1
Quilter Mechanic	8584.166	11	10
Quilting Machine Fixer	8584.166	11	10
Radiation Monitor	1176.130	15	5
Radiation-Contamination Monitor	1176.130	15	5
Radio Astronomer	2113.114	18	1
Radiographer, Industrial	9916.110	11	3
Radiotherapy Technician	3155.118	11	10
Railway Engineer	2143.146	18	5
Railway Car Inspector	8586.142	15	3
Rate Reviewer	4139.114	11	1
Re-Recording Mixer	9555.118	15	5
Reader, First (Pub.)	3359.114	11	1
Reader, Script	3353.130	11	1
Record Process Equipment Repairman	8584.218	11	10
Record-Systems Analyst	1173.126	11	3
Recording Director	3330.178	15	3
Records Management Specialist	1173.126	11	3
Reference Librarian	2351.110	15	3
Refrigeration Operator	9533.114	15	5
Refrigeration Engineer	2147.142	18	5
Refrigeration Mechanic	8333.118	15	1
Regulator, Piano-tone	8599.250	11	1
Rehabilitation Specialist	2399.110	18	5
Remedial Gymnast	3137.130	11	18
Remote Sensing Technician	2169.112	15	5
Repairer, Shop	8735.146	11	3
Repairer, Video Equipment	8535.123	11	1
Repairer, Electronic Music Equipment	8535.124	15	1
Repairer, Small Engines	8589.144	15	5
Repairer, Electronic Games	8535.136	11	1
Repairer, Process-Control Equipment	8535.109	15	1
Repairer, New-car	8581.162	11	1
Repairer, Motorcycle	8581.158	11	1
Repairer Roller, Textile	8391.114	15	1
Repairer, Automotive-brake	8581.166	11	1
Repairer Test Equipment, Oil Exploration	8539.114	11	1
Repairer, Car	8583.110	15	1
Repairer, Photoelectric-Sorting Machine	8539.118	11	1
Repairer, Carburator	8581.150	11	1
Repairer, Body (motor Vehicle)	8581.142	15	1
Repairer, Recreation-Vehicle	8581.132	11	1
Repairer, Rug	8569.114	11	1
Repairer, Automotive-radiator	8581.170	11	1

Repairer, Stringed-instrument	8549.226	15	1
Repairer, Roller	8579.114	11	1
Repairer, Mechanical-unit	8581.138	11	1
Repairer, Truck-trailer	8581.140	11	1
Repairer, Mine-hoist	8584.350	15	10
Repairer, Transformer	8739.138	15	1
Repairer, Power-transformer	8739.134	15	1
Repairer, Salvage	8739.146	11	1
Repairer, Pump	8589.134	15	5
Repairer, Electric-meter	8739.122	15	1
Repairer, Oil Tool	8584.178	11	10
Repairer, Hydraulic-unit	8589.162	11	1
Repairer, Pneumatic-tube	8589.154	11	5
Repairer, Speedometer	8588.146	11	5
Repairer, Punched-card Machines	8585.114	15	1
Repairer, Wind-instrument	8599.238	15	1
Repairer and Installer, Pump	8589.126	11	5
Repairer, Piano	8599.230	15	1
Repairer and Tuner, Pipe-organ	8599.222	15	1
Repairer, Musical-instrument	8599.218	18	1
Repairer, Accordion	8599.226	15	1
Repairer, Engine (motor vehicle)	8581.114	15	1
Repairer-Tester Relay (elec.)	8739.126	15	1
Repairman Air Conditioner	8533.162	11	1
Repairman Electric Tool	8533.166	11	1
Repairman Electric Motor	8533.122	15	1
Repairman Portable Appliance	8533.170	11	1
Repairman Major Appliance	8533.126	15	1
Repairman Electrical Instruments	8533.142	15	1
Repairman, Television-Camera	8535.126	11	1
Repairman, Radio-Communication Equipment	8535.122	11	1
Repairman, Electronic-Equipment	8535.114	15	1
Repairman, Telecine-Equipment	8535.126	11	1
Repairman, Electronic Organ	8535.114	15	1
Repairman, Electrical	8533.110	15	1
Repairman, Appliances	8533.126	15	1
Repairman, Clock	3313.146	18	1
Repairman, Boilerhouse	8584.146	11	10
Repairman, Air-Compressor	8589.178	11	5
Repairman, Hearing-Aid	8535.142	11	1
Repairman, Nucleonic-Controller	8535.134	11	1
Repairman, Automated-Processing Equipment	8535.138	11	1
Repairman, Television-Studio Equipment	8535.126	11	1
Repairman, Communications-Equipment	8535.114	15	1
Repairman, Major Appliances	8533.126	15	1
Repairman, Portable Appliance	8533.170	11	1
Reporter	3351.174	15	3
Research Nutritionist	3152.110	11	1
Research Engineer, Electrical and Electronic	2144.114	18	5

Research Officer, Social Welfare	2339.110	18	5
Research Assistant	9919.108	11	1
Researcher, Program (Broadcast)	3353.128	15	1
Reserves Clerk	4135.190	11	1
Reservoir Engineer, Petroleum	2154.118	15	5
Residential Energy Adviser	5131.144	11	1
Resource Economist	2311.152	18	1
Respiratory Technologist	3159.134	11	10
Restorer, Antique-car	8581.111	18	1
Restorer, Equipment	2353.126	11	1
Rewrite Man	3351.182	15	3
Rheologist	2113.138	18	1
Rigger	8592.130	15	1
Roll Setter	8584.242	11	10
Roll Builder	8584.242	11	10
Rural-Telephone Maintainer	8735.114	15	3
Safety Director	2145.118	18	5
Safety-And-Sanitary Inspector	1176.110	15	5
Safety Inspector	1176.110	15	5
Safety Coordinator	1176.122	11	5
Sailmaker	8551.110	15	1
Sales Representative, Garments and other Textile Products	5133.134	11	1
Sales Representative, Plastic Products	5133.146	11	1
Sales Representative, Food Products	5133.130	11	2
Sales Representative, Canvas Products	5133.122	11	1
Sales Representative, Rubber Products	5133.154	11	1
Sales Representative, Petroleum Products	5133.142	11	1
Sales Representative, Pulp and Paper Products	5133.150	11	1
Sales Representative, Textbooks	5133.118	11	1
Sales Representative, Light, Heat and Power	5131.146	11	1
Sales Engineer, Light, Heat and Power	5131.110	18	1
Sales Representative, Motor Vehicles and Equipment	5133.138	11	1
Sales Representative, Wine, Beer and Spirits	5133.132	11	1
Sales Representative, Comm/Ind. Equipment and Supplies	5133.126	11	1
Sales Representative, Freight Forwarding Services	5177.121	11	1
Sales Representative, Hotel Services	5177.114	15	1
Sales Representative, Employment Services	5177.120	11	1
Sales Representative, Credit Bureau	5177.130	11	1
Sales Representative, Telephone Service	5177.118	11	1
Sales Engineer, Oil-Well Services	5177.110	18	1
Sales Representative, Trade Association	5177.126	11	1
Sales Representative, Collection Agency	5177.130	11	1
Sales Representative, Financial Services	5177.130	11	1
Sales Representative, Telecommunications	5177.118	11	1
Sales Representative, Freight Services	5177.122	11	1

Sales Representative, Printing	5177.134	11	1
Sales-Promotion Administrator	1179.154	15	1
Sales-Promotion Manager	1179.154	15	1
Salesman, Advertising	5174.118	11	3
Salesman, Signs and Displays	5174.114	11	3
Salesman, Radio or Television Time	5174.122	11	3
Salesman, Art	5174.110	15	3
Salesman, Drug Supplies	5133.114	15	1
Salesperson, Musical Instruments and Supplies	5135.122	11	3
Salesperson, Livestock	5135.120	11	3
Salesperson, Parts	5135.126	11	3
Salesperson, Wood Burning Appliances	5135.124	11	3
Salesperson, Art	5135.121	11	3
Salesperson, Motor Vehicles	5135.110	11	3
Salesperson, Sewing Machines	5135.114	11	3
Salesperson, Computers	5135.116	11	3
Salesperson, Hearing Aids	5135.118	11	3
Salvager, Machinery	8589.158	11	5
Sample Maker Household Appliances	8313.166	15	1
Scale Mechanic	8589.170	11	5
Scale Repairman	8589.170	11	5
Schedule Analyst	9113.126	11	1
Scientific Illustrator	3314.126	11	3
Scientist, Agricultural	2131.110	18	1
Scientist, Animal	2131.114	18	1
Screen Reporter	3315.174	15	1
Seamer Machine Repairman	8584.222	11	10
Secretarial Stenographer	4111.110	11	5
Secretary	4111.110	11	5
Securities Counsellor	1171.182	18	1
Seismologist	2112.138	18	1
Sericulturist	2133.114	18	1
Serologist	2133.162	18	1
Service-Station Inspector	1176.134	11	5
Service Representative	4192.114	15	3
Service Representative, Field	8589.110	15	5
Service Technician, Consumer Products	8537.112	11	1
Serviceman, Dictating and Transcribing Machines	8585.122	11	1
Serviceman, Office-Machine	8585.118	11	1
Serviceman, Typewriter	8585.118	11	1
Serviceman, Appliances	8533.126	15	1
Serviceman, Radio	8537.114	11	1
Serviceman, Television Repair	8537.110	15	1
Serviceman-Salesman, Sewing Machines	5135.114	11	3
Servicer, Electronic Cash Register	8585.124	11	1
Servicer, Photocopying-Machine	8585.120	11	1
Servicer, Word and Information Processing Equipment	8585.121	11	1

Servicer, Fuel-injection Unit	8589.130	11	5
Servicer, Safe-and Vault	8589.142	15	5
Servicer, Automotive-Maintenance Equipment	8589.114	15	5
Set Designer	3313.122	18	1
Set-Up Man, Honing Machine	8313.142	15	1
Set-Up Man, Screw Machine Production	8313.142	15	1
Set-Up Man, Lathe	8313.142	15	1
Set-Up Man, Grinder	8313.142	15	1
Set-Up Man, Threading Machine	8313.142	15	1
Set-Up Operator, Rotary-head-milling Machine	8313.174	15	1
Set-Up Man, Milling Machine	8313.142	15	1
Setter, Machine-Tool	8313.142	15	1
Setter, Lens-Grinder-Polisher	8373.206	15	1
Setter, Rope-Machine	8263.110	11	1
Setter, Metal-Can Machine	8339.130	11	1
Setter, Precious Stone	8591.126	15	1
Sewer	8553.146	11	1
Sewer, Women's Garments Alterations	8553.150	11	1
Sewing Machine Mechanic	8584.198	11	10
Sewing Machine Repairman	8584.198	11	10
Sewing Instructor	2797.128	15	1
Shaper, Steel Plate	8337.150	11	1
Shearing Machine Fixer	8584.234	11	10
Ship's Electrician	8533.134	15	1
Ship-Construction Engineer	2159.122	18	5
Shipwright, Wood	8592.118	18	1
Shipwright, Metal	8592.114	18	1
Shoe Designer	3313.142	18	1
Shoe Repairman	8561.114	15	1
Shoemaker	8561.114	15	1
Shoemaker, Custom	8561.110	15	1
Sight-Effects Man	3339.118	15	1
Sign Designer	3313.182	15	1
Sign Language Interpreter	3355.116	15	1
Signal Engineer	2144.154	18	5
Silversmith	8591.210	15	1
Skinner, Animal	8215.122	11	1
Small-Arms Repairman	8589.122	15	5
Social Worker, Group	2331.130	15	5
Social Worker	2331.124	15	5
Social-Work Supervisor	2331.110	18	5
Social Worker, Case Work	2331.126	15	5
Sociologist	2313.114	18	1
Soil Engineer	2143.150	18	5
Soil Scientist	2131.126	18	1
Sound Mixer	9555.110	15	5
Sound Effects Technician	9555.130	11	5
Special Librarian	2351.118	15	3
Special-Endorsement Clerk	4135.122	11	1

Specialist, Optical-Instrument	2113.142	18	1
Specialist, Tune-up	8581.134	11	1
Specialist, Optical-Instrument	2113.146	18	1
Spectroscopist, Optical	2113.118	18	1
Spectroscopist, Chemical	2113.118	18	1
Speech Pathologist	3137.114	15	10
Stage Manager	3330.166	15	3
Stage-Scenery Designer	3313.122	18	1
Stained-Glass Artist	3313.126	18	1
Stained-Glass Window Designer	3313.126	18	1
Stamping Die Maker, Bench	8311.118	15	1
Standards Specialist	1173.112	18	3
Station Repairer	8735.126	15	3
Station Agent	9113.124	15	1
Stations-Relations Administrator	1179.194	11	1
Statistician, Vital	2181.154	18	1
Statistician, Biological and Agricultural Science	2181.138	18	1
Statistician, Applied	2181.134	18	1
Statistician, Physical Science and Engineering	2181.146	18	1
Statistician, Mathematical	2181.114	18	1
Statistician, Social Science	2181.150	18	1
Statistician, Business and Economics	2181.142	18	1
Steam Operator	9533.124	15	5
Steam Plant Maintenance Man	8584.146	11	10
Stereo Tape Editor	9555.114	15	5
Stereoplotter	2169.118	15	5
Storekeeper Drilling Rig	4155.111	11	3
Story Board Artist	3314.112	15	3
Structural-Design Engineer	2143.114	18	5
Structural Engineer	2143.114	18	5
Student Loan Officer	1171.200	15	3
Student Awards Officer	1171.200	15	3
Student Scholarship Officer	1171.200	15	3
Student-Activities Adviser	2339.114	11	5
Stylist, Copy	3319.166	11	1
Substation Inspector	9531.114	15	1
Suggestion-Program Clerk	4199.162	11	3
Supervisor, Accountants	1171.110	18	3
Supervisor, Art	3314.110	18	3
Supervisor, Auditors	1171.158	18	3
Supervisor, Organization/Methods Analyst	1173.110	18	3
Supervisor, Wardrobe	3339.114	15	1
Surgeon, Tree	7195.110	11	1
Surveyor	2161.114	15	1
Surveyor, Provincial-land	2161.114	15	1
Surveyor, Topographic	2161.114	15	1
Surveyor, County	2161.114	15	1
Surveyor, Hydrographic	2161.110	15	1
Surveyor, Mine	2161.114	15	1

Surveyor, Geophysical Prospecting (Oil and Nat. Gas)	2161.118	15	1
Surveyor, Dominion-Land	2161.114	15	1
Switcher	9551.126	15	5
System Analyst Business, Electronic Data-Processing	2183.110	18	10
Systems Analyst Eng/Scientific, Electronic Data-Proc.	2183.114	13	10
Systems-Software Programmer	2183.116	18	10
Tailor, Made-to-measure Garments	8553.110	18	1
Tailor, Ready-to-wear Garments	8553.114	11	1
Tailor, Men's Garments Alterations	8553.118	11	1
Tannery Machinery Repairman	8584.158	11	10
Taster, Tea	8226.194	15	1
Taster and Buyer, Beverages	8226.194	15	1
Taster, Coffee	8226.194	15	1
Tax Economist	2311.154	18	1
Taxidermist	2353.118	15	1
Taxonomist, Plant	2133.114	18	1
Taxonomist, Animal	2133.126	18	1
Teaching Homemaker	2333.117	11	5
Technical Illustrator	2163.176	15	1
Technical Producer	3330.122	18	3
Technical Salesman, Medical-Dental Equipment and Supplies	5131.138	15	1
Technical Salesman, Metals	5131.154	11	1
Technical Salesperson, Heavy Equipment	5131.132	15	1
Technical Salesman, Aircraft	5131.118	15	1
Technical Salesman, Chemicals	5131.150	11	1
Technical Salesman, Ind. Machinery and Equipment	5131.134	15	1
Technical Salesman, Construction Equipment and Supplies	5131.126	15	1
Technical Salesman, Agriculture Equipment and Supplies	5131.122	15	1
Technical Salesman, Electronic Equipment	5131.130	15	1
Technical Secretary (Clerical)	4111.115	11	5
Technical Salesman, Railroad Equipment and Supplies	5131.142	15	1
Technical Salesman, Electronic-Data Processing	5131.114	18	1
Technical-Service Consultant	1179.158	15	1
Technical Writer	3351.178	15	3
Technician, CADD/CAM Repair	8535.106	15	1
Technician, Electronic Drilling Rig	8535.105	15	1
Technician, Computer Equipment Repair	8535.108	15	1
Technician, Traffic	9113.128	11	1
Technician, Robotics	8535.107	15	1
Technician, Electrical Engineering	2165.226	11	1

Technician, Building Systems	9533.128	11	5
Technician, Agricultural Engineering	2165.214	11	1
Technician, Resource Management	2135.268	15	1
Technician, Food-Bacteriological	2135.240	11	1
Technician, Wildlife	2135.252	11	1
Technician, Botanical	2135.248	11	1
Technician, Automotive, Engine Fuel System Repairs	8581.119	15	1
Technician, Mammalogy	2135.252	11	1
Technician, Metrology	2165.228	11	1
Technician, Drilling-fluid Offshore Drilling Rig	2165.225	11	1
Technician, Planning	2319.142	11	1
Technician, Conservation and Restoration	2353.128	11	1
Technician, Stage Production	3339.124	11	1
Technician, Plastics Moulding	8573.108	15	1
Technician, Bacteriological	2135.240	11	1
Technician, Light	3339.120	15	1
Technician, Industrial-Bacteriological	2135.240	11	1
Technician, Plant-Pathology	2135.248	11	1
Technician, Automotive, Front-end Systems	8581.120	15	1
Technician, Poultry	2135.220	11	1
Technician, Soil-Bacteriological	2135.240	11	1
Technician, Quality Control (dairy)	8226.110	11	1
Technician, Horticultural	2135.248	11	1
Technician Automotive, Automatic Transmissions	8581.121	15	1
Technician, Statistical	2189.114	15	1
Technician, Fishery-Bacteriological	2135.240	11	1
Technician, Laboratory (confection)	8226.110	11	1
Technician, Microbiological	2135.240	11	1
Technician, Library	2353.134	11	1
Technician, Laboratory	8256.110	11	1
Technician, Laboratory (fish process)	8226.110	11	1
Technician, Field Crop	2135.220	11	1
Technician, Special-effects	3339.116	15	1
Technician, Forest	2135.272	11	1
Technician, Zoological	2135.252	11	1
Technician, Aquatic-Biology	2135.244	11	1
Technician, Ecological	2135.244	11	1
Technician, Agricultural	2135.220	11	1
Technician, Fish-Roe	8226.111	11	1
Technician, Laboratory Veterinary	3156.130	11	5
Technician, Ornithological	2135.252	11	1
Technician, Vaccine	2135.244	11	1
Technician, Biological	2135.244	11	1
Technician, Civil-Engineering	2165.222	11	1
Technician, Soil-Science	2135.248	11	1
Technician, Ichthyological	2135.252	11	1
Technician, Mycological	2135.248	11	1

Technician, Entomological	2135.252	11	1
Technologist, Architectural	2165.114	15	1
Technologist, Electrical Engineering	2165.126	15	1
Technologist, Mammalogy	2135.142	15	1
Technologist, Food	2135.166	15	1
Technologist, Food-process	2135.166	15	1
Technologist, Electron Microscopy	3156.116	15	5
Technologist, Biochemistry	3156.110	15	5
Technologist, Soil-Bacteriological	2135.130	15	1
Technologist, Histology	3156.118	15	5
Technologist, Plant-Pathology	2135.138	15	1
Technologist, Soil Science	2135.138	15	1
Technologist, Food-product	2135.166	15	1
Technologist, Ornithological	2135.142	15	1
Technologist, Zoological	2135.142	15	1
Technologist, Quality-control Food Processing	2135.166	15	1
Technologist, Ichthyological	2135.142	15	1
Technologist, Entomological	2135.142	15	1
Technologist, Industrial-Bacteriological	2135.130	15	1
Technologist, Cytogenetics	3156.112	15	5
Technologist, Wildlife	2135.142	15	1
Technologist, Pilot-plant Food Products	2135.166	15	1
Technologist, Forest	2135.199	15	1
Technologist, Virology	2135.146	15	1
Technologist, Fish-farm	2135.162	15	1
Technologist, Immunology	3156.123	15	5
Technologist, Mycological	2135.138	15	1
Technologist, Aquatic-Biology	2135.134	15	1
Technologist, Fishery-Bacteriological	2135.130	15	1
Technologist, Biological	2135.134	15	1
Technologist, Food-Bacteriological	2135.130	15	1
Technologist, Medical-Laboratory	3156.122	15	5
Technologist, Bacteriological	2135.130	15	1
Technologist, Immunohematology	3156.124	15	5
Technologist, Home Economics	2319.134	15	1
Technologist, Civil-Engineering	2165.122	15	1
Technologist, Horticultural	2135.138	15	1
Technologist, Poultry	2135.110	15	1
Technologist, Botanical	2135.138	15	1
Technologist, Field-Crop	2135.110	15	1
Technologist, Microbiology	3156.126	15	5
Technologist, Ecological	2135.134	15	1
Technologist, Sea-farm	2135.162	15	1
Technologists, Agricultural	2135.110	15	1
Telecommunications Specialist Computers	2183.162	15	10
Telecommunications-Equipment Installer	8735.166	11	3
Telegraph-Equipment Repairer	8735.134	15	3
Telephone Engineer	2144.158	18	5
Telephone-Station Installer	8735.162	11	3

Terminal and Repeater Tester	8736.138	11	5
Tester, Ultrasonic	9916.114	11	3
Tester and Regulator	8736.126	15	5
Tester, Systems	8536.122	15	1
Tester, Beer	8226.198	11	1
Tester, Cable	8526.274	11	1
Tester, Control-Panel	8536.110	18	1
Tester, Laboratory	8256.110	11	1
Tester, Hydraulic	8526.258	11	1
Tester, Tensile-Strength	8526.274	11	1
Textile Technologist	2117.130	15	1
Textile Designer	3313.146	18	1
Textile Technician	2117.268	11	1
Theorist, Experimentary-particle	2113.126	18	1
Time-Study Engineer	2145.122	18	5
Title Examiner	2349.126	11	1
Tobacco Machine Adjuster	8584.226	11	10
Tool Maker, Bench	8311.130	15	1
Tool Engineer	2147.114	18	5
Tool-Maintenance man	8584.178	11	10
Tool Maker, Carbide	8311.134	15	1
Tool and Die Inspector	8316.110	15	5
Tool and Die Maker	8311.110	15	1
Tool Programmer, Numerical Control	2183.126	18	10
Tour Operator	1179.139	15	1
Toxicologist	2133.213	18	1
Traffic Engineer	2159.150	18	5
Traffic Inspector	1176.126	11	5
Train Dispatcher	9135.110	15	1
Training Representative	2797.142	15	1
Training Specialist, Computers	2797.120	15	1
Transit Man	2161.118	15	1
Translator	3355.122	11	1
Translator, Scientific Documents	3355.114	15	1
Transmission Engineer	2144.162	18	5
Transmission Tester	8736.142	11	5
Transport Economist	2311.156	18	1
Travel Agent	1179.140	15	1
Travel-Accommodation Appraiser	1176.146	11	5
Treatment Plant Mechanic	8584.186	11	10
Trust Officer (Bank and Finance)	1171.190	15	3
Turbine Operator Steam	9531.142	15	1
Typographer-Proofer	3319.166	11	1
Unit Operator	8165.110	15	10
Upholsterer	8562.110	15	1
Upholsterer All Around	8562.110	15	1
Utility Clerk, Bank	4135.182	11	1
Utilization Engineer	2147.134	18	5
Vehicle Upholstery Repairman	8562.114	11	1

Appendix C

Veterinarian	3115.110	18	1
Video and Sound Recorder	9555.122	15	5
Video Console Operator	9551.118	15	5
Video Recording Equipment Operator	9555.126	15	5
Videotex Page Designer	3314.135	15	3
Virologist	2133.244	18	1
Virologist, Veterinary	2133.242	18	1
Voicer, Organ-pipe	8599.242	15	1
Watch Adjuster	8587.110	15	1
Watch Repairman	8587.110	15	1
Watchmaker	8587.110	15	1
Water-Purification Technician	2117.244	11	1
Water-Resources Engineer	2143.154	18	5
Waterworks and Water-Supply Engineer	2143.154	18	5
Weather Forecaster	2114.122	18	1
Weight Analyst, Aerospace Vehicles	2155.114	18	5
Weight and Balance Engineer	2155.114	18	5
Weld Inspector	8336.110	15	1
Welder Setter, Resistance	8335.110	15	1
Welder, Combination (gas and arc)	8335.126	15	1
Welder, Pipeline	8335.120	15	1
Welder, Tool and Die	8335.118	15	1
Welder, Drilling Rig	8335.112	15	1
Welder, Arc	8335.138	11	1
Welder, Laser-beam	8335.119	11	1
Welder, Pressure Vessels	8335.122	15	1
Welder, Gas	8335.142	11	1
Welder, Fitter	8335.114	15	1
Welding Engineer	2159.142	18	5
Welding Equipment Repairman	8584.190	15	10
Welding Machine Operator, Metal-Inert Gas	8335.130	11	1
Welding Machine Operator, Gas-shielded Arc	8335.130	11	1
Welding Machine Operator, Tungsten-Inert Gas	8335.130	11	1
Welding Machine Operator, Automatic	8335.134	11	1
Welding Machine Operator, Submerged Arc	8335.134	11	1
Welding Technician	8335.334	15	1
Wheel and Axle Inspector	8586.150	11	3
Women's Fashion Designer	3313.162	15	1
Wood Carver	8549.246	18	1
Work-Study Analyst	1173.130	11	3
Worker, Canvas	8569.110	15	1
Worker, Airport-maintenance	8589.138	15	5
Worker, Art-Metal	8339.110	15	1
Worker, Sheet-Metal	8333.118	15	1
Working Sous-Chef	6121.123	18	10
Writer, Script (Broadcast)	3353.122	15	1
Writer, Gag	3359.110	15	1
Writer, Continuity (Broadcast)	3353.122	15	1

Writer, News Or Script Int'l Broadcasting	3353.126	15	1
Writer-Announcer, Int'l Broadcasting	3353.126	15	1
Zoologist	2133.126	18	1
Zoologist, Invertebrate	2133.126	18	1

Appendix D
Immigration Application Processing Fee and Right of Landing Fee

INTRODUCTION

Canada has imposed Processing Fees and Right of Landing Fees on several categories of applications. The following details were correct as at 1 July 1996. However, the fees frequently change and you should ascertain the correct fee at the time you submit your application.

APPLICATION PROCESSING FEE

Principal applicant:	Independent Skilled Workers or Assisted Relatives	Cdn$500
Principal applicant:	Investor, Entrepreneur or Self-employed	Cdn$825

Accompanying spouse and *each* accompanying dependant
19 years of age or over   Cdn$500

Each accompanying dependant under 19 years
of age: Cdn$100

The amount of the fee is determined by the age of your dependants on the date the application is submitted. The fee is payable only for those dependants who are accompanying you to Canada. If any accompanying dependants are added after the application is submitted, an additional fee is payable based on the age of the dependant on the date the dependant is added to the application. No refunds will be given for dependants who decide at a later date not to accompany you to Canada.

- **Refunds will not be issued to unsuccessful applicants.**

RIGHT OF LANDING FEE

This is a second fee, **in addition** to the Processing Fee outlined above.

All permanent resident applicants, their spouses and accompanying depandants 19 years of age or older on the date of application must each pay a Right of Landing Fee of Cdn$975. Dependant children under the age of 19 do not pay this fee.

Unlike the Processing Fee which is non-refundable, the Right of Landing Fee will be refunded to you if your application is not approved.

HOW TO PAY

Payment procedures vary from office to office and you should receive specific instructions from the visa office when you request an Application for Permanent Residence in Canada. Generally speaking, all payments must be made in Canadian dollars or local currency. Payment may be made by banker's or cashier's cheques, postal money order or bank draft, usually made payable to 'The Receiver General for Canada'.

Cash is not always accepted but where cash is accepted, it will only be accepted in person.

Personal cheques are not accepted.

WHEN TO PAY

For all applications, both the Processing Fee and the Right of Landing Fee must be paid at the time the application is submitted.

Any application submitted without the fees will simply be returned to the applicant.

GENERAL

If you are being sponsored by a relative in Canada, the fee will usually be paid by your sponsor in Canada. Only one fee is required.

You will see that the immigration process has become an expensive proposition. For example, a married couple with two dependent children under 19 will have to submit a total of Cdn$3150 with their application to be considered, and only a portion of this money will be refunded if the application is not approved. It is therefore very important to assess your prospects carefully before submitting an application.

Appendix E
Sample CCDO Job Descriptions

2143-118 Civil Engineer, General (prof. & tech.)
Studies design proposals and advises on works and facilities; such as, roads, railways, bridges, dams, disposal systems and buildings, and supervises their construction and maintenance by performing any combination of the following duties:

Studies project proposal, accumulates and analyses basic data; such as, topography and geology for highways, run-off history of a river, population growth statistics, laboratory analysis of cement, soil and water. Prepares preliminary plans for the project applying knowledge of mathematics and engineering design to superstructures, structural frames and infrastructure. Prepares estimate of project to ensure economy of cost in relation to service required. Supervises preparation of detail design drawings and specifications for contractors and consults with other specialists such as mechanical, chemical and electrical engineers and architects regarding technical and aesthetic requirements. Secures approval of plans from client, management and other authorities. Inspects project during construction and certifies, on completion, that it has been built in accordance with specifications. Supervises the maintenance and repair of civil engineering projects such as, transportation systems, water systems, pipelines or water-resource developments. Conducts studies into improving maintenance practices and the use of new materials to keep completed facilities in service. Supervises and co-ordinates the work of technologists and technicians.
  May work as a consultant or collaborate with engineers in other disciplines and advise clients for a fee.

2183-110 System Analyst Business, Electronic Data-Processing (prof. & tech.), commercial-systems analyst

Analyzes business problems, such as development of integrated production and inventory control, cost analysis, selects appropriate equipment and develops programs for electronic data-processing systems:

Confers with department heads or project directors to ascertain specific management information requirements; such as, nature and degree of summarization, identification of items and format for presentation of results. Analyzes systems, procedures and methods used in various operations selected for conversion, determines feasibility and extent of conversion, and prepares process flow-charts and diagrams. Develops new applications and long-range plans for customer utilization of electronic-data-processing system, and analyzes capabilities and limitations of computers and peripheral equipment. Devises means of deriving input data to select a feasible and economic method for personnel operating equipment. Tests and eliminates errors in computer programs, to prepare final system of operations. Assists sales personnel of electronic-data-processing services in preparation and presentation of proposals to customer, in a non-technical language. Prepares cost estimates and summary of savings resulting from proposed systems. Maintains accurate records and documentation of system analysis to facilitate follow-up action. Prepares instruction manuals covering use, operation, routine maintenance and technical specifications of key-punch machines, sorters, and other related tabulator equipment, and trains operating and supervisory personnel. Designs new forms and other documents relating to computer operation. Supervises and coordinates the work of programmers.

May write programs, using computer coding symbols in language processable by computer. May specify power-supply requirements and recommend purchase of air-conditioning equipment to control temperature, humidity and dust. May select and design forms of use in program.

2331-124 Social Worker (social wel.)

Counsels and assists individuals, families and groups to understand and resolve their social and behavioural problems:

Interviews clients to determine nature, extent and causes of problems. Interviews family or acquaintances of client or requests completion of forms to obtain further information regarding clients. Assesses clients' situation using information obtained in interviews and from completed forms. Determines type of assistance required and develops plan to assist clients to deal with their problems and meet their needs. Counsels clients on ways of dealing with problems. Assists clients to modify attitudes and patterns of behaviour and to develop skills necessary to deal with problems. Refers clients to community agencies and other organizations and arranges for provision of appropriate assistance. Follows progress of clients after immediate problems have been solved. Prepares records and reports. Discusses cases with professionals from other disciplines to share insights and methods of dealing with clients.

4111-110 Secretary (clerical), secretarial stenographer.
Schedules appointments, gives information to callers, takes dictation and relieves employer of clerical work and minor administrative and business details, performing any of the following duties:

Reads and routes incoming mail. Locates and attaches appropriate file to correspondence to be answered by employer. Takes dictation in shorthand or on stenotype machine, and transcribes on typewriter from notes or voice recordings. Composes and types correspondence. Files correspondence and other records. Answers telephone and gives information to caller, or routes call to appropriate official, and places outgoing calls. Schedules appointments for employer and reminds him when they are due. Greets visitors, ascertains nature of business and conducts visitors to employer or to appropriate person. Compiles and types statistical reports. Records minutes of meetings.

May keep confidential personnel records. May arrange travel schedules and reservations. May be designated according to type of work performed; for example:

Appointments Secretary
Legal Secretary
Medical Secretary
Social Secretary

4111-111 Executive Secetary (clerical)
Performs secretarial and administrative duties for office executive:

Performs duties similar to those of **4111-110 Secretary (clerical)** utilizing secretarial experience and knowledge of office administration and public relations. Arranges conferences and other meetings and researches and compiles information for employer. Acts on routine matters affecting day to day operations of organization, in employer's absence. May perform other duties including supervising office workers.

4131-114 Bookkeeper (clerical)
Keeps complete records of financial transactions of establishment or undertaking:

Verifies accuracy of documents and records relating to payments, receipts and other financial transactions, and makes necessary calculations. Makes and checks entries from items, such as sales slips, invoices and cheque stubs, and totals ledgers at regular intervals. Compiles reports at specified intervals to show items; such as, receipts, payments, balances of accounts owing to or by the establishment of undertaking, and other financial information.
    May prepare financial statements and accounts for the year or other specified period, calculate and arrange payment of wages, prepare and mail statements of accounts to customers, and perform various tasks related to bookkeeping.

5135-116 Salesperson, Computers (ret. trade)
Demonstrates and sells microcomputers and peripherals in retail outlet:

Performs duties as described under master title, 01-230 SALESPERSON (ret. trade; whole. trade). Advises consumer on selection of personal computer best suited for in-home use. Assists business customers in selecting appropriate microcomputer system for office use. Quotes prices, and discusses credit and discount terms. Arranges deliveries. Provides service information. Sells computer hardware, software, drives, input devices, accessories, furniture, books and magazines, games and other related items.

8313-154 Machinist, general (mach., weld. & forg.)
machinist, all-round; machinist, fitter; machinist, precision
Sets up and operates various machine-tools, such as lathes, millers, shapers and grinders, and fits and assembles parts to make or repair mechanisms, tools or machines, applying knowledge of mechanics, shop mathematics, metal properties, lay-out and machining procedures:

Studies specifications and drawings or sample parts and plans sequence of operations. Computes dimensions and tolerances and prepares working sketches from general descriptions and by examining parts and their mating surfaces. Measures, marks and scribes center lines, dimensions and reference points on workpiece, using measuring and marking instruments, to lay out workpiece for machining. Positions workpiece in machine by securing it onto machine table or fixture, into chuck or collet or between centers, manually or using hoist, dial indicator, shims, parallel blocks or clamps. Selects and installs cutting tools in machines. Sets controls and gears to facilitate indexing of workpiece, cutting speed and depth of cut according to type of materials. Starts machine and observes machining progress, and frequently verifies conformance of part to specifications, using measuring instruments; such as, scales, calipers, micrometers and fixed gauges. Finishes and fits parts to mechanisms by filing, grinding, scraping and polishing. Verifies dimensions and alignment, using instruments; such as, micrometers, height gauges, surface plate and gauge blocks.

May operate assembled or repaired mechanism to test performance.

Appendix F
Canadian Immigration Offices Abroad

There are over 100 Canadian Embassies, High Commissions, Consulates and Missions, etc. abroad, but not all are involved in the full processing of immigration applications.

You should request immigration applications for completion from one of the Full Processing Missions. Here is a list of all the countries, dependencies and territories, etc. in the world, and the name of the Full Processing Mission handling applications for permanent residence from these areas.

Following this is a list of the name, address, telephone and fax number of each of the Full Processing Missions:

Country	**Full processing mission**
Abu Dhabi	Riyadh
Afghanistan	Islamabad
Agalega Island	Nairobi
Ajman	Riyadh
Albania	Belgrade
Aldabra	Nairobi
Alderney	London
Algeria	Paris
American Samoa	Sydney
Andaman	New Delhi
Andorra	Paris
Anegada	Port of Spain
Angola	Pretoria
Anguilla	Port of Spain
Antigua and Barbuda	Port of Spain
Argentina	Buenos Aires
Armenia	Moscow
Aruba	Bogota
Ascension	Abidjan
Assumption Island	Nairobi
Australia	Sydney
Azerbaijan	Ankara

Austria	Vienna
Azores	Lisbon
Bahamas Islands	Kingston
Bahrain	Riyadh
Balearic Islands	Paris
Bangladesh	Bangkok
Barbados	Port of Spain
Belarus	Moscow
Belgium	Paris
Belize	Kingston
Benin	Abidjan
Bequia Island	Port of Spain
Bermuda	New York
Bhutan	New Delhi
Bolivia	Lima
Bonaire	Bogota
Bora Bora	Sydney
Bosnia-Hercegovina	Belgrade
Botswana	Pretoria
Brazil	Sao Paulo
Brechou	London
British Indian Ocean Territory	Nairobi
Brunei	Singapore
Bulgaria	Belgrade
Burkina-Faso	Abidjan
Burundi	Nairobi
Cambodia	Bangkok
Cameroon	Abidjan
Canary Islands	Paris
Canouan Island	Port of Spain
Cape Verde	Accra
Carriacou Island	Port of Spain
Cayman Island	Kingston
Central African Rep.	Abidjan
Chad	Abidjan
Chagos Archipelago	Nairobi
Channel Islands	London
Chile	Buenos Aires
China	Beijing
Choiseul	Sydney
Christmas Island	Sydney
Cocos (Keeling) Isl.	Sydney
Colombia	Bogota
Comoros	Nairobi
Congo	Abidjan
Cook Islands	Sydney
Costa Rica	Guatemala City
Croatia	Vienna
Cuba	Havana

Appendix F

Curacao	Bogota
Cyprus	Tel Aviv
Czech Republic	Vienna
Denmark	London
Desroches	Nairobi
Diego Garcia	Nairobi
Djibouti	Nairobi
Dominica	Port of Spain
Dominican Republic	Port-au-Prince
Dubai	Riyadh
Easter Island	Buenos Aires
Ecuador	Bogota
Egypt	Cairo
El Salvador	Guatemala City
England	London
Equatorial Guinea	Accra
Eritrea	Nairobi
Estonia	London
Ethiopia	Nairobi
Faroe Islands	London
Falkland Islands	Buenos Aires
Farquhar	Nairobi
Fiji	Sydney
Finland	London
France	Paris
French Guyana	Port of Spain
French Polynesia	Sydney
Fujairah	Riyadh
Gabon Republic	Abidjan
Gambia	Accra
Gambier Islands	Sydney
Georgia	Moscow
Germany-Federal Republic of	Bonn
Ghana	Accra
Gibraltar	Paris
Great Britain	London
Greece	Rome
Greenland	London
Grenada	Port of Spain
Guadalcanal	Sydney
Guadeloupe	Port-au-Prince
Guam	Tokyo
Guatemala	Guatemala City
Guernsey	London
Guinea-Republic of	Abidjan
Guinea-Bissau	Accra
Guyana	Port of Spain
Haiti	Port-au-Prince
Holy See	Rome

Honduras	Guatemala City
Hong Kong B.C.C.	Hong Kong
Huahine	Sydney
Hungary	Budapest
Iceland	London
India	New Delhi
Indonesia	Singapore
Iran	Damascus
Iraq	Damascus
Ireland	London
Isle of Man	London
Israel	Tel Aviv
Italy	Rome
Ivory Coast	Abidjan
Jamaica	Kingston
Japan	Tokyo
Jersey	London
Johnston Atoll	Tokyo
Jordan (except west Bank)	Damascus
Jordan (west Bank)	Tel Aviv
Jost Van Dyke	Port of Spain
Kazakhstan	Moscow
Kenya	Nairobi
Kerguelen Archipelago	Nairobi
Kiribati	Sydney
Korea (North)	Seoul
Korea (South)	Seoul
Kosrae	Tokyo
Kuwait	Riyadh
Kyrgyzstan	Moscow
Laos	Bangkok
Latvia	London
Lebanon	Damascus
Lesotho	Pretoria
Liberia	Accra
Libya	Rome
Liechtenstein	Paris
Lithuania	London
Lord Howe Island	Sydney
Loyalty Islands	Sydney
Luxembourg	Paris
Lacao	Hong Kong
Macedonia (FYR)	Belgrade
Madeira	Lisbon
Maio	Sydney
Malagasy Republic	Nairobi
Malawi	Pretoria
Malaysia	Singapore
Maldives	Colombo

Mali Republic	Abidjan
Malta	Rome
Marie Galante	Port-au-Prince
Marquesas Islands	Sydney
Marshall Islands	Tokyo
Martinique	Port-au-Prince
Maupiti	Sydney
Mauritania	Abidjan
Mauritius	Nairobi
Mayotte	Nairobi
Mayreau	Port of Spain
Mexico	Mexico City
Micronesia	Tokyo
Midway Island	Tokyo
Moldova	Bucharest
Monaco	Paris
Mongolian People's Republic	Moscow
Montserrat	Port of Spain
Moorea	Sydney
Morocco	Paris
Mozambique	Pretoria
Mustique	Port of Spain
Namibia	Pretoria
Nauru	Sydney
Nepal	New Delhi
Netherlands	London
Nevis	Port of Spain
New Caledonia	Sydney
New Georgia	Sydney
New Ireland	Sydney
New Zealand	Sydney
Nicaragua	Guatemala City
Nicobar Islands	New Delhi
Niger	Abidjan
Nigeria	Accra
Niue Island	Sydney
Norfolk Island	Sydney
Northern Ireland	London
Northern Mariana Islands	Tokyo
Norway	London
Oman	Riyadh
Orkney Islands	London
Pakistan	Islamabad
Palau	Tokyo
Palestine	Tel Aviv
Panama	Guatemala City
Papua New Guinea	Sydney
Paraguay	Buenos Aires
Peru	Lima

Philippines	Manila
Pitcairn Island	Sydney
Poland	Warsaw
Ponape	Tokyo
Portugal	Lisbon
Puerto Rico	Port of Spain
Qatar	Riyadh
Raiatea	Sydney
Ras Al Khaimah	Riyadh
Redonda	Port of Spain
Reunion	Nairobi
Rodrigues	Nairobi
Romania	Bucharest
Russia	Moscow
Rwanda	Nairobi
Saba	Port-au-Prince
Sabah	Singapore
St Barthelemy	Port-au-Prince
St Brandon Group	Nairobi
St Croix	Port of Spain
St Eustatius	Port-au-Prince
St Helena	Accra
St John	Port of Spain
St Kitts-Nevis	Port of Spain
St Lucia	Port of Spain
St Martin	Port-au-Prince
St Maarten	Port-au-Prince
St Pierre et Miquelon	Paris
St Thomas	Port of Spain
St Vincent and the Grenadines	Port of Spain
Saharawi Arab Democratic Republic	Paris
San Marino	Rome
Santa Isabel	Sydney
Sao Tome e Principe	Accra
Sarawak	Singapore
Sark	London
Saudi Arabia	Riyadh
Scotland	London
Senegal	Abidjan
Seychelles	Nairobi
Sharjah	Riyadh
Sierra Leone	Accra
Singapore	Singapore
Slovakia	Vienna
Slovenia	Vienna
Society Archipelago	Sydney
Solomon Islands	Sydney
Somali Republic	Nairobi
South Africa	Pretoria

Spain	Paris
Sri Lanka	Colombo
Sudan	Cairo
Suriname	Port of Spain
Swaziland	Pretoria
Sweden	London
Switzerland	Paris
Syria	Damascus
Tadjikistan	Moscow
Tahaa	Sydney
Tahiti	Sydney
Taiwan	Taipei
Tanzania	Nairobi
Thailand	Bangkok
Tibet	Peking (Beijing)
Togo	Abidjan
Tokeleau Islands	Sydney
Tonga	Sydney
Tortola	Port of Spain
Trinidad and Tobago	Port of Spain
Tristan da Cunha	Abidjan
Truk Island	Tokyo
Tuamotu Archipelago	Sydney
Tunisia	Paris
Turkey	Ankara
Turkmenistan	Moscow
Turks and Caicos Islands	Kingston
Tuvalu	Sydney
Uganda	Nairobo
Ukraine	Kiev
Umm Al Qaiwan	Riyadh
United Arab Emirates	Riyadh
Union Island	Port of Spain
Union of Myanmar	Bangkok
United States of America	(see below)
Uruguay	Buenos Aires
U.S. Trust Terr. of the Pacific Islands	Tokyo
Uzbekistan	Moscow
Vanuatu	Sydney
Vatican City State	Rome
Venezuela	Bogota
Vietnam	Bangkok
Virgin Gorda	Port of Spain
Virgin Islands, British	Port of Spain
Virgin Islands, U.S.	Port of Spain
Wake Island	Tokyo
Wales	London
Wallis and Futuna	Sydney
Western Samoa	Sydney

Yap Island   Tokyo
Yemen, Republic of   Riyadh
Yugoslavia   Belgrade
Zaire   Abidjan
Zambia   Pretoria
Zimbabwe   Pretoria

UNITED STATES OF AMERICA

Alabama   Buffalo*/New York**
Alaska   Seattle
Arizona   Los Angeles
Arkansas   Buffalo*/New York**
California   Los Angeles
Colorado   Los Angeles
Connecticut   New York
Delaware   New York*/Washington**
District of Columbia New York*/Washington**
Florida   New York
Georgia   New York
Hawaii   Los Angeles
Idaho   Seattle
Illinois   Buffalo*/Detroit**
Indiana   Buffalo*/Detroit**
Iowa   Buffalo*/Detroit**
Kansas   Los Angeles
Kentucky   Buffalo*/Detroit**
Louisiana   Buffalo*/New York**
Maine   New York
Maryland   New York*/Washington**
Massachusetts   New York
Michigan   Buffalo*/Detroit**
Minnesota   Buffalo*/Detroit**
Mississippi   Buffalo*/New York**
Missouri   Buffalo*/Detroit**
Montana   Seattle
Nebraska   Seattle
Nevada   Los Angeles
New Hampshire   New York
New Jersey   New York
New Mexico   Los Angeles
New York   New York and Buffalo[1]
North Carolina   New York
North Dakota   Seattle
Ohio   Buffalo*/Detroit**
Oklahoma   Los Angeles
Oregon   Seattle

Pennsylvania	New York*/Washington**
	—Eastern part of state
	Buffalo—Western part of state
Rhode Island	New York
South Carolina	New York
South Dakota	Seattle
Tennessee	Buffalo*/New York**
Texas	Los Angeles
Utah	Los Angeles
Vermont	New York
Virginia	New York*/Washington**
Washington	Seattle
West Virginia	New York*/Washington**
Wisconsin	Buffalo*/Detroit**
Wyoming	Los Angeles

[1]New York (Southeastern New York), Buffalo (Western and Northern New York)
*Immigrant applications
**Visitor Visa, employment and student authorization, returning resident permit applications

FULL IMMIGRATION PROCESSING MISSIONS ABROAD

ABIDJAN—Republic of Côte d'Ivoire
Street address: Immeuble Trade Center, 23 av. Nogues.
Postal address: The Canadian Embassy, 01 C.P. 4104, Abidjan 01, Côte d'Ivoire. Tel.: 21-20-09. Fax: 011-255-21-77-28.
ACCRA—Republic of Ghana
Street address: 42 Independence Ave.
Postal address: The Canadian High Commission, P.O. Box 1639, Accra, Ghana. Tel.: (011-233-21) 77-37-91. Fax: 011-233-21-77-37-92.
ANKARA—Republic of Turkey
Street address: The Canadian Embassy, Nenehatun Caddesi, No. 75, Gaziosmanpasa, Ankara, Turkey. Tel.: 436-12-75/76/77/78/79. Fax: 011-90-312-446-1761.
BANGKOK—Kingdom of Thailand
Street address: Boonmitr Bldg., 11th Floor, 138 Silom Road, Bangkok 10500.
Postal address: The Canadian Embassy, P.O. Box 2090, Bangkok 10500, Thailand. Tel.: 238-4452. Fax: 011-66-2-236-7467.
BEIJING (PEKING)—People's Republic of China
Street address: The Canadian Embassy, 19 Dong Zhi, Men Wai Street, Beijing, China. Tel.: 532-3031. Fax: 011-86-10-532-1684.
BELGRADE—Socialist Federal Republic of Yugoslavia
Street address: The Canadian Embassy, Kneza Milosa 75, 11000 Belgrade, Yugoslavia. Tel.: 644-666. Fax: 011-381-11-641-343.
BOGOTA—Republic of Colombia
Street address: The Canadian Embassy, Calle 76, No. 11-52.

Postal address: The Canadian Embassy, Immigration Section, P.O. Box 53531, Bogota 2, Colombia. Tel.: 313-1355. Fax: 011-57-1-313-3047.
BONN—Federal Republic of Germany
Street address: The Canadian Embassy, Immigration Office, Godesberger Allee 119, 53175, Bonn 2. Tel.: (011-49-228) 812-0. Fax: 011-49-228-812-34-58.
BUCHAREST—Socialist Republic of Romania
Street address: 36 Nicolae Iorga, 71118, Bucharest.
Postal address: The Canadian Embassy, Post Office No. 22, Bucharest, Romania. Tel.: 222-9845. Fax: 011-40-1-311-3128.
BUDAPEST—Republic of Hungary
Street address: The Canadian Embassy, Budakeszi ut. 32, 1121 Budapest, Hungary. Tel.: (011-361) 275-1200. Fax: (011-361) 275-1215.
BUENOS AIRES—Argentine Republic
Street address: Tagle 2828, 1425 Buenos Aires.
Postal address: The Canadian Embassy, Casilla de Correo 1598, Buenos Aires, Argentina. Tel.: 805-3032. Fax: 011-54-1-806-1212.
BUFFALO—United States of America
Street address: The Consulate General of Canada, Suite 3000, 1 Marine Midland Centre, Buffalo, New York 14203-2884. Tel.: (716) 858-9501. Fax: 81-716-852-2477.
CAIRO—Arab Republic of Egypt
Street address: Arab African International Bank Building, 5 Maidan El Saray Al Kobra, 3rd Floor, Garden City, Cairo.
Postal address: The Canadian Embassy, P.O. Box 1667, Cairo, Egypt. Tel.: 354-3110. Fax: 011-20-2-354-4224.
COLOMBO—Democratic Socialist Republic of Sri Lanka
Street address: 6 Gregory's Road, Cinnamon Gardens, Colombo 7.
Postal address: The Canadian High Commission, P.O. Box 1006, Colombo, Sri Lanka. Tel.: 69-58-45. Fax: 011-94-1-68-7815.
DAMASCUS—Syrian Arab Republic
Street address: Lot 12, Mezzeh Autostrade, Damascus.
Postal address: The Canadian Embassy, P.O. Box 3394, Damascus, Syria. Tel.: 2236-851-892. Fax: 011-963-11-2228-034.
GUATEMALA CITY—Republic of Guatemala
Street address: Edyma Plaza, 8th Floor, 13 Calle 8-44, Zone 10.
Postal address: The Canadian Embassy, P.O. Box 400, Guatemala, C.A. Tel.: 33-6104/07/40. Fax: 011-502-2-33-61-53.
HAVANA—Republic of Cuba
Street address: The Canadian Embassy, Calle 30 No. 518 Esquina a7a, Miramar, Havana, Cuba.
Postal address: The Canadian Embassy, P.O. Box 6125, Havana, Cuba. Tel.: 33-25-16/17/27. Fax: 33-10-69.
HONG KONG
Street address: Exchange Square, Tower One, 11/14 Floors, 8 Connaught Place.
Postal address: Office of the Commission for Canada, P.O. Box 11142 G.P.O., Hong Kong. Tel.: 847-7484. Fax: 011-852-847-7493.
ISLAMABAD—Islamic Republic of Pakistan
Street address: Diplomatic Enclave, Sector G-5.

Postal address: The Canadian Embassy, G.P.O. Box 1042, Islamabad, Pakistan. Tel.: 211-104. Fax: 011-92-51-823-466.
KIEV—Ukraine
Street address: 31 Yaroslaviv Val St – Kiev, 252034.
Postal address: The Canadian Embasssy, P.O. Box 200, Kiev, 252001, Ukraine. Tel.: 212-3550, 212-2235. Fax: 011-7-044-2251305.
KINGSTON—Jamaica
Street address: 30-36 Knutsford Blvd, Kingston 5.
Postal address: The Canadian High Commission, P.O. Box 1500, Kingston 10, Jamaica. Tel.: 926-1500/1/2/3/4/5/6/7. Fax: 1-809- 968-7159.
LIMA—Republic of Peru
Street address: Calle Libertad 130, Miraflores.
Postal address: The Canadian Embassy, Casilla 18-1126, Lima, 18 Peru. Tel.: 011-(51-1) 444-4015. Fax: 011-(51-1) 445-5555.
LISBON—Portuguese Republic
Street address: The Canadian Embassy, Immigration Section, Avenida Da Liberdade 144/56, 2nd Floor, Lisbon 1200, Portugal. Tel.: 347-4892. Fax: 011-351-1-347-6466.
LONDON—United Kingdom of Great Britain and Northern Ireland
Street address: The Canadian High Commission, Immigration Section, 38 Grosvenor St., London, W1X 0AA. England, U.K. Tel.: (01) 258-6600. Fax: 8011-441-258-6506.
LOS ANGELES—United States of America
Street address: The Consulate General of Canada, Immigration Section, 10th Floor, 300 South Grand Avenue, Los Angeles, CA 90071. Tel.: (213) 346-2700. Fax: 1-213-625-7154.
MANILA—Republic of the Philippines
Street address: 9th Floor, Allied Bank Centre, 6754 Ayala Ave., Makati, Metro Manila.
Postal address: The Canadian Embassy, Immigration Section, P.O. Box 2098, Makati, Central P.O., Manila, Philippines. Tel.: 810-8861. Fax: 011-63-2-810-4659.
MEXICO CITY—United Mexican States
Street address: Calle Schiller No. 529 (Rincon del Bosque), Colonia Polanco, 11580 Mexico D.F.
Postal address: Apartado Postal 105-05, 11580 Mexico, D.F. Tel.: 724-7900. Fax: 011-525-724-7983.
MOSCOW—Union of Soviet Socialist Republics
Street address: The Canadian Embassy, 23 Starokonyushenny Pereulok, Moscow, U.S.S.R. Tel.: 956-6666. Fax: 011-7-095-241-5676.
NAIROBI—Republic of Kenya
Street address: Comcraft House, Hailé Sélassie Ave.
Postal address: The Canadian High Commission, P.O. Box 30481, Nairobi, Kenya. Tel.: 214-804. Fax: 011-254-2-21-54-39.
NEW DELHI—Republic of India
Street address: 7/8 Shantipath, Chanakyapuri, New Delhi 110021.
Postal address: The Canadian High Commission, Immigration Section, P.O. Box 5209, Dew Delhi, India. Tel.: 687-6500. Fax: 011-91-11-687-6736.
NEW YORK—United States of America

Street address: The Consulate General of Canada, 22nd Floor, 1251 Ave. of the Americas, New York, N.Y. 10020-1175. Tel.: (212) 596-1600. Fax: 1-212-596-1791.
PARIS—French Republic
Street address: The Canadian Embassy, 35, av. Montaigne, 75008 Paris VIIIe. Tel.: 44.43.29.00. Fax: 011-33-1-44-43-29-93.
PORT-AU-PRINCE—Republic of Haiti
Street address: Edifice Banque Nova Scotia, Route de Delmas.
Postal address: The Canadian Embassy, C.P. 826, Port-au-Prince, Haiti. Tel.: (011-509) 23-2358. Fax: 011-509-22-7007.
PORT OF SPAIN—Republic of Trinidad and Tobago
Street address: 1st Floor, Huggins Bldg., 72-74 South Quay.
Postal address: The Canadian High Commission, Immigration Section, P.O. Box 565, Port of Spain, Trinidad and Tobago. Tel.: 623-7254. Fax: 1-809-625-6734.
PRETORIA—Republic of South Africa
Street addresss: Canadian High Commission of Pretoria 1103 Arcadia, Hatfield, 0083 Pretoria, Republic of South Africa.
Postal address: Canadian High Commission, Visa Section, Private Bag X14, Hatfield 0028, South Africa. Tel.: (0110-27-12) 342-6923. Fax: (011-27-12) 342-3839.
RIYADH—Kingdom of Saudi Arabia
Street address: Diplomatic Quarter, Riyadh.
Postal address: The Canadian Embassy, P.O. Box 94321, Riyadh 11693, Saudi Arabia. Tel.: (011-966-1) 488-2288. Fax: 011-966-1-488-1361.
ROME—Italian Republic
Street address: The Canadian Embassy, Immigration Section, Via Zara 30, 00198 Rome, Italy. Tel.: 44-59-81 or 3029. Fax: 011-39-6-44-598-905.
SAO PAULO—Federative Republic of Brazil
Street address: Edificio Elijass Gliksamanis, Av. Paulista 1106, 1st Floor.
Postal address: The Canadian Consulate General, Visa/Immigration Section, Av. Paulista 1106-1 andar, 01310-100, Sao Paulo, Brazil. Tel.: 011-55-11-285-5099. Fax: 011-55-11-285-5659.
SEATTLE—United States of America
Street address: The Consulate General of Canada, 412 Plaza 600, Sixth and Stewart, Seattle, Wash. 98101-1286. Tel.: (206) 443-1777. Fax: 1-206-441-7838.
Code: 6054.
SEOUL—Republic of Korea
Street address: 10th Floor, Kolon Building, 45 Mugyo-Dong, Jung-Ku.
Postal Address: P.O. Box 6299, Seoul 100, Korea. Tel.: 753-6685/5. Fax: 011-82-2-776-0974.
SINGAPORE—Republic of Singapore
Street address: 80 Anson Road, 15-01, IBM Towers, Singapore 079907.
Postal address: The Canadian High Commission, Robinson Road, P.O. Box 845, Singapore 901645, Singapore. Tel.: 011-65-325-3200. Fax: 011-65-325-3297.
SYDNEY—Commonwealth of Australia
Street address: Level 5, Quay West Bldg., 111 Harrington St., Sydney, N.S.W. 2000, Australia. Tel.: 364-3000. Fax: 011-61-2-364-3099.
TAIPEI—Taiwan
Street address: Canadian Trade Office, Visa Facilitation Section, 13th Floor,

365 Fu Hsing N. Road, Taipei, Taiwan. Tel.: 011-886-2-514-0056. Fax: 011-852-5-514-0067.

TEL AVIV—State of Israel
Street address: The Canadian Embassy, Visa and Consular Section, 07 Havakuk Street, Tel Aviv 63505.
Postal address: The Canadian Embassy, Immigration Section, P.O. Box 6410, Tel Aviv 61063, Israel. Tel.: 544-28-81. Fax: 011-972-3-544-5686.

THE HAGUE—The Netherlands
Street address: Canadian Embassy, Immigration Section, Sophialaan 7, 2514 JP The Hague, The Netherlands. Tel.: 31-(0) 70 311-1600. Fax: 31-(0) 70 311-1697.

TOKYO—Japan
Street address: The Canadian Embassy, Visa Section, 3-38, Akasaka 7-chome, Minato-ku, Tokyo 107, Japan. Tel.: 3408-2101. Fax: 011-81-3-34-3-8357.

VIENNA—Republic of Austria
Address: The Canadian Embassy, Immigration Section, Laurenzerberg, 2, A-1010 Vienna, Austria. Tel.: 011-43-1-531-38-3010. Fax: 011-43-1-531-38-3911.

WARSAW—Polish People's Republic
Street address: The Canadian Embassy, Piekna 2/8, Warsaw 00-481, Poland. Tel: 29-80-51/59. Fax: 29-64-57.

Other Useful Addresses

CANADIAN IMMIGRATION COUNSELLING

M. J. Bjarnason & Associates Co. Ltd., 3 Harshaw Avenue, Toronto, Ontario, Canada M6S 1X7. Tel: (416) 766-2313. Fax: (416) 766-8263

Far East Office
Bjarnason & Associates Limited, Bank of America Tower, Suite 803, 8th Floor, 12 Harcourt Road, Central, Hong Kong. Tel: (852) 2723-6158. Fax: (852) 2530-0484.

TRAVEL

All-Canada Travel & Holidays Ltd, 90 High Street, Lowestoft, Suffolk, NR3 1XN. Tel: (01502) 585825
Canada Connections, 7 York Way, Lancaster Road, High Wycombe, Bucks HP12 3PY. Tel: (01345) 045904
Canadian Airlines International Ltd, 62 Trafalgar Square, London WC2N 5DS. Tel: (0171) 930 3501.
Canadian National Railways, 17 Cockspur Street, London SW1Y 5BL. Tel: (0171) 930 2150.
Canadian Pacific Hotels & Resorts, 62-65 Trafalgar Square, London WC2N 5DY. Tel: (0171) 798 9898.
Canadian Ski Holidays Ltd, 6 Kew Green, Richmond, Surrey. Tel: (0181) 948 4333.
Canadian Universities Travel Services (UK) Ltd, 295a Regent Street, London W1R 7YA. Tel: (0171) 255 2191.
Canadians Abroad, 20 Craven Terrace, London W2 3QH. Tel: (0171) 706 2798.

FINANCIAL SERVICES

Canadian Imperial Bank of Commerce, Cottons Centre, Cotton Land, London SE1 2QG. Tel: (0171) 234 6000.
Toronto-Dominion Bank, Triton Court, Finsbury Square, London EC2A 1DB. Tel: (0171) 920 0272.

OTHER

Alberta House, 1 Mount Street, London W1Y 5AA. Tel: (0171) 491 3430.
British Columbia House, 1 Regent Street, London SW1Y 4NS. Tel: (0171) 930 6857.
Canadian Broadcasting Corporation, 43 Great Titchfield Street, London W1P 7FJ. Tel: (0171) 580 0336.
Canadian University Society, 59 Pall Mall, London SW1Y 3JH. Tel: (0171) 839 8993.
Canadian Women's Club, Alberta House, 1 Mount Street, London W1Y 5AA. Tel: (0171) 408 2459.
Ontario Government Office, 21 Knightsbridge, London SW1. Tel: (0171) 245 1222. Fax: (0171) 259 6661.
Quebec House, 59 Pall Mall, London SW1Y 5JH. Tel: (0171) 930 8314.

OTHER USEFUL ORGANIZATIONS

Accounting
Canadian Association of Certified Executive Accountants, PO Box 43038, Ottawa, Ontario K1J 9M4. Tel: (613) 745 5762.
Canadian Institute of Chartered Accountants, 277 Wellington Street West, Toronto, Ontario M5V 3H2. Tel: (416) 977 3222.
Society of Management Accountants of Canada, No. 850, 120 King Street West, PO Box 176, Hamilton, Ontario L8N 3C3. Tel: (416) 525 4100.

Agriculture and farming
Canadian Federation of Agriculture, No. 1101, 75 Albert Street, Ottawa, Ontario K1P 5E7. Tel: (613) 236 3633.
National Farmers Union, 250C-2 Avenue South, Saksatoon, Saskatchewan S7K 2M1. Tel: (306) 652 9465.

Animals
Canadian Veterinary Medical Association, 339 Booth Street, Ottawa, Ontario K1R 7K1. Tel: (613) 236 1162.
Canadian Wildlife Federation, 2740 Queensway Drive, Ottawa, Ontario K2B 1A2. Tel: (613) 721 2286.

Architecture
Royal Architectural Institute of Canada, No. 330, 55 Murray Street, Ottawa, Ontario K1N 5M3. Tel: (613) 232 7165.

Automotive
Canadian Automobile Association, 1775 Courtwood Crescent, Ottawa, Ontario K2C 3J2. Tel: (613) 226 7631.

Broadcasting
Canadian Association of Broadcasters, PO Box 626, Station B, Ottawa, Ontario K1P 5S2. Tel: (613) 233 4035.

Building and construction
Canadian Construction Association, 85 Albert Street, 10th Floor, Ottawa, Ontario K1P 6A4. Tel: (613) 236 9526.

Business
Canadian Association of Family Enterprise, No. 803, 121 Bloor Street East, Toronto, Ontario M4W 3M8. Tel: (416) 961 1673.
Canadian Association of Professional Salespeople, No. 200, 251 Midpark Boulevard South East, Calgary, Alberta T2X 1S3. Tel: (403) 259 8464.
Canadian Council of Better Business Bureaus, No. 219, 2180 Steeles Avenue West, Concord, Ontario L4K 2Z5. Tel: (416) 669 1248.
Canadian Institute of Marketing, 41 Capital Drive, Nepean, Ontario K2G 0E7. Tel: (613) 727 0954.
Canadian Organization of Small Business Inc, Box 11246, MPO, Edmonton, Alberta T5H 3J5. Tel: (403) 423 2672.
Canadian Professional Sales Association, No. 310, 145 Wellington Street West, Toronto, Ontario M5J 1H8. Tel: (416) 408 2685.
Home Business Network (1986), 195 Markville Road, Unionville, Ontario L3R 4V8. Tel: (416) 470 7930.

Chemical industry
The Chemical Institute of Canada, No. 550, 130 Slater Street, Ottawa, Ontario K1P 6E2. Tel: (613) 232 6252.

Children & youth
Boys & Girls Clubs of Canada, No. 703, 7030 Woodbine Avenue, Markham, Ontario L3R 6G2. Tel: (416) 477 7272.
Canadian Council on Children & Youth, 55 Parkdale Road, 3rd Floor, Ottawa, Ontario K1Y 1E5. Tel: (613) 722 0133.
Girl Guides of Canada, 50 Merton Street, Toronto, Ontario M4S 1A3. Tel: (416) 487 5281.

Citizenship & immigration
Calgary Canadian Citizenship Council, PO Box 4171, Station C, Calgary, Alberta T2T 5N1. Tel: (403) 246 8748.
Canadian Citizenship Federation, No. 402, 396 Cooper Street, Ottawa Ontario K2P 2H7. Tel: (613) 235 1467.
Canadian Immigration Historical Society, PO Box 9502, Ottawa, Ontario K1G 3V2. Tel: (613) 824 3035.
Citizenship Council of Manitoba Inc., 406 Edmonton Street, Winnipeg Manitoba R3B 2M2. Tel: (204) 943 9158.
Greater Victoria Citizenship Council, 1117 May Street, Victoria, British Columbia V8V 2S6. Tel: (604) 385 0238.
Jewish Immigrant Aid Services of Canada, No. 325, 4600 Bathurst Street, Willowdale, Ontario M2R 3V3. Tel: (416) 630 6481.
Montreal Citizenship Council, Cp 438, Succ. Beaubien, Montreal, Quebec H3G 3E1. Tel: (514) 334 2009.
National Organization of Immigrants & Visible Minority Women of Canada, No. 506, Bank Street, Ottawa, Ontario K2P 1X3. Tel: (613) 232 0689.
Ontario Council of Agencies Serving Immigrants, No. 201, 579 St Clair Avenue West, Toronto, Ontario M6C 1A3. Tel: (416) 657 8777.
Organization of Professional Immigration Consultants, Scotia Plaza, No. 6200, 40 King Street West, Toronto, Ontario M5H 3Z7. Tel: (416) 495 7965.

Consumers
Consumers' Association of Canada, 49 Auriga Drive, Nepean, Ontario K2E 8A1. Tel: (613) 723 0187.

Cultural

Association of Canadian Clubs, 237 Nepean Street, Ottawa, Ontario K2P 0B7. Tel: (613) 236 8288.

English-Speaking Union of Canada, No. 306, 40 St Clair Avenue East, Toronto, Ontario M4T 1M9. Tel: (416) 925 7860.

The Royal Commonwealth Society, Commonwealth House, 18 Northumberland Avenue, London WC2N 5BJE, United Kingdom. Tel: (0171) 930 9705.

Society for Educational Visits & Exchanges in Canada, 57 Auriga Drive, Nepean, Ontario K2E 8B2. Tel: (613) 998 3760.

Disability

Canadian Disability Rights Council, No. 208, 428 Portage Avenue, Winnipeg, Manitoba R3C 0E4. Tel: (204) 943 4787.

Economics

Canadian Economics Association, Stephen Leacock Building, Department of Economics, McGill University, 855 Sherbrooke Street West, Montreal, Quebec H3A 2T7. Tel: (514) 398 4830.

Education

Association of Student Councils (Canada), 171 College Street, Toronto, Ontario M5T 1P7. Tel: (416) 977 3703.

Association of Universities & Colleges of Canada, 151 Slater Street, Ottawa, Ontario K1P 5N1. Tel: (613) 563 1236.

Canadian Federation of Students, No. 600, 170 Metcalfe Street, Ottawa, Ontario K2P 1P3. Tel: (613) 232 7394.

Canadian Home & School & Parent-Teacher Federation, 331 Somerset Street West, Ottawa, Ontario K2P 0J8. Tel: (613) 234 7292.

Canadian Teachers' Federation, 110 Argyle Street, Ottawa, Ontario K2P 1B4. Tel: (613) 232 1505.

Employment & human resources

Association of Professional Placement Agencies & Consultants, No. L-109, 114 Richmond Street East, Toronto, Ontario M5C 1P1. Tel: (416) 362 0983.

Canadian Institute of Employee Benefit Specialists, 253 Sheppard Avenue West, North York, Ontario M2N 1N2. Tel: (416) 225 2870.

Federation of Temporary Help Services, No. 409, 1 Eva Road, Etobicoke, Ontario M9C 4Z5. Tel: (4165) 626 7130.
Personnel Association of Ontario, No. 600, 2 Bloor Street West, Toronto, Ontario M4W 3E2. Tel: (416) 923 2324.
Senior Talent Bank Association of Ontario, No. 806, 163 Eglinton Avenue East, Toronto, Ontario M4P 1J4. Tel: (416) 483 2626.

Energy
Canadian Institute of Energy, No. 229, 640-5 Avenue South West, Calgary, Alberta T2P 0M6. Tel: (403) 262 6969.

Engineering
Canadian Council of Professional Engineers, No. 401, 116 Albert Street, Ottawa, Ontario K1P 5G3. Tel: (613) 232 2474.
Heating, Refrigerating & Air Conditioning Institute of Canada, No. 308, 5468 Dundas Street West, Etobicoke, Ontario M9B 6E3. Tel: (416) 239 8191.

Events
Canadian Association of Festivals & Events, PO Box 398, Station A, Ottawa, Ontario K1N 8V4. Tel: (613) 220 1552.
Canadian Film Institute, 2 Daly, Ottawa, Ontario K1N 6E2. Tel: (613) 232 6727.
Canadian Film & Television Production Association, No. 404, 663 Yonge Street, Toronto, Ontario M4Y 2A4. Tel: (416) 927 8942.
Federation of Canadian Music Festivals, 1034 Chestnut Avenue, Moose Jaw, Saskatchewan S6H 1A6. Tel: (306) 693 7087.

Finance
Association of Canadian Venture Capital Companies, No. 600, 1881 Yonge Street, Toronto, Ontario M4S 1Y6.
Canadian Association of Individual Investors, No. 401, 3284 Yonge Street, Toronto, Ontario M4N 3M7. Tel: (416) 489 3500.
Canadian Association of Investment Clubs, No. 0116, 65 Ford Street West, PO Box 174, Toronto, Ontario M5J 1E6. Tel: (416) 488 2242.
Canadian Bankers' Association, The Exchange Tower, No. 600, 2 First Canadian Place, PO Box 348, Toronto, Ontario M5X 1E1. Tel: (416) 362 6092.

Society of Mortgage Finance of Canada, 951 Wilson Avenue, Unit 8, Downsview, Ontario M3K 2A7. Tel: (416) 631 0320.

Health & medical
Canadian Dental Association, 1815 Alta Vista Drive, Ottawa, Ontario K1G 3Y6. Tel: (613) 523 1770.
Canadian Medical Association, 1867 Alta Vista Drive, PO Box 8050, Ottawa, Ontario K1G 3Y6. Tel: (613) 731 9331.
Canadian Nurses Association, 50 The Driveway, Ottawa, Ontario K2P 1E2. Tel: (613) 237 2133.

Human Rights & civil liberties
Amnesty International, Canadian Section, No. 900, 130 Slater Street, Ottawa, Ontario K1P 6E2.
Canada Council on Human Rights & Race Relations, The Guardian Tower, No. 1202, 181 University Avenue, Toronto, Ontario M5H 3M7. Tel: (416) 594 3291.
Canadian Civil Liberties Association, No. 403, 229 Yonge Street, Toronto, Ontario M5B 1N9. Tel: (416) 363 0321.

Information management
Computer Science Association, No. 205, 430 King Street West, Toronto, Ontario M5V 1L5. Tel: (416) 593 4040.
Information Technology Association of Canada, No. 402, 2800 Skymark Avenue, Mississauga, Ontario L4W 5A6. Tel: (416) 602 8345.

Insurance industry
Association of Canadian Insurers, No. 2000, 390 Bay Street, Toronto, Ontario M5H 2Y2. Tel: (416) 362 5286.

International cooperation
Canadian Council for International Cooperation, No. 300, One Nicholas Street, Ottawa, Ontario K1N 7B7. Tel: (613) 236 4547.

Other Useful Addresses

Friends of the Earth, No. 701, 251 Laurier Avenue West, Ottawa, Ontario K1P 5J6. Tel: (613) 230 3352.

Management & administration
Institute of Chartered Secretaries & Administrators, No. 301, 250 Consumers Road, Willowdale, Ontario M2J 4Y6. Tel: (416) 494 3757.

Professional Secretaries International, 10502 North West Ambassador Drive, PO Box 20404, Kansas City, Missouri MO 64195-0404 USA. Tel: (816) 891 6600.

Manufacturing & industry
Canadian Manufacturers' Association, No. 1400, One Yonge Street, Toronto, Ontario M5E 1J9. Tel: (416) 363 7261.

Real estate
The Canadian Real Estate Association, Place de Ville, Tower A, No. 2100, 320 Queen Street, Ottawa, Ontario K1R 5A3. Tel: (613) 234 3372.

Restaurants, bars, food services
Canadian Restaurant & Foodservices Association, No. 1201, 80 Bloor Street West, Toronto, Ontario M5S 2V1. Tel: (416) 923 8416.

Senior citizens
Canadian Association of Retired Persons, No. 1304, 27 Queen Street East, Toronto, Ontario M5C 2M6. Tel: (416) 363 8748.

Taxation
Canadian Federation of Tax Consultants, No. 502, 161 Eglinton Avenue East, Toronto, Ontario M4P 1J5. Tel: (416) 488 5404.

Tourism & travel
Tourism Industry Association of Canada, No. 1016, 130 Albert Street, Ottawa, Ontario K1P 5G4. Tel: (613) 238 3853.

Further Reading

Canada News, Outbound Newspapers, 1 Commercial Road, Eastbourne, East Sussex BN21 3XQ. Tel: (01323) 412001. News and features for visitors and migrants to Canada.

Can-UK Link, magazine of the Canada-UK Chamber of Commerce, British Columbia House, 3 Regent Street, London SW1Y 4NZ. Tel: (0171) 930 7711. Fax: (0171) 930 9703.

Canadabooks International, The Warehouse, Old Mead Road, Elsenham, Bishops Stortford, Hertfordshire. Tel: Bishops Stortford 814228.

Directory of Associations in Canada, Micromedia Ltd, 20 Victoria Street, Toronto M5C 2N8. Comprehensive reference source which costs in excess of Can.$200.

Directory of Canadian Companies Overseas, Overseas Employment Services, PO Box 460, Town of Mount Royal, Quebec H3P 3C7.

Directory of Canadian Employment Agencies, Overseas Consultants, PO Box 152, Douglas, Isle of Man.

Directory of Canadian Firms Overseas, Overseas Consultants, PO Box 152, Douglas, Isle of Man.

Toronto Globe & Mail, 444 Front Street West, Toronto, Ontario. Leading national newspaper.

Toronto Star Newspapers, UK office, 60 Great Titchfield Street, London W1P 7AE. Tel: (0171) 637 7187.

Working Abroad, Jonathan Golding, International Venture Handbooks, Plymbridge House, Estover Road, Plymouth PL6 7PZ. Tel: (01752) 202301. Essential financial advice for prospective British expatriates and their employers, covering tax, offshore investment, contract negotiation and similar matters.

Index

accountants, 129
age, 49
Alphabetical Listing of Occupations, 67
appeals, 125
Application for Permanent Residence, 18, 37, 41, 87, 91–112
appointments secretary, 202
arranged employment, 47
assessment criteria, 43–50
assets, 106
Assisted Relatives, 13, 105

bookkeeper, 202
business proposals, 70

children, 14–15
citizenship, 100, 123
civil engineers, 200
clearance checks, 117
clubs/memberships, 106
conditional visa, 70
Confirmation of Offer of Employment, 47
consultants, immigration, 109, 111, 125–26
convictions (criminal), 107
Customs, 122

date of birth, 100
debts (obligations), 106
Demographic Factor, 49

dental hygienists, 129
dependants, 14–15
Designated Occupations, 16, 47, 48, 67
destination, 106
documents, 87

education, 43, 51, 102–4
engineering technologists, 129
engineers, 129
entrepreneurs, 12, 52, 53, 69
executive secretary, 202
experience, 46

family members, 13
Federal Court of Appeals, 126
fees, government, 34, 42, 197–9
financial evaluation, 18

General Occupations List, 67

health, 107,

Immigrant Visa, 19
Immigration Appeal Board, 38, 126
immigration counselling, 218
Immigration Offices abroad, 205–17
Independent Applicants, 11, 40–68
intended occupation, 104
interview, 38, 113–16

investors, 12, 52, 53, 72

job descriptions, 110

language ability, 102
languages (English, French), 49, 52
Levels Control, 49
licensing requirements, 129
Low Income Cut-Off, 37

machinist, 204
medical examination, 19, 117–18
medical secretary, 202

name (other names), 100
nurses, 129

Occupational Demand, 46, 52
occupational therapists, 129
Officers, Immigration, 205–17

Parents' particulars, 106
passport, 102
personal suitability, 49, 52
photographs, 108
physiotherapists, 129
Point System, 43
port of entry, 122
present occupation, 104
priority system, 113
processing fees, 197–9
processing time, 108

Quebec, 54–65

Record of Landing, 19, 37
refugees, 125
relationship, 105
relatives, 50
Retirement Category, 13
right of appeal, 38
Right of Landing Fees, 197–9

salesperson, computers, 203
secretarial stenographer, 202
secretary, 202
security checks, 110, 117
self-employed, 12, 13, 71
skilled immigrants, 12
Social Insurance Number, 122
social secretary, 202
social worker, 201–2
Specific Vocational Preparation, 45, 66–8
Sponsored Dependants, 11, 18–39
Sponsorship Kit, 20
students, 15
systems analyst, 201

third party involvement, 126

unconditional visa, 69
Undertaking of Assistance, 18, 30, 31, 37

Visa, Immigrant, 119

war crimes, 108
work history, 105

FINDING WORK OVERSEAS
How and where to contact international recruitment agencies, consultancies and employers
Matthew Cunningham

This is an essential reference guide for all overseas job hunters and recruiters. Part 1 explains how to write and present a CV for an overseas job, how to plan and manage a successful overseas job search campaign, and how to deal with healthcare, domestic and offshore finance, travel, dependents, social/cultural survival and other matters. Part 2 lists more than 1,500 key recruitment agencies, international consultancies and employers, who can offer international employment opportunities. The data is presented in a consistent, clear and user-friendly format, summarising each organisation's recruitment specialties, full contact details, and work locations abroad. Matthew Cunningham is a professional coporate manpower planner.

208pp. illus. 1 85703 409 0.

HOW TO EMIGRATE
Your complete guide to a successful future overseas
Roger Jones

Would you like to pack your bags, and make a completely new life for yourself overseas? According to a recent poll, thousands of people would, dreaming of a better lifestyle, new horizons and a more rewarding future. But how do you actually go about it? Which countries should you consider, and what visas and permits will you need? In practical steps, this book will set you on the right path, with essential advice and information on weighing up your prospects, choosing the right location, coping with immigration, the actual move, housing, employment and settling in successfully to your new life overseas. Written by a leading writer of books on living and working overseas. 'Very practical and entertaining—I would recommend it.' *Phoenix/Association of Graduate Careers Advisory Services.*

176pp. illus. 1 85703 101 6.

Other titles in this series

HOW TO FIND TEMPORARY WORK ABROAD
A world of opportunities for everyone

Nick Vandome

Would you like the chance to work abroad—perhaps to expand your horizons, finance an extended holiday, or use some 'time between'? Whatever your aims and interests, this practical book has something for you. It explains where to find the opportunities suited to your own particular interests, how to apply and be selected, how to manage money, passports, permits, insurance and accommodation, and how to get the most out of your experience overseas. Whether you plan to stay abroad for a couple of weeks or most of the year, this is the book for you, packed with valuable employment advice and contacts. Nick Vandome is a young freelance writer who has spent a year abroad on three occasions, in France, Australia, Africa and Asia. His articles have appeared in *The Guardian, The Scotsman, The Daily Telegraph* and elsewhere. He is also author of *How to Get a Job in Australia* in this series.

160pp. illus. 1 85703 109 1.

HOW TO GET A JOB ABROAD
A handbook of opportunities and contacts

Roger Jones

Now in a fourth fully revised edition, this top-selling title is essential for everyone planning to spend a period abroad. It contains a big reference section of medium and long-term job opportunities and possibilities, arranged by region and country of the world, and by profession/occupation. There are more than 100 pages of specific contacts and leads, giving literally hundreds of updated addresses and much hard-to-find information. There is a classified guide to overseas recruitment agencies, and even a multi-lingual guide to writing application letters. 'A fine book for anyone considering even a temporary overseas job.' *The Evening Star.* 'A highly informative and well researched book . . . containing lots of hard information and a first class reference section . . . A superb buy.' *The Escape Committee Newsletter.* 'A valuable addition to any careers library.' *Phoenix/Association of Graduate Careers Advisory Services.* 'An excellent addition to any careers library . . . Compact and realistic . . . There is a wide range of reference addresses covering employment agencies, specialist newspapers, a comprehensive booklist and helpful addresses . . . All readers, whether careers officers, young adults or more mature adults, will find use for this book.' *Newscheck/Careers Services Bulletin.* Roger Jones has himself worked abroad for many years and is a specialist writer on expatriate and employment matters.

272pp. illus. 1 85703 182 2. 4th edition.

How To Books

How To Books provide practical help on a large range of topics. They are available through all good bookshops or can be ordered direct from the distributors. Just tick the titles you want and complete the form on the following page.

- ___ Apply to an Industrial Tribunal (£7.99)
- ___ Applying for a Job (£7.99)
- ___ Applying for a United States Visa (£15.99)
- ___ Be a Freelance Journalist (£8.99)
- ___ Be a Freelance Secretary (£8.99)
- ___ Be a Local Councillor (£8.99)
- ___ Be an Effective School Governor (£9.99)
- ___ Become a Freelance Sales Agent (£9.99)
- ___ Become an Au Pair (£8.99)
- ___ Buy & Run a Shop (£8.99)
- ___ Buy & Run a Small Hotel (£8.99)
- ___ Cash from your Computer (£9.99)
- ___ Career Planning for Women (£8.99)
- ___ Choosing a Nursing Home (£8.99)
- ___ Claim State Benefits (£9.99)
- ___ Communicate at Work (£7.99)
- ___ Conduct Staff Appraisals (£7.99)
- ___ Conducting Effective Interviews (£8.99)
- ___ Copyright & Law for Writers (£8.99)
- ___ Counsel People at Work (£7.99)
- ___ Creating a Twist in the Tale (£8.99)
- ___ Creative Writing (£9.99)
- ___ Critical Thinking for Students (£8.99)
- ___ Do Voluntary Work Abroad (£8.99)
- ___ Do Your Own Advertising (£8.99)
- ___ Do Your Own PR (£8.99)
- ___ Doing Business Abroad (£9.99)
- ___ Emigrate (£9.99)
- ___ Employ & Manage Staff (£8.99)
- ___ Find Temporary Work Abroad (£8.99)
- ___ Finding a Job in Canada (£9.99)
- ___ Finding a Job in Computers (£8.99)
- ___ Finding a Job in New Zealand (£9.99)
- ___ Finding a Job with a Future (£8.99)
- ___ Finding Work Overseas (£9.99)
- ___ Freelance DJ-ing (£8.99)
- ___ Get a Job Abroad (£10.99)
- ___ Get a Job in America (£9.99)
- ___ Get a Job in Australia (£9.99)
- ___ Get a Job in Europe (£9.99)
- ___ Get a Job in France (£9.99)
- ___ Get a Job in Germany (£9.99)
- ___ Get a Job in Hotels and Catering (£8.99)
- ___ Get a Job in Travel & Tourism (£8.99)
- ___ Get into Films & TV (£8.99)
- ___ Get into Radio (£8.99)
- ___ Get That Job (£6.99)
- ___ Getting your First Job (£8.99)
- ___ Going to University (£8.99)
- ___ Helping your Child to Read (£8.99)
- ___ Investing in People (£8.99)
- ___ Invest in Stocks & Shares (£8.99)
- ___ Keep Business Accounts (£7.99)
- ___ Know Your Rights at Work (£8.99)
- ___ Know Your Rights: Teachers (£6.99)
- ___ Live & Work in America (£9.99)
- ___ Live & Work in Australia (£12.99)
- ___ Live & Work in Germany (£9.99)
- ___ Live & Work in Greece (£9.99)
- ___ Live & Work in Italy (£8.99)
- ___ Live & Work in New Zealand (£9.99)
- ___ Live & Work in Portugal (£9.99)
- ___ Live & Work in Spain (£7.99)
- ___ Live & Work in the Gulf (£9.99)
- ___ Living & Working in Britain (£8.99)
- ___ Living & Working in China (£9.99)
- ___ Living & Working in Hong Kong (£10.99)
- ___ Living & Working in Israel (£10.99)
- ___ Living & Working in Japan (£8.99)
- ___ Living & Working in Saudi Arabia (£12.99)
- ___ Living & Working in the Netherlands (£9.99)
- ___ Lose Weight & Keep Fit (£6.99)
- ___ Make a Wedding Speech (£7.99)
- ___ Making a Complaint (£8.99)
- ___ Manage a Sales Team (£8.99)
- ___ Manage an Office (£8.99)
- ___ Manage Computers at Work (£8.99)
- ___ Manage People at Work (£8.99)
- ___ Manage Your Career (£8.99)
- ___ Managing Budgets & Cash Flows (£9.99)
- ___ Managing Meetings (£8.99)
- ___ Managing Your Personal Finances (£8.99)
- ___ Market Yourself (£8.99)
- ___ Master Book-Keeping (£8.99)
- ___ Mastering Business English (£8.99)
- ___ Master GCSE Accounts (£8.99)
- ___ Master Languages (£8.99)
- ___ Master Public Speaking (£8.99)
- ___ Obtaining Visas & Work Permits (£9.99)
- ___ Organising Effective Training (£9.99)
- ___ Pass Exams Without Anxiety (£7.99)
- ___ Pass That Interview (£6.99)
- ___ Plan a Wedding (£7.99)
- ___ Prepare a Business Plan (£8.99)
- ___ Publish a Book (£9.99)
- ___ Publish a Newsletter (£9.99)
- ___ Raise Funds & Sponsorship (£7.99)
- ___ Rent & Buy Property in France (£9.99)
- ___ Rent & Buy Property in Italy (£9.99)
- ___ Retire Abroad (£8.99)
- ___ Return to Work (£7.99)
- ___ Run a Local Campaign (£6.99)
- ___ Run a Voluntary Group (£8.99)
- ___ Sell Your Business (£9.99)

How To Books

- Selling into Japan (£14.99)
- Setting up Home in Florida (£9.99)
- Spend a Year Abroad (£8.99)
- Start a Business from Home (£7.99)
- Start a New Career (£6.99)
- Starting to Manage (£8.99)
- Starting to Write (£8.99)
- Start Word Processing (£8.99)
- Start Your Own Business (£8.99)
- Study Abroad (£8.99)
- Study & Learn (£7.99)
- Study & Live in Britain (£7.99)
- Studying at University (£8.99)
- Studying for a Degree (£8.99)
- Successful Grandparenting (£8.99)
- Successful Mail Order Marketing (£9.99)
- Successful Single Parenting (£8.99)
- Survive at College (£4.99)
- Survive Divorce (£8.99)
- Surviving Redundancy (£8.99)
- Take Care of Your Heart (£5.99)
- Taking in Students (£8.99)
- Taking on Staff (£8.99)
- Taking Your A-Levels (£8.99)
- Teach Abroad (£8.99)
- Teach Adults (£8.99)
- Teaching Someone to Drive (£8.99)
- Travel Round the World (£8.99)
- Use a Library (£6.99)
- Use the Internet (£9.99)
- Winning Consumer Competitions (£8.99)
- Winning Presentations (£8.99)
- Work from Home (£8.99)
- Work in an Office (£7.99)
- Work in Retail (£8.99)
- Work with Dogs (£8.99)
- Working Abroad (£14.99)
- Working as a Holiday Rep (£9.99)
- Working in Japan (£10.99)
- Working in Photography (£8.99)
- Working in the Gulf (£10.99)
- Working on Contract Worldwide (£9.99)
- Working on Cruise Ships (£9.99)
- Write a CV that Works (£7.99)
- Write a Press Release (£9.99)
- Write a Report (£8.99)
- Write an Assignment (£8.99)
- Write an Essay (£7.99)
- Write & Sell Computer Software (£9.99)
- Write Business Letters (£8.99)
- Write for Publication (£8.99)
- Write for Television (£8.99)
- Write Your Dissertation (£8.99)
- Writing a Non Fiction Book (£8.99)
- Writing & Selling a Novel (£8.99)
- Writing & Selling Short Stories (£8.99)
- Writing Reviews (£8.99)
- Your Own Business in Europe (£12.99)

To: Plymbridge Distributors Ltd, Plymbridge House, Estover Road, Plymouth PL6 7PZ.
Customer Services Tel: (01752) 202301. Fax: (01752) 202331.

Please send me copies of the titles I have indicated. Please add postage & packing (UK £1, Europe including Eire, £2, World £3 airmail).

☐ I enclose cheque/PO payable to Plymbridge Distributors Ltd for £ _____

☐ Please charge to my ☐ MasterCard, ☐ Visa, ☐ AMEX card.

Account No. _____

Card Expiry Date ____ 19 ____   ☎ **Credit Card orders may be faxed or phoned.**

Customer Name (CAPITALS) ....

Address ....

.... Postcode ....

Telephone .... Signature ....

Every effort will be made to despatch your copy as soon as possible but to avoid possible disappointment please allow up to 21 days for despatch time (42 days if overseas). Prices and availability are subject to change without notice.

Code BPA